DEALMAKING IN THE FILM & TELEVISION INDUSTRY

Other books by Mark Litwak

Reel Power
Courtroom Crusaders
Contracts for the Film and Television Industry

DEALMAKING
IN THE
FILM
&
TELEVISION
INDUSTRY
FROM NEGOTIATIONS
TO FINAL CONTRACTS

BY MARK LITWAK

SILMAN-JAMES PRESS
LOS ANGELES

First Edition

10 9 8 7 6 5 4

Library of Congress Cataloging-in-Publication Data

Litwak, Mark.
Dealmaking in the film and television industry / by Mark Litwak
p.   cm.
Includes bibliographical references and index.
1. Performing arts—Law and legislation—United States—
Popular works. 2. Motion pictures—Law and legislation—
United States—Popular works. 3. Entertainers—
Legal status, laws, etc.—United States—Popular works. I. Title.
KF4290.Z9L58 1994   343.73'0787902—dc20   94-1939
[347.303787902]

ISBN: 1-879505-15-0

Cover design by Heidi Frieder

Printed and bound in the United States of America

SILMAN-JAMES PRESS
distributed by
Samuel French Trade
7623 Sunset Blvd.
Hollywood, CA 90046

To my sons, David and Michael

DISCLAIMER

This book is designed to help non-lawyers understand legal issues frequently encountered in the entertainment industry. It will provide readers with an understanding of basic legal principles, enabling them to communicate better with their attorneys.

Nothing in this book should be construed as legal advice. The information provided is not a substitute for consulting with an experienced entertainment attorney and receiving counsel based on the facts and circumstances of a particular transaction. Many of the legal principles mentioned are subject to exceptions and qualifications that may not be noted. Futhermore, case law and statutes are subject to change and may not apply in every state.

ACKNOWLEDGEMENTS

I am grateful for the assistance of Phil Hacker, Tiiu Lukk, Gary Salt and Lon Sobel for reading and critiquing early drafts of this work. Thanks also to Lawrence Young and Danielle Casselman for checking case citations and facts.

My thanks to Elliott Williams, General Counsel to the Directors Guild of America, and Vicki Shapiro, Assistant Hollywood Executive Director-Legal Affairs, Screen Actor's Guild, for reviewing portions of the chapters pertaining to their members and guild rules.

I am also indebted to my publishers, Gwen Feldman and Jim Fox, for their helpful suggestions.

CONTENTS

CONTRACTS[1]

---

[1] All of the contracts in this book are available on computer disc. See page 349 for information on how to order.

CASE SUMMARIES

PREFACE

After the publication of my book *Reel Power* in 1986, I was invited to lecture at many universities in the United States and abroad. On numerous occasions I was asked to recommend a guide to entertainment legal issues. I have never been able to recommend such a guide because I did not know of one.

While there are several texts on entertainment law, none are addressed to the general reader. These books are written by lawyers for lawyers and are confusing, if not impenetrable, to everyone else.

Eventually I resolved to write a layperson's guide to entertainment law, and this is that book. I have attempted to explain complex legal ideas as simply as possible, avoiding jargon and explaining terms of art. I have taken a practical, problem-solving approach, rather than explore theoretical issues of interest to academicians.

Of course there is a danger in trying to simplify complex information. Important exceptions and qualifications may be overlooked. The unwary reader may be misled into thinking he knows more than he does. It is well to recall the maxim that a little knowledge can be dangerous. So I caution readers to consult an experienced entertainment lawyer before making decisions with legal ramifications.

DEALMAKING
IN THE
FILM AND
TELEVISION
INDUSTRY

xviii

While this book is not a substitute for consulting an attorney, it does familiarize the reader with entertainment law and industry practice. It will impart to the neophyte some wisdom of showbiz veterans, enabling newcomers to protect themselves from exploitation as they learn to become savvy dealmakers.

Moreover, this guide can save readers thousands of dollars in legal fees. Entertainment attorneys generally charge $200 to $400 an hour for their time. Armed with this guide, laypeople won't need to ask their attorney to explain basic legal concepts and common deal structures. The lawyer and client can work more efficiently. Moreover, as the reader becomes more knowledgeable about his rights, he can take measures to prevent legal problems from arising in the first place.

I welcome comments and suggestions from readers. You can contact me at: Law Offices of Mark Litwak, P.O. Box 3226, Santa Monica, CA 90408, (310) 450-4500, fax (310) 450-9956.

I hope this guide will prove useful to you.

Mark Litwak
January, 1994

CHAPTER 1

INTRODUCTION

Before delving into the details of dealmaking, it is important for the reader to understand the context in which deals are made and the motivation of the players. Shrewd dealmakers know how to structure a deal to meet the needs, often unexpressed, of all the parties.

The following section provides background information on the social, legal and technological forces that have influenced, and continue to influence, the industry. Readers can gain additional insight by reading the books in the recommended reading list in the Appendix.

THE AMERICAN FILM INDUSTRY

The United States motion picture and television industry is a uniquely successful enterprise. In those countries that allow American films to be freely exhibited, they usually dominate the marketplace. Hollywood's films succeed in the world to an extent unrivaled by other American products. In 1992, they earned total export revenues of $7.7 billion and brought the United States a net trade surplus of $4 billion.[1]

---

[1] According to the Motion Picture of America Association (MPAA).

Yet the industry is extremely volatile, risky and beset with problems. Managements frequently change, profits are erratic, and smaller production and distribution companies regularly go bust. A typical major studio movie now costs about $29 million to produce and another $11 million to market. Many movies are expensive flops. Most television pilot programs don't become series or recoup their production costs.

Every year American distributors release more than 400 feature films.[1] Major studios only distribute about 150 of those films, yet earn more than 90% of all box office revenues. Upon further examination, one discovers that a relative handful of movies earn most of the revenues. In 1992, there were only thirty-six motion pictures with rentals[2] of $20 million or more. Of any ten major theatrical films produced, on the average, six or seven are unprofitable,[3] and one will break even, according to Harold Vogel, entertainment analyst for Merrill Lynch and Co. Thus while Hollywood dominates the world market with its product, it is hardly an efficient producer of popular entertainment.

THE MOVIE INDUSTRY THEN AND NOW

The movie industry was founded by European immigrants. They were an unsophisticated and uneducated lot. Adolph Zukor, the builder of Paramount, was a furrier from Hungary. Universal's Carl Laemmle was a clothing-store manager from Germany. These pioneers were modestly successful small businessmen who decided to invest their capital in a fledgling industry.

Business barons of the era expressed little interest in the movie industry. The public's fascination with the medium was considered a fad and the enterprise deemed risky. Besides, movies were entertainment for the unwashed masses, not for educated individuals who patronized plays and operas.

---

[1] For 1992 there was a total of 431 new releases, with 141 pictures released by the seven major studios.

[2] Rentals are the amount of money paid by the exhibitor to the distributor. Rentals are roughly half of box office gross revenues.

[3] However, most films earn substantial additional revenue from ancillary markets such as home video and cable television.

Los Angeles became the center of the industry because labor was cheap, the weather good and the location far from the Edison Company and the Motion Picture Patents Company which controlled the patents for moviemaking. These companies contended that producers who made movies without their permission were outlaws operating illegally.

The founders of the industry became known as the "moguls." While they had a great love of movies, they were foremost tough businessmen out to make a buck. They made some high-quality pictures but mostly churned out grade-B movies like *Son of Dracula* and *Abbott and Costello Meet Frankenstein*. Fox's biggest moneymaker was Shirley Temple. Rin Tin Tin kept Warner Bros. afloat.

Unabashed tyrants, the moguls ran their studios with an iron hand. They would change the names of their stars, tell them what their next movie would be, and loan them to one another like chattel. One year David Selznick made $425,000 lending out Ingrid Bergman—she received $60,000. Anyone who dared object would be suspended without pay, and no other studio would employ them.

Many of the abuses the moguls were famous for no longer exist in Hollywood. The mogul's practice of seducing actresses on "casting couches" is not acceptable behavior in the more corporate atmosphere that now prevails.[1] Writers, directors and stars are no longer indentured servants working under long-term contracts. They have unions, agents and attorneys to protect their interests.

Nowadays the studios are run by college-educated men and women, many of whom have MBAs or law degrees. Generally bright, hard-working and liberal-minded, they try to make decisions rationally and have invested in state-of-the-art technology that has vastly improved picture quality. They have many types of market research to help them, and they promote films with sophisticated ads, merchandising tie-ins and slick music videos.

But observers note that today's movies are not any better—artistically or commercially—than those produced by the mo-

---

[1] Of course, there is plenty of sexual activity in the industry and numerous instances of sexual harassment in the workplace.

guls. In 1988, despite a record-high domestic gross of $4.46 billion, the theatrical box office rentals from all the MPAA companies were $1.5 billion less than the total cost of making those films. Were it not for the large revenues from ancillary and foreign markets, Hollywood would have gone belly up.[1]

THE END OF THE STUDIO SYSTEM

The motion picture industry has undergone a remarkable transformation over the past forty years. Major changes began in 1948 when the United States Supreme Court upheld the Justice Department's anti-trust suit against the studios, which divested the studios of their theater chains. In the early 1950s a fierce new competitor, television, came on the scene, drastically reducing attendance at movies. This, in turn, reduced the level of studio production and ultimately led to the end of long-term contracts and the studio system.

Eventually the studios began producing for television. They diversified into related areas such as amusement parks and music recording. Cable television and home video created new markets for films and additional sources of revenue. The studios became conglomerates or were acquired by conglomerates. Recently several studios were purchased by foreign investors.

There has also been a sea change in the attitude of the captains of industry. The moguls, for all their failings, were entrepreneurs. They built an industry based on gut instinct— perhaps because they lacked market research, but also because they were inclined to take chances.

"The great gamblers are dead," Steven Spielberg commented several years ago, "and I think that's the tragedy of Hollywood today. In the old days, the Thalbergs and the Zanucks and the Mayers came out of nickelodeon vaudeville, they came out of borscht-belt theater, and they came with a great deal of showmanship and esprit de corps to a little citrus grove in California [Los Angeles]. They were brave. They were gamblers. They were high rollers.

"There is a paranoia today. People are afraid. People in high

---
[1] *Daily Variety*, February 15, 1989.

positions are unable to say 'okay' or 'not okay,' they're afraid to take the big gamble. They're looking for the odds-on-favorite. And that's very very hard when you're making movies. All motion pictures are a gamble. Anything having to do with creating something that nobody's seen before, and showing it, and counting on ten or twenty million people, individuals, to go into the theater to make or break that film—that's a gamble. And I just think in the old days, in the golden age of Hollywood, gambling was just taken for granted. Today gambling is a no-no. And I'm sorry to see that go."[1]

The primary drive of many studio executives, as with businesspeople in much of corporate America, is risk avoidance. They try to make films they can justify to their boards of directors. If they develop a story similar to a recent hit and attach a successful director and a couple of stars, they will have an impressive-looking package with some "insurance." Should the picture flop, they can exclaim, "Look, I got you Kevin Costner in a project like *E.T.*, directed by the guy who made *Top Gun*." And the board of directors will be sympathetic, chalk up the loss to a fickle public, and the executive is less likely to be fired.

The desire of executives to play it safe has induced them to devise complex schemes to reduce the financial risks of moviemaking. By entering pre-sale agreements with cable and home-video companies, or by cutting deals with outside investors, a studio can eliminate much risk.

Perhaps that is why the most-prized executives are often the top dealmakers. When these executives go beyond business and financial matters, however, interjecting themselves into the creative process, problems can arise because they lack filmmaking knowledge and training. Most executives today have little hands-on filmmaking experience.

It is important to bear in mind that, in spite of the financial acumen of contemporary executives, today's studios are no more profitable than in the days of the studio system. Because the studios compete so heavily for the services of a small pool of stars and big-name directors, the price of these commodities has risen dramatically. According to the Motion Picture Associa-

[1] Spielberg quote: Michael Ventura, "Spielberg on Spielberg," *L.A. Weekly*, December 9-15, 1983, p. 12.

tion of America (MPAA), between 1972 and 1981 the cost of films distributed by major studios rose at a compound annual rate of 21.5%. From 1980 to 1987 the average cost rose by 113.7%, or $10.7 million per film. From 1987 to 1992 costs rose another 44%.

A UNIQUE PRODUCT

Hollywood suffers from many of the same problems that plague other American industries. Professional managers have taken the reins of control. They are better-educated than their predecessors but often lack their entrepreneurial zeal and willingness to take risks.

Entrepreneurs who start businesses often don't have the desire or management skills to run a large organization. Inventors, like Stephen Wozniak, may find it more satisfying to tinker in their garages and invent new products than attend board-of-directors meetings and manage a large bureaucracy. While these entrepreneurs may function well as lone operators or in small groups, when called upon to supervise large enterprises their shortcomings can prevent the organization from prospering. So the entrepreneurs stand aside—or are shoved aside—and the managers take over.

But the movie and television industry is different from other industries. The commodity being sold is creativity. Movies don't lend themselves easily to assembly-line manufacturing. It's not like making soap, where once you devise the right formula you can churn out the same product time and again. A consumer who finds a brand of soap he likes may stick with it for a long time. He doesn't want the tenth bar to be any different from the first. He doesn't expect the product to entertain him or provide a new experience.

But people don't find one movie they like and watch it repeatedly. Moviegoers always want something different. They want to be taken where they haven't been before. They want fresh situations, plots and characters—not a rehash of last week's hit.

Consequently, the movies that do best are often those that are distinctly original. *Star Wars* was a breakthrough film because of its wonderful special effects, unusual setting and fresh characters. Moviegoers had never seen anything like it before.

Unfortunately, the atmosphere prevalent at many major studios today is not conducive to creative filmmaking because executives are so risk adverse. United Artists and Universal rejected *Star Wars* before Alan Ladd Jr. at Twentieth Century-Fox decided to back it. Often filmmakers can't find a single executive willing to gamble on anything that is offbeat or unusual. It took director Oliver Stone ten years to produce *Platoon*, and then he succeeded only because an independent company provided the financing.

Many intelligent, provocative and innovative movies—like *The Crying Game, Roger and Me, Sex, Lies and Videotape, Hollywood Shuffle, Kiss of the Spider Woman,* and *Blood Simple*—have been made with independent financing. Some of these independently-made pictures are enormously profitable, such as *Rocky* and *Platoon*, and many have received Academy Award nominations for Best Picture. Such critically-acclaimed films as *The Mission, A Room with a View, Amadeus, The Killing Fields, A Passage to India, Chariots of Fire,* and *Gandhi* were made outside Hollywood. The public is generally unaware of how many of the best movies are only distributed by a major studio.

Due to the risk-adverse climate in Hollywood, a common failing of studio movies today is that they are derivative of other movies. *Flashdance* spawns *Footloose. Animal House* is reworked into *Meatballs* and *Police Academy*. Any movie that is the least bit profitable is the basis for one or more sequels. The studios try to squeeze as much as possible from every successful property they own.

COPING WITH RISK

Because of their aversion to risk, the studios have largely withdrawn from producing films in house. While many maintain production lots, which are rented to anyone needing a soundstage, the studios essentially function as specialized banks, lending money to produce worthy projects and then distributing the finished product.

Like banks, they evaluate proposals submitted to them but rarely initiate projects. After borrowing money from large banks or obtaining investment funds, the studios decide which producers to back. The producer and director make the movie, with oversight by the studio concerned about protecting its investment. Once the picture is complete, the studio markets it, creating an advertising campaign and duplicating and distributing prints. Finally, the studio uses its clout to collect receipts from exhibitors.

There are some exceptions to this modus operandi. At Disney and some independent production entities like Castle Rock Entertainment and Imagine Entertainment, the executives who run the company are more involved in creating product.

But most studios are run by dealmaking, not filmmakers. Many executives rise to the top based on their relationships with big-name talent and their dealmaking prowess, not because of their understanding of what makes a good script or of their filmmaking ability.

Other problems have arisen because the studios have relinquished much of their creative authority. Increasingly, executives make decisions based on market research, demographic trends and minimizing financial risks. It has become much more of a lawyer-agent game, with less showmanship, according to producer Martin Ranshohoff (*The Jagged Edge*). "Picture-making itself had a better shot under the old moguls. They were basically movie guys. Not conglomerate or bank-endorsed people."

The old studio staff producers have been replaced by creative-affairs executives. "They function as staff producers but without the public shame and responsibility that comes from having your name on the picture," says industry analyst A. D. Murphy. "They exercise authority but remain anonymous. And when you have a lot of faceless people who are not out there naked next to their films, you have a lot of copping out and log rolling."

Large talent agencies like CAA and William Morris exercise considerable influence in developing and packaging projects. Agents conceive ideas for movies, discover new talent and decide which writers, directors and stars shall work together in the packages they create. In the old days, the studios performed these creative tasks.

MANAGING A CREATIVE ENTERPRISE

In many ways the atmosphere for creative moviemaking was better during the era of the moguls. More than fifty million Americans went to the theater every week in the days before television. Admissions reached an all-time high of four billion in 1946.[1] Because films cost less and there was no competition from television, videogames and the like, even mediocre films stood a better chance of making a profit. Since the moguls owned the studios they ran, they were more secure in their positions and could afford to take more risks—if a picture flopped, it might hurt their pocketbook but they wouldn't lose their job.

Some studios have belatedly realized the importance of creativity in moviemaking. Burned by expensive star-studded flops based on agency packages, these studios have hired executives who can play a more creative role in filmmaking.

In 1984, after *Rhinestone* (starring Sylvester Stallone and Dolly Parton) bombed, Twentieth Century-Fox fired Alan Hirschfield and Joe Wizan and hired Barry Diller. Diller was head of the much-vaunted Paramount team (Diller/Eisner/Katzenberg/Mancuso) that insisted on developing projects itself rather than accepting agency packages. Disney also lured two other members of that Paramount team, Michael Eisner and Jeff Katzenberg, to replace the more business-oriented Ron Miller.[2]

In each of these instances, studios replaced executives with backgrounds in finance and dealmaking with people known for their creative abilities. This may be a new trend, with studio boards of directors no longer willing to hire agents and lawyers to run the shop.

---

[1] With the advent of television the numbers dropped to one billion where they have remained relatively steady.

[2] Disney has generally avoided big-budget star packages, and after its release of *Dick Tracy*, which earned relatively modest returns, Katzenberg cautioned his staff to be wary of expensive star packages.

CHAPTER 2

DEALMAKING

There is more dealmaking activity in the movie business today than ever before. Late in his career director Billy Wilder complained "Today we spend 80% of the time making deals and 20% making pictures."[1] Indeed most people who work in the industry devote far more time to dealmaking than filmmaking. It wasn't always this way; in the golden age of Hollywood, when the moguls ran the industry, the emphasis was just the reverse.

Dealmaking increased with the end of the studio system. With talent no longer tied to long-term contracts, the studios dismantled their rosters of stars and stables of writers. Nowadays talent is hired on an ad-hoc, picture-by-picture basis, and as a result, many more deals need to be negotiated.

Imagine a football game where the players' employment must be renegotiated after every play. The referee blows the whistle and the agents and attorneys rush onto the field to consult with their clients and begin bargaining with management. This would change the game as we know it—perhaps at halftime the lawyers could march in precision drill teams to entertain the fans. Well, the process has not become quite that unwieldy in Hollywood, but you get the idea.

---

[1] Billy Wilder quote: *The Book of Hollywood Quotes*, compiled by Gary Herman (London/New York/Sydney/Tokyo/Cologne: Omnibus Press, 1979), p. 118.

Dealmaking has become more complex as well. Methods of financing films have multiplied. Under the old studio system, films were funded from current revenues or bank loans. The studios didn't rely on intricate Wall Street investment schemes, pre-sale deals or foreign co-productions.

Other complications have arisen as new markets developed. Today deals must take account of revenue from cable television, home video, syndication, network sales, merchandising, soundtrack albums and foreign sales. As studios began to share "profits" with talent, other problems arose. Studios and profit participants often disagreed on accounting methods and interpretation of contracts. To avoid ambiguity, net profit's definitions grew. One studio attaches an eighteen-page, single-spaced definition of the term.

Because of these industry changes, an understanding of dealmaking has become vital for anyone interested in filmmaking. It is always important to remember, however, that the final product is the film. In the heat of negotiations, parties may forget that audiences don't care about the deal. Can you imagine moviegoers watching deal memos projected on the screen as they exclaim: "Wow, look at deal point five" or "Isn't that an interesting definition of gross?" No, the viewer only cares about the story. Since a good deal does not necessarily produce a good movie, attorneys and agents must take care not to put their clients into projects that stand little chance of success because the deals didn't leave enough money to produce a good film.

DISINCENTIVES TO GOOD FILMMAKING

The Pay-or-Play Clause

Dealmakers need to be aware of disincentives to good moviemaking. Certain deals can encourage bad moviemaking. For example, a pay-or-play deal may induce a studio to produce a poorly written screenplay.

A pay-or-play provision is often demanded by actors and directors in return for their commitment to participate in a project. Essentially, the deal guarantees talent their salary even if the movie ultimately does not get made. The desire for such a deal is reasonable for sought-after talent, although it may put a producer or studio in a bind. To understand the dynamics of such a deal, let us consider a hypothetical scenario:

You are a filmmaker with an idea for a movie. You want Barbra Streisand to star in your picture. Somehow you gain access to her, tell her the idea and she responds favorably. She will not, however, commit to the project based on a mere idea. No star in their right mind would commit to a film at this stage. So Barbra tells you that if you can produce an acceptable script, she would love to star in your film.

You write a script, or hire a writer to create one, and after several rewrites incorporating Barbra's suggestions, she is satisfied with the screenplay and decides she wants to be in the film. You ask her to commit to the project. She, or her agent, wants to know if this film is really going to happen. She does not want to block out three months of her summer schedule and hold herself available to make your film if it is not a sure thing.

Once Barbra commits contractually to star in your movie, she must turn down other projects that may be offered to her that will shoot at the same time. She knows that there are many reasons why, despite your great efforts and talent, you may not succeed in getting the script produced. Perhaps you can't secure financing, or obtain the right co-star, or attract a studio-acceptable director. So her agent tells you that she will not commit to the project until you have all the other elements in place. The problem is the other elements feel the same way. No one wants to commit first.

To obtain talent commitments, a pay-or-play clause, guaranteeing the talent's salary, may be needed. If the salary is large, this can be a very risky commitment to make. Suppose you are an executive who has made such a deal with a star and you cannot surmount all the obstacles to production. In the realm of feature films, perhaps one out of ten projects that are developed get produced.[1] So as your start date rapidly approaches, you become increasingly agitated. You are faced with a terrible

---

[1] For television movies, a much larger percentage of projects that are developed ultimately get produced.

dilemma: Do you go forward and produce the project under less-than-ideal circumstances or should you write off the pay-or-play commitment?

This is exactly what happened with *Villa Rides*. The studio was committed to pay Yul Brynner and Robert Mitchum regardless of whether the film was made. Let's suppose that the studio was on the hook for $1 million on pay-or-play deals, and it would cost another million to make the film. In such a case it might make sense financially, if not artistically, to go forward in the hope that the movie could recoup its budget before bad word-of-mouth killed it. On the other hand, if you scrap the project, you can't possibly recoup your investment. You may also find it difficult to explain to your board of directors why you spent $1 million of their money and have nothing to show for it.

Have you ever wondered as you watched a terrible movie: "How could a studio produce this piece of dreck? Couldn't the executives discern from the script that this story was flawed? Are these executives brain-dead?" Well, the answer may be that the executives knew full well that the project was third-rate, but it may have made financial sense to go forward.

Another disincentive to good filmmaking occurs when agents push clients into making movies they shouldn't. Sometimes agents are more interested in earning their 10% commission than in furthering the client's long-range career goals. After all, if a client is making $2 million a picture, an agent has a powerful incentive to keep her working. The attitude of some agents is to grab as much as you can when the client is hot, because who knows if you will be representing her two years from now.

Overall Development Deals

Producers who enter overall development deals with studios sometimes have an incentive to make their films at other studios.

There are several types of overall development deals, including EXCLUSIVE, FIRST LOOK and HOUSEKEEPING deals.

Studios enter overall development deals with producers to ensure a steady flow of product. Keeping the pipeline full satisfies exhibitors and helps the studio amortize certain fixed overhead expenses, such as the cost of the marketing staff.

Producers benefit in several ways from overall development deals. The producer often receives an office on the studio lot, a secretary and perhaps a development person or two. The studio agrees to pay for development expenses, such as hiring writers to develop the producer's projects. Also, the studio pays the producer a fee for every project produced, and often provides an advance.

For a top producer, the advance may be hundreds of thousands of dollars per year. The money is paid out in monthly or weekly installments like a salary and is non-recoupable—it doesn't have to be repaid, even if the producer doesn't produce anything. Essentially, the overall development deal takes the financial risk of producing off a producer's shoulders and places it with the studio.

When a producer enters an EXCLUSIVE development deal, he agrees to distribute all his projects through one studio. He may be exclusive for features or television or both, but whatever the parameters, the producer is essentially a hostage of that studio and cannot produce his projects elsewhere.

A FIRST-LOOK deal, on the other hand, simply gives the studio first look, or first crack, at the producer's projects. If the studio passes on a project, the producer can develop it elsewhere. Most deals allow the studio several weeks to decide if they want a project, and if no decision is made, the producer automatically has the right to take it to another studio.

A HOUSEKEEPING DEAL is one in which the producer receives an office and development expenses but no advance. Typically this deal is offered to novice producers. The studio wants to have an ongoing relationship without incurring a lot of expense. The producer gets to set up housekeeping on the studio lot and cover his overhead expenses. The producer may gain credibility within the industry by being able to use the studio stationery and switchboard. Agents promptly return his phone calls, the producer can network with others on the lot, and most importantly, he can take his parents to the commissary when they visit.

Obviously, producers prefer first-look deals. The producer

likes to have alternative sources of financing and distribution available. Savvy producers also know that a first-look deal gives one leverage within the studio decision-making bureaucracy. You can force the studio to make up its mind on a project or risk losing it. On the other hand, if you have an exclusive deal, the studio knows you can't take a project elsewhere, and consequently there may be no urgency to make a decision.

Studios prefer exclusive deals. They will argue that since they are paying an advance and overhead expenses, it is only fair that the producer spend her time developing projects for the studio and not for others. Another reason studio executives prefer exclusive deals is to avoid the embarassment of passing on a project on a first-look basis and later see it become a blockbuster hit for another studio. In such a case, the studio's board of directors may ask the executive, "Isn't Producer X one of ours?" And, "Why is X making films for our competitor while we pay his expenses?" The chagrined executive may be forced to admit that he foolishly passed on a hit project.

The problem with overall development deals is that they create disincentives. Let's say a producer has entered such a deal with studio A. It's a three-year deal and the producer receives a $100,000 advance each year, paid out in monthly installments. This advance is against producer fees of $400,000 per picture.

After one year, the producer is about to produce his first project. Thus he is entitled to a fee of $400,000, less the $100,000 advance, or $300,000. However, if the project goes into turnaround,[1] the producer could obtain a larger producer fee from studio B, which hasn't invested anything in the film's development or the producer. Thus the producer has a financial incentive to produce his film at a studio other than his home base.

Most producers realize that a bird in the hand is worth ten in the bush, and they would not purposely sabotage a deal in the hope of earning more elsewhere. But, this has been known to happen.

---

[1] A turnaround clause gives the producer the option of taking the project to a second studio if the first shelves it. The right to take the project elsewhere is often predicated on reimbursing the first studio its development expenses.

TYPES OF CONTRACTS

Contracts can be either WRITTEN or ORAL. Contrary to popular belief, oral contracts may be valid and binding. Most states have a law, known as the Statute of Frauds,[1] requiring that certain kinds of agreements be in writing to be valid. For example, you cannot transfer real estate orally. Other kinds of agreements may be made orally, but oral contracts can be difficult to enforce.

Let's assume you made an oral agreement with a buyer to sell your car for $3,000. You shake hands on the deal but don't put anything in writing. One month later there is a dispute and you eventually end up in small claims court.

The buyer informs the judge that you offered to sell him your car. You agree. The buyer then claims you promised to tune up the car before delivery. You disagree. There are no documents or witnesses or evidence that the judge can review to figure out the terms of the agreement. In this situation, whom should the judge believe? The judge may simply throw up her hands and refuse to enforce the contract because she cannot ascertain its terms.

So while the law does not require that all contracts be in writing, it is usually advantageous to have something in writing, if only for the sake of creating evidence. Otherwise, you risk ending up with an unenforceable deal.

Another way to classify contracts is as EXPRESS or IMPLIED contracts. When parties make an express contract, it is explicit that they are making an agreement. Typically, they sign a piece of paper or shake hands.

An implied contract is a contract implied from facts or from the law. It may be implied from the behavior of the parties. Let's suppose that you enter a store and pick up a candy bar. Without saying a word to anyone, you remove the wrapper and begin eating it. Then you head for the door. The proprietor says, "Hey, wait a minute, you didn't pay for the candy bar." You reply, "I never agreed to pay for it." Under these circumstances, a court would imply that an agreement exists, based on your conduct. It is understood that when a person consumes a candy

---

[1] See e.g. California Civil Code § 1624.

bar under these circumstances, he has agreed to buy it.

Sometimes implied contracts are not based on behavior but are implied by law in the name of equity and fairness, or to prevent the unjust enrichment of one party at the expense of another.

CONTRACT LAW AS A REMEDY FOR STORY THEFT

The law of oral and implied contracts can provide the basis for a successful lawsuit for story theft. A basic tenet of copyright law is that ideas are not copyrightable because they are not considered an "expression of an author." As courts sometimes observe, "Ideas are as free as the air." Similarly, concepts, themes and titles are not protected by copyright law.

A copyright does protect embellishments upon ideas, however. So while a single word cannot be copyrighted, the particular manner in which a writer organizes words—his craft, his approach—is protected. While other writers remain free to create their own work based on the same topic, theme or idea, they cannot copy the particular expression of any other writer.

Since one cannot protect an idea under copyright law, a writer who pitches a story idea to another is vulnerable to theft. But there is another way to protect ideas. Ideas can be the subject of a contract. A writer can protect himself by getting the recipient of the idea to agree to pay for it.

The best way for the writer to protect himself would be to use a written agreement. However, it may be awkward to begin a meeting by asking a producer to sign a contract, even a short one. Such a request might offend some producers or make them uncomfortable. They might worry about liability and might want to consult a lawyer. Since writers often have difficulty getting in the door to see powerful producers, asking for a written agreement may not be practicable.

A less-threatening approach would be to make an oral agreement. The writer begins the meeting by simply saying: "Before I tell you my idea, I want to make sure you understand that I am telling you this idea with the understanding that if you decide to use it, I expect to receive reasonable compensation." The producer most likely will nod his head yes, or say, "Of course," in which case you have a deal. If the producer indicates he does not agree to these terms, don't pitch your story and leave.

Since this contract is oral, there might be a problem proving its existence and terms. That is why it's a good idea to have a witness or some documentation. You could bring a co-writer, agent or associate along to the meeting, and you could send a letter after the meeting to the producer reiterating your understanding. The letter should be cordial and non-threatening. You could write: "It was really a pleasure meeting with you to discuss my story about. . . . As we agreed, if you decide to exploit this material, I will receive reasonable compensation." If the terms set forth in your letter are not disavowed by the recipient, the letter could be used as evidence of your agreement.[1]

But what if the producer listening to your pitch doesn't steal your story but repeats it to another producer who uses it? You can protect yourself against this peril by saying: "I am telling you my idea with the understanding that you will keep it confidential and will not tell it to anyone else without my permission." If the producer nods his head okay or says yes, you have a deal, and you can sue if he breaches his promise.

The following case illustrates how contract law has been applied in a story-theft dispute.

DESNY V. WILDER (1956)[2]

FACTS: In 1949, P (plaintiff) telephoned Billy Wilder's office on the Paramount lot and spoke to his secretary, saying that he wished to see Wilder. She insisted that P explain his purpose. P told her about a story based on the life of a boy, Floyd Collins, who had been trapped in a cave. The incident had been the subject of widespread news coverage for several weeks back in the 1920s.

The secretary liked the story, but when she learned of its length (sixty-five pages), she said that Wilder would not read it. She offered to send the story to the script

---

[1] Since the letter has not been signed by the producer, his agreement to the terms is merely implied if he does not object. Of course, if the writer has a letter from the producer confirming these terms, that would be much better evidence.

[2] 46 Cal. 2d 715, 299 P.2d 257 (1956).

department to be put in synopsis form. P said that he preferred to condense it himself. He did so and called back two days later. The secretary asked him to read her a three-page outline over the phone, and he did so. She took the story down shorthand and said she would discuss it with Wilder. P then told her that he expected to be paid for the story if Wilder used it.

Later P discovers that Paramount has made a movie about the boy, including a fictionalized incident that P created. P sues.

ISSUES: Can P sue for the theft of a story based on a true story in the public domain?

Does it matter that P never directly spoke or met with Wilder or Paramount?

Can there be an implied contract between the parties?

Can P recover even though he didn't ask for compensation until the second conversation?

HOLDING: P prevails.

RATIONALE: Literary property can be created out of historical events in the public domain. Paramount had the right to go back to the historical record and prepare its own story. P has no hold over public-domain material or the idea of doing a screenplay about this subject. But if the defendants used P's research and work, there may be an implied agreement to compensate him.

The P in this case didn't sue for copyright infringement because his story was largely a true historical incident in the public domain. Writers cannot gain rights to stories in the public domain. However, a writer can incorporate public-domain material into his own literary work, which can be copyrighted (although the public-domain material remains in the public domain).

In other words, ten different authors can draw upon public-domain material to write biographies of George Washington. Each possesses a copyright to his book, but the copyright is limited to the author's expression, his approach in arranging and organizing the facts. The author cannot prevent others from using the same facts in their work.

While the writer in the Wilder case may not be able to sue for copyright infringement, he may have a remedy under contract law. The court sent the case back to the trial level so a jury could decide if Paramount relied on P's synopsis in making the film. In other words, the court held that an implied contract could exist. A contract could be implied from the conversations between the writer and the secretary. Ultimately, a jury upon retrial would decide if the facts show that such an agreement did exist.

While P never spoke to Wilder or any Paramount executives, he could still successfully sue them. The secretary was considered an agent of Wilder and Paramount to the extent that she acted within the scope of her duties. A secretary has the authority to accept stories and manuscripts for her employer. If she had made commitments beyond her authority ("I'll give you a two-picture deal"), they would not be binding on Wilder or Paramount.

Nevertheless, how could there be a contract when the writer didn't ask to get paid until the end of the second conversation? Didn't the writer give the idea away and then ask to be paid for it?

No, said the court. The two conversations should be construed as one. Courts sometimes bend over backwards to help victims.

What should you remember from *Desney v. Wilder*? Although you don't have a written agreement, you may have a legal remedy. Now, consider the following case:

BLAUSTEIN V. BURTON (1970)[1]

FACTS: Plaintiff (P), a producer, conceives the idea of producing a movie based on Shakespeare's play *The Taming of the Shrew*, starring Richard Burton and Elizabeth Taylor with Franco Zeffirelli as director. P approached the Burtons' agent about their availability and suggested he had something in mind for them. The agent said he would like to hear P's idea and P disclosed it. The agent liked the idea, and P later met with the Burtons, who said they would like to do the movie.

Later, the Burtons made the movie with Zeffirelli but without P's participation. P sues, alleging that the circum-

---

[1] 9 Cal. App.3d 161, 88 Cal. Rptr. 319 (1970).

stances surrounding the disclosure of his idea were such as would imply a contract.

ISSUE: Can a contract be implied under these circumstances?

HOLDING: Yes, P wins. Case remanded to trial court to decide if the circumstances created an implied-in-fact contract.

Here the P didn't have a story idea; he just had some casting ideas and a suggestion for director. Shakespeare's story is in the public domain, and the Burtons have just as much right to it as P. Moreover, there was never an explicit agreement among the parties that P would get to produce the project. P didn't tell the agent: "I'll disclose my idea if you agree that I can produce the project."

The producer contends that such an understanding is implied from the fact that he is a veteran producer contacting an agent for the Burtons. The court agrees that such an agreement could exist, implied from the behavior of the parties.

But what if P wasn't a veteran producer? Suppose a carpenter on the checkout line at the supermarket sees a picture of Cher on the cover of *The National Enquirer.* She writes Cher a fan letter suggesting that Cher star in a movie version of *Hamlet.* Cher reads the letter, thinks this is a wonderful idea and makes the movie. Now the carpenter contacts Cher and says, "Remember me? I sent you the idea for the *Hamlet* movie. I want compensation, a producer credit and a piece of the profits."

Is Cher obligated to pay? No, the circumstances are different. There are no facts to suggest that the carpenter submitted the idea with a reasonable expectation of receiving anything in return. It appears she was making a gift. Similarly, if a veteran producer at a social function casually mentions to Elizabeth Taylor that she would be wonderful in *Taming of the Shrew,* no obligation would arise.

In summary, if you think someone has ripped you off, don't assume you are without a legal remedy. Consult an attorney.

Let us now turn to an examination of some industry contracts.

TYPES OF DEALS

Option Contracts

Option contracts are not unique to the movie and television industry. For many enterprises they provide a useful way for parties to share risk.

Perhaps you have heard friends in the industry talk about "optioning a book" to be made into a movie. When you take an option on a literary property, you are buying the exclusive right to purchase the movie rights in the future.

Suppose you are a producer and you read a wonderful novel written by Alex. You would like to make a movie based on this book. Since a movie based on the book is considered a derivative work, and since Alex owns the copyright to his book, you cannot make a movie without his permission.

You approach Alex and offer to buy the movie rights. He, or his agent, says, "Fine, we would like $50,000 for the rights." You cannot afford to pay $50,000 at this time. Even if you could afford the expense, it would be very risky to buy the movie rights outright. What if you couldn't get a good screenplay written? Or get the right director? Or obtain financing for the film? There are many obstacles to getting a movie produced, and if you buy the movie rights to Alex's book and cannot get the movie made, you have bought something you ultimately don't need.

A better way for you to approach the situation would be to offer a different kind of deal to Alex. Instead of buying the movie rights outright, you offer to take an option to purchase them.

Let's say you offer Alex $5,000 for a one-year option. During that one-year period you have the exclusive right to EXERCISE the option and buy the movie rights. Let's also suppose that the purchase price is $50,000. As a rule of thumb, options are often 10% of the full purchase price, but the amount is negotiable. Sometimes sellers are willing to give a "free" option or an option for a nominal sum (e.g., "for ten dollars"). Of course, a seller is not required to option his movie rights, and if you are dealing with the author of a best seller, he may refuse to sell an option and insist on an outright sale.

The option period can be any length of time but the initial option period is often a year. The buyer may seek certain RIGHTS OF RENEWAL, which allows him to extend the option upon payment of an additional sum. Let's suppose that you have taken a one-year option for $5,000 and have a right of renewal to extend the option for a second year for $6,000. The right of renewal must be exercised before the initial option period expires. The parties could agree to second and/or third renewal periods to allow the buyer to extend the option further.

Renewals let the purchaser extend an option without exercising it. Assume Alex has sold you a one-year option that is about to expire. You have commissioned a screenplay, which you are pleased with, and you have the interest of an important director. But you don't have a star attached to your project and your financing is not in place. At this time, you don't want to buy Alex's movie rights for $50,000, but you also don't want to lose the right to buy those rights in the future. If you have a right of renewal in your agreement, you can extend the option. Generally, buyers don't want to purchase movie rights until the first day of principal photography, when they know for sure that a movie will be produced.

Note that an option gives the buyer the exclusive right to purchase movie rights within the option period. No one else can buy the movie rights during that time. The seller can do nothing that would interfere with the buyer purchasing those rights during the option period.

Once the option expires, however, the writer retains not only the option money but all movie rights as well. Some writers have repeatedly sold options on the same property because the earlier options were never exercised. Of course, once the option is exercised, the buyer owns the movie rights outright, and the writer can't sell or option what he no longer owns.

The option payments, and any payments for rights of renewals, can be APPLICABLE or NON-APPLICABLE. If the payments are applicable, they count as an advance against the purchase price. If they are non-applicable, they do not apply against the purchase price. For example, if an option was for $5,000 applicable against a purchase price of $50,000, a buyer wanting to exercise the option would pay $45,000 to the writer. If the

$5,000 option was non-applicable, the buyer would pay $50,000 because the $5,000 option payment would not count against the purchase price.

The most important point to remember when taking (purchasing) an option is that you must simultaneously negotiate the terms of the purchase agreement. Usually the option contract is a two- or three-page document with a literary purchase agreement attached as an exhibit. When the option is exercised, the literary purchase agreement automatically kicks in. A buyer who enters an option agreement without negotiating the underlying literary purchase agreement has purchased a WORTHLESS OPTION. All you have bought is the right to haggle with the buyer should you choose to buy the movie rights. The buyer is under no obligation to sell on the terms you propose.

For example, you purchase an option for $500 for one year but don't work out the terms of the literary purchase agreement. Nine months later you decide to exercise the option and buy the movie rights. You send a check for $10,000 to the writer, but she objects. She wants $20,000. Since the parties have not agreed to this essential term of the sale, the contract is unenforceable. You have a worthless option, and the time and money you spent developing the project may be wasted. The writer now has you over the barrel and can demand any amount she wants for the rights.

Step Deals

Producers often use step deals to hire writers. Suppose you are a producer interested in hiring Marcia, a novice writer. You have read a wonderful action/adventure script that she wrote, and now you want her to write a comedy. Since you're a Writer's Guild signatory, you must pay Marcia Writer's Guild scale, about $57,000.[1] However, you are not entirely confident that Marcia can produce an acceptable script because she has no experience in this genre. You want to reduce your financial risk. One way is to hire her on a step deal.

---

[1] The MBA flat deal for a non-original screenplay, including treatment, is $57,084 for a high-budget film for the period of 5/2/92 to 5/1/93.

A step deal proceeds, step by step, with the producer having the option after each step to stop the writer's services. For the first step you agree to pay Marcia $20,000 to write a treatment. If you like the treatment, you pay her an additional sum to go to the second step and write a first draft. If you like the first draft, you can take additional steps for rewrites and polishes. The Writer's Guilds sets minimums for each step, and the total paid to her will be at least the minimum she would receive if you had hired her to write a completed script from the outset.

The step deal allows the producer to bail out of his commitment to the writer early. If upon completion of the treatment the producer has lost confidence in the writer or isn't happy with the direction the story has taken, he is not obligated to continue employing the writer. As the owner of all the work created by the writer, the producer can shelve the project or bring in a new writer. The writer retains the payments received for the work completed.

In a step deal, the producer has "reading periods," usually a couple of weeks, in which to decide whether to go to the next step. When a producer decides not to go onto the next step, or fails to make a decision within the reading period, the writer is free to accept other work. This prevents the producer from endlessly stringing along the writer. During the reading period, the writer must hold herself available to continue working for the producer if he should choose to go to the next step.

Of course, top writers can decline to be hired on a step deal, and producers cannot force them to accept such a deal.

Merchandising Deals

Movie merchandising has earned studios money and promoted their movies for some time. Walt Disney made a fortune selling toys, Mickey Mouse ears and other products, not to mention the enormous revenue generated from his theme parks.

Recently, there has been a renaissance of merchandising activity. You may recall that when the movie *E.T.* was released in 1982, it contained a scene in which the friendly alien was fed some candy by a child. That candy was Reese's Pieces, and as a result of showing that candy in the film, sales shot up 65%. This bonanza delighted the makers of Reese's Pieces, but distressed the executives at M&M's who had rejected Steven Spielberg's request to use their candy. Some marketing genius figured that having an alien eating M&M's would reflect unfavorably on the product—one of the greatest marketing blunders of all time.

This incident was widely reported in the trade press, encouraging manufacturers to place their products in films. They realized that product placement in a film could be more reward-

ing than television advertising, which cost a great deal and often produces meager results.

Because of this interest, a new breed of agent arose: the product-placement agent. These agents don't represent people; they represent products. One agent might represent several non-competing products: Mars bars for candy, Dr. Pepper for soda, Coors for beer, Ford for cars, and so forth.

The product-placement agent spends her time looking for scripts in which to place products. Of course, not every placement is desirable. Coca Cola would not want their soda to be consumed by a character who then vomits and goes into convulsions. But assuming the placement is in a neutral or positive light, the manufacturer will probably be interested.

DEALMAKING TIME LINE

A. DEVELOPMENT
  A) RETAINER AGREEMENT WITH ATTORNEY AND/OR AGENT
  B) LITERARY ACQUISITION AGREEMENT
  C) WRITER EMPLOYMENT AGREEMENT

B. PRE-PRODUCTION
  A) ACTOR, DIRECTOR AND CREW EMPLOYMENT AGREEMENTS
  B) COMPLETION BOND AGREEMENT
  C) ERRORS & OMISSIONS INSURANCE [1]
  D) WORKER'S COMPENSATION, NEGATIVE FILM AND OTHER INSURANCE
  E) LOCATION RELEASES AND PERMITS
  F) SIGNATORY AGREEMENTS WITH UNION AND GUILDS
  G) FINANCING AND PRODUCING AGREEMENTS

C. POST-PRODUCTION
  A) DISTRIBUTION AGREEMENT, IF NOT ALREADY OBTAINED.
  B) MUSIC PERMISSIONS
  C) FILM AND TAPE CLIP PERMISSIONS
  B) DISTRIBUTOR/EXHIBITOR AGREEMENTS

[1] Errors and Omissions Insurance covers the insured against judgments, costs and attorneys' fees incurred as a result of a successful or unsuccessful suit involving defamation, invasion of privacy and copyright infringment. It does not cover breach of contract.

The law does not always require a release to show a product in a film. Assuming you don't disparage the product, it is unlikely a manufacturer could successfully sue simply because its product was shown without consent.

If the product is momentarily on the screen and not identifiable, you don't need to get a release.[1] No director who shoots a scene in a supermarket is going to obtain releases for every product in the background. Still, a release never hurts, even if not legally required. Remember that your distributor and insurance carrier may want to see releases for every identifiable product.

To induce filmmakers to insert products in movies, the product-placement agent can offer several inducements:

1) Release forms: You won't have to bother writing to the manufacturer for permission.

2) Freebies: Agents will give producers cartons of candy bars, free airline tickets, a truckload of beer. These freebies can help a producer lower his production costs by eliminating the need to buy props and food. If an item is expensive, such as a car, a mink stole or fine jewelry, often the agent will lend it for the duration of the shoot.

3) Promotion: If McDonald's agrees to distribute millions of *Roger Rabbit* cups to its customers, and spend additional millions of dollars to advertise the promotion, the movie benefits from increased public awareness. For distributors, promotional campaigns are often the most alluring aspect of a product-placement deal.

4) Cash: Sometimes cash is part of a placement deal. Nabisco paid $100,000 to have its Baby Ruth candy bar displayed in *The Goonies*. The company also agreed to provide $1.5 million of network advertising and to give away free movie posters with the purchase of its candy from displays in 37,000 stores.

Usually manufacturers offer multi-million dollar cross-promotional deal and cash payments to major studio releases. How-

---

[1] You should always have a lawyer review your script before production to determine what releases may be required.

ever, they also provide freebies to independent low-budget filmmakers.

Besides product-placement deals, studios license the right to sell spin-off products to manufacturers. In most of these deals there is no risk to the studio because the licensees incur all manufacturing and distribution expenses. The studio receives an advance per product and royalty payments (often between 5% and 10% of gross revenues) from retailers (i.e. the wholesale price). If the movie flops and the products don't sell, the manufacturer absorbs the loss.

Musicals such as *Saturday Night Fever, Grease, Flashdance,* and *Dirty Dancing* can earn substantial revenues from sound-track recordings. Moreover, a hit song can effectively promote a film. Similarly, music videos have become important marketing tools.

Keep in mind that few films lend themselves to extensive merchandising. Movies that can spin off toys, posters and similar items have the greatest potential. But with a film like *Falling in Love,* starring Robert DeNiro and Meryl Streep, there are limited merchandising possibilities.

ARBITRATION

It is wise to consider adding an arbitration clause to any contract you make. Such a provision requires that disputes be resolved through binding arbitration, not litigation. Arbitration is a much quicker, more informal and less expensive method of resolving disputes than litigation. Conflicts can be settled within a matter of months, rules of evidence don't apply and costs are much less.

It is particularly important to provide for arbitration if the party you are contracting with is wealthier than you; in such a case the other party may prevail in litigation simply because it can finance a protracted court battle and you cannot. With an arbitration clause the playing field is more level.

Here are some sample arbitration clauses:

> ARBITRATION: Any controversy or claim arising out of or relating to this agreement or any breach thereof shall

be settled by arbitration according to the Rules of the American Arbitration Association; and judgment upon the award rendered by the arbitrators may be entered in any court having jurisdiction thereof. The prevailing party shall be entitled to reimbursement for costs and reasonable attorneys' fees.

ARBITRATION: This Agreement shall be interpreted and construed according to the laws of the State of New York, applicable to contracts made and entirely performed therein. The parties select the American Arbitration Association, expedited arbitration using one arbitrator, to be a disinterested attorney specializing in entertainment law, as the sole forum for the resolution of any dispute between them. The venue for arbitration shall be either New York City or Los Angeles, California, to be determined by the party who first files a demand for arbitration. The determination of the arbitrator in such proceeding shall be final, binding and non-appealable.

It is important to provide that the prevailing party shall be entitled to reimbursement for costs and reasonable attorneys' fees. Otherwise, the prevailing party usually cannot recoup these expenses.

Binding arbitration awards are difficult to overturn. There are limited grounds for appeal. If the losing party does not voluntarily comply with the arbitration award, the prevailing party can go to court to seek confirmation of the award. Once confirmed, the award is no different from a court judgment. A judgment creditor can have the sheriff seize the judgment debtor's assets to satisfy the award.

CHAPTER 3

PERMISSION TO PORTRAY PEOPLE AND PLACES

DEPICTION & LOCATION RELEASES

PURCHASING THE RIGHTS TO A PERSON'S LIFE STORY

Do you need to buy the rights?

Before you decide to purchase the rights to a person's life story, it is worth considering what you are buying. When you buy the rights to portray someone in film or television, you are buying a bundle of rights. These rights include protection from suits based on defamation, invasion of privacy and the right to publicity. You may also be buying the cooperation of the subject and his family or heirs. Perhaps you want access to diaries and letters that are not otherwise available to you.

If the subject of the life story is deceased, much of the rationale for buying these rights disappears, since defamation and invasion of privacy actions protect personal rights that do not descend to the estate.[1] In other words, people can spread lies and falsehoods about the dead, reveal their innermost secrets, and their heirs cannot sue for defamation or invasion of privacy. A writer could publish a revisionist history of George Washington, portraying our first President as a child molester and a thief, and his heirs would have no remedy. So when a subject is deceased, a producer has less need for a depiction release.

It is also important to consider whether the subject of your film is a private individual or a public official or public figure. As we will discuss later in Chapters 14 and 15, public officials and figures have opened more of their lives to public scrutiny, and consequently more of their lives can be portrayed without invading their privacy. Moreover, public officials and figures must meet a much higher burden of proof in order to establish defamation or invasion of privacy. They must prove that the defamer intentionally spread a falsehood or acted with reckless disregard of the truth.

One should also consider the possibility of fictionalizing a true story. If you change the names of the individuals involved, change the location and make other alterations so that the real-life people are not recognizable to the public, you could avoid the necessity of a depiction release.

Keep in mind, however, that the story's appeal may be predicated on the fact that it is a true story. In such a case, fictionalization is not a good alternative. Suppose you wanted to do the Jessica McClure story, describing how a Texas community rallied to the rescue of a young girl who fell down a well hole. Here you would want to bill the movie as *The Jessica McClure Story*. That is why viewers would tune in.

Terms of the Agreement

In negotiating for life-story rights, there are a number of important issues that need to be resolved. At the outset, the parties must determine the extent of the rights granted. Does the

---

[1] The right of publicity may or may not descend, depending on which state's laws apply.

grant include remakes, sequels, television series, merchandizing, novelization, live-stage rights and radio rights? Are the rights worldwide? Buyers will usually want as broad a grant as possible. The seller may insist on retaining certain rights.

The buyer must also consider other releases that may be needed. What about the subject's spouse, children, friends, etc.? Will these people consent to be portrayed? Will the subject ask his friends and relatives to cooperate? Can these secondary characters be fictionalized? If the producer is planning an ensemble piece about a basketball team, it makes no sense to sign up players one by one, hoping to get them all. A smart producer will gather the team in a room and either buy all the rights or none.

Another issue is whether the rights can be assigned to a studio or production company. If the buyer is a producer she will often need to assign such rights to a studio or network later as part of a financing/distribution agreement.

The purchase of life-story rights can be structured as either an option/purchase deal or as an outright sale, often with a reversion clause. A reversion clause would essentially provide that in the event the rights are not exploited within a certain number of years (i.e., the movie is not made), then all rights would revert to the subject. This provision protects the subject if he has sold rights to his life story to a producer who never uses them, and some time later another producer is interested in making such a film.

The agreement should recite the consideration exchanged. Consideration is a legal term of art. Consideration is that which is given in exchange for a benefit received. It is a necessary element for the existence of a contract. A contract is only binding with consideration. It is what distinguishes a contract from a gift, which may be revocable.

Consideration is usually money, but it can be anything of value. As a general principle, courts do not review the adequacy of consideration. In other words, should you be foolish enough to agree to sell your brand-new car, worth $15,000, for only $5,000, don't expect a judge to rescue you from the results of your poor judgment. Unless there was some sort of fraud or duress involved, the contract will be enforced, although it may be unfair to one party.

To ensure that a contract is binding, agreements often recite: "For ten dollars and other valuable consideration." This clause establishes that there has been an exchange of value, even if it is nominal consideration. Make sure the consideration is actually paid. It is wise to pay by check so that you will have the cancelled check as proof of payment.

There are some exceptional circumstances where courts will throw out a contract with nominal consideration if the contract is unconscionable. Mutually exhanged promises can be adequate consideration. For example, a producer's efforts to develop a project could be deemed adequate consideration for an option. But to be sure their contracts are enforceable, producers may want to pay some money for the option.

There are other ways to compensate a subject of a life story besides a flat fixed fee. You could give the subject points (percentage of net profits), consulting fees, and/or bonuses to be paid when the film is exploited in ancillary markets.

An important part of any depiction agreement is the "Warranties and Representations" clause. A warranty is a promise. The buyer will want the seller to promise never to sue for an invasion of his rights of publicity and privacy, or for defamation. The warranties must cover all fifty states and all conceivable situations. No one wants to buy a lawsuit.

There will also be a provision that gives the buyer the right to embellish, fictionalize, dramatize and adapt the life story in any way he chooses. This is a frequent sticking point in negotiations. The subject is delighted to be asked to have her story told on the silver screen, but when you present her with a depiction release she becomes concerned. She asks, "This document says you can change my story any way you like and I can't sue for defamation. How do I know you won't portray me as a monster?"

A producer may reply: "Trust me, trust me." Sometimes that will work. But the subject may respond: "I have no intention of trusting any of you charming Hollywood types. I want script approval. Write your script, and if I like it, I'll sign the release."

Can a producer give a subject script approval? No sane producer would. No producer is going to expend a lot of time and money developing a script only to find that the subject has changed her mind or is unreasonably withholding approval.

If the subject refuses to give the producer carte blanche, are any compromises possible? Yes. The subject could have approval over the treatment or selection of the writer. Perhaps the subject will figure that if she approves only a classy writer, her portrayal will be acceptable.

Alternatively, the producer could offer to make the subject a creative or technical consultant to the production. "You'll be right there by the side of the director," says the producer, "giving him advice and suggestions to ensure that everything is authentic." The producer may not mention that the director doesn't want the subject on the set and is not required to accept any suggestions.

Another possible compromise could limit the subject matter and period portrayed. Perhaps the subject is primarily concerned that an embarrassing incident in her life not be re-enacted in Panavision. The release could say that certain incidents (e.g., a divorce) are not included in the release. Or the release could cover limited periods of the subject's life (e.g., only those incidents that occurred before 1947).

Finally, the subject might have the right to determind screen notice. He could decide if the film will be billed as a true story or a dramatized account. Alternatively, he could decide whether real names are used for the characters.

The following case illustrates the problem that can arise when portraying another without a depiction release.

BETTE MIDLER V. FORD MOTOR COMPANY[1]

FACTS: Ford Motor Company and its ad agency designed a series of television commercials. Bette Midler (P) was asked to sing the song "Do You Want To Dance" for the advertisement. Midler had performed the song on her 1973 album.

When Midler declined to participate, the ad agency hired one of Midler's former backup singers to record the song, imitating Midler's voice and style. When the advertisements were run, many listeners thought the song had been sung by Midler. The ad agency obtained permission to use the song from its copyright owner but did not have Midler's consent to imitate her voice.

---

[1] *Bette Midler v. Ford Motor Company*, 849 F.2d 460 (9th Cir., 1988).

ISSUE: Does this imitation of Midler's voice infringe upon her rights?

HOLDING: Yes.

RATIONALE: The court said that when a distinctive voice of a professional singer is widely known and is deliberately imitated in order to sell a product, a tort has been committed in California. The court limited the holding to the facts, and cautioned that not every imitation of a voice to advertise merchandise is necessarily actionable.

A voice is not copyrightable because it is not fixed in a tangible medium of expression. The defendants didn't infringe

DEPICTION RELEASE *CHECKLIST*

A. WHAT ARE YOU PURCHASING?
    1. PROTECTION AGAINST A SUIT BASED ON RIGHT TO PUBLICITY.
    2. PROTECTION AGAINST A SUIT FOR INVASION OF PRIVACY.
    3. PROTECTION AGAINST A SUIT FOR DEFAMATION.
    4. COOPERATION OF SUBJECT AND HIS FAMILY.

B. WHO ARE YOU PURCHASING THE RELEASE FROM?
    1. A PRIVATE PERSON WHO HAS DONE SOMETHING NEWSWORTHY.
    2. A CELEBRITY WHO WANTS TO PROTECT HER RIGHT OF PUBLICITY.
    3. A PUBLIC PERSON (E.G., POLITICIAN) WHOSE ACTIVITIES MAY BE IN THE PUBLIC DOMAIN.

C. DO YOU NEED THE RIGHTS?
    1. CAN YOU FICTIONALIZE THE STORY?
    2. DO YOU NEED THE SUBJECT'S COOPERATION TO OBTAIN FACTS?
    3. HOW MUCH IS IN THE PUBLIC DOMAIN?
    4. IS THE SUBJECT DECEASED?

D. THE EXTENT OF RIGHTS OBTAINED.
    1. WHAT ABOUT REMAKES, SEQUELS, TELEVISION SERIES, MERCHANDISING, NOVELIZATION, LIVE-STAGE RIGHTS, RADIO RIGHTS? ARE THEY WORLDWIDE?
    2. CAN THE RIGHTS BE ASSIGNED TO A STUDIO OR PRODUCTION COMPANY?
    3. SHOULD THE RIGHTS REVERT TO THE OWNER AT SOME FUTURE TIME?

E. DEAL STRUCTURE.
    1. OPTION
    2. OUTRIGHT PURCHASE

CONTINUED

the copyright in any of Midler's recordings because her recordings were not copied. Midler's voice was not misappropriated under California Civil Code 3344 because the backup singer's voice was used, not Midler's. However, the court held Midler had a common-law (i.e., not based on a statute) right to protect her identity. Here, the impersonation was deemed to be an unlawful appropriation of her identity.

Section 3344 of the California Civil Code affords damages for appropriations of another person's "name, voice, signature, photograph or likeness" to promote a product without the subject's consent. The Midler case is interesting because it extends protection to an imitation of a voice. Thus, at least in California, this type of imitation is considered an appropriation of another's identity.

DEPICTION RELEASE *CHECKLIST*
(CONTINUED)

F. CONSIDERATION
1. OPTION MONEY
2. PURCHASE PRICE
3. OTHER FORMS OF COMPENSATION: POINTS, CONSULTING FEES, BONUSES.

G. WARRANTIES AND REPRESENTATIONS.
BROAD ALL-INCLUSIVE RELEASE OF OWNER'S RIGHTS TO PUBLICITY, INVASION OF PRIVACY AND DEFAMATION.
1. MUST COVER ALL STATES AND CONCEIVABLE SITUATIONS.
2. WARRANTIES BY OWNER OF ORIGINALITY AND TRUTH.
3. PURCHASER GIVEN RIGHT TO EMBELLISH, FICTIONALIZE, DRAMATIZE AND ADAPT STORY.

H. OTHER CHARACTERS?
1. RELEASES FROM OTHER PEOPLE WHO APPEAR IN STORY: SPOUSE, CHILDREN, FRIENDS, ETC.

I. CREATIVE APPROVAL
1. NO SCRIPT APPROVAL.
2. POSSIBLE CONCESSIONS:
   A. APPROVAL OF TREATMENT AND/OR WRITER.
   B. OWNER OF RIGHTS BECOMES CREATIVE CONSULTANT.
   C. LIMIT SUBJECT MATTER AND PERIOD PORTRAYED.
   D. OWNER TO DETERMINE SCREEN NOTICE: BASED ON A TRUE STORY OR DRAMATIZED ACCOUNT.

DEPICTION RELEASE
(Outright Grant with Reversion Clause)

CONSENT AND RELEASE[1]

To: Very Big Productions, Inc., a California Corporation

I understand that you desire to use all or parts of the events of my life in order to have one or more teleplays or screenplays written, and to produce, distribute, exhibit and exploit one or more television programs and/or motion pictures of any length in any and all media now known or hereafter devised and sound recordings in any and all media now known or hereafter devised. I have agreed to grant you certain rights in that connection. This Consent and Release confirms our agreement as follows:

1. CONSIDERATION; GRANT OF RIGHTS: In consideration of your efforts to produce my story, payment to me of $_____, upon the beginning of principal photography of a full-length feature film, and/or $_____ upon the beginning of production of a television movie, and/or $_____ upon the beginning of production of a pilot program and a royalty of $_____ for each episode, and for other valuable consideration, with full knowledge I hereby grant you, perpetually and irrevocably, the unconditional and exclusive right throughout the world to use, simulate and portray my name, likeness, voice, personality, personal identification and personal experiences, incidents, situations and events which heretofore occurred or hereafter occur (in whole or in part), based upon or taken from my life or otherwise in and in connection with motion pictures, sound recordings, publications and any and all other media of any nature whatsoever, whether now known or hereafter devised. Without limiting the generality of the foregoing, it is understood and agreed that said exclusive right includes theatrical, television, dramatic stage, radio, sound recording, music, publishing, commercial tie-up, merchandising, advertising and publicity rights in all media of every nature whatsoever, whether now known or hereafter devised.

---

[1] See page 349 for information on how to obtain the contracts in this book on computer disk.

I reserve no rights with respect to such uses. (All said rights are after this called the "Granted Rights.") It is further understood and agreed that the Granted Rights may be used in any manner and by any means, whether now known or unknown, and either factually or with such fictionalization, portrayal, impersonation, simulation and/or imitation or other modification as you, your successors and assigns, determine in your sole discretion. I further acknowledge that I am to receive no further payment with respect to any matter referred to herein. Any and all of the Granted Rights shall be freely assignable by you.

2. PAYMENT OF CONSIDERATION; REVERSION OF RIGHTS: I understand that you shall make the payments mentioned in Paragraph 1 only if you begin production of a feature film or television movie or television pilot. In the event that you do not begin such a production within three years of the date this agreement was executed, all rights granted by me under this agreement shall revert to me. I understand that if you do begin production within three years of the date this agreement was executed, all rights granted by me under this agreement shall be perpetual.

3. RELEASE: I agree hereby to release and discharge you, your employees, agents, licensees, successors and assigns from any and all claims, demands or causes of actions that I may now have or may hereafter have for libel, defamation, invasion of privacy or right of publicity, infringement of copyright or violation of any other right arising out of or relating to any utilization of the Granted Rights or based upon any failure or omission to make use thereof.

4. NAME-PSEUDONYM: You have informed me and I agree that in exercising the Granted Rights, you, if you so elect, may refrain from using my real name and may use a pseudonym that will be dissimilar to my real name, however, such agreement does not preclude you from the use of my real name should you in your sole discretion elect and that in connection with it I shall have no claim arising out of the so-called right of privacy and/or right of publicity.

5. FURTHER DOCUMENTS: I agree to execute such further documents and instruments as you may reasonably request to effectuate the terms and intentions of this Consent and Release, and in the event I fail or am unable to execute any such documents or instruments, I hereby appoint you as my irrevocable attorney-in-fact to execute any such documents and instruments, if said documents and instruments shall not be inconsistent with the terms and conditions of this Consent and Release. Your rights under this Clause 5 constitute a power coupled with an interest and are irrevocable.

6. REMEDIES: No breach of this Consent and Release shall entitle me to terminate or rescind the rights granted to you herein, and I hereby waive the right, in the event of any such breach, to equitable relief or to enjoin, restrain or interfere with the production, distribution, exploitation, exhibition or use of any of the Granted Rights granted, it being my understanding that my sole remedy shall be the right to recover damages with respect to any such breach.

7. PUBLIC-DOMAIN MATERIAL: Nothing in this Consent and Release shall ever be construed to restrict, diminish or impair the rights of either you or me to use freely, in any work or media, any story, idea, pilot, theme, sequence, scene, episode, incident, name, characterization or dialogue which may be in the public domain from whatever source derived.

8. ENTIRE UNDERSTANDING: This Consent and Release expresses the entire understanding between you and me, and I agree that no oral understandings have been made with regard thereto. This Consent and Release may be amended only by written instrument signed by you and me. I acknowledge that in granting the Granted Rights I have not been induced to do so by any representations or assurances, whether written or oral, by you or your representatives concerning the manner in which the Granted Rights may be exercised, and I agree that you are under no obligation to exercise any of the Granted Rights and agree I have not received any promises or inducements other than as herein set forth. The provisions hereof shall be binding upon me and my heirs,

executors, administrators and successors. I acknowledge that you have explained to me that this Consent and Release has been prepared by your attorney and that you have recommended to me that I consult with my attorney concerning this Consent and Release. This Consent and Release shall be construed according to the laws of the State of California applicable to agreements which are fully signed and performed within the State of California, and I hereby waive any rights I may have, known or unknown, pursuant to Section 1542 of the California Civil code, which provides:

"A general release does not extend to claims which the creditor does not know or suspect to exist in his favor at the time of executing the release, which if known by him must have materially affected his settlement with the debtor."

In witness hereof and in full understanding of the foregoing, I have signed this Consent and Release on this day of   , 19__.

_____

(Signature)

_____

(Name, please print)

_____

(Address)

AGREED:

_____

DEPICTION RELEASE
(Option to Purchase Rights Format)

_____
(date)

Mr. John Doe
242 Beverly Hills Lane
Beverly Hills, CA

Dear John:

It was a pleasure speaking to you recently. As I mentioned, I am interested in producing a television program or feature film about your life story.

This letter is intended to set forth the basic terms of our agreement regarding acquisition of the exclusive right and option to purchase all motion picture, television and allied rights concerning your life story. Please feel free to consult an entertainment attorney or an agent before signing this document.

Our agreement is as follows:

1) In consideration of the mutual promises contained herein, and other valuable consideration, you grant my company, Very Big Productions, Inc. ("Big"), the exclusive and irrevocable right to option the motion picture, television and all allied, ancillary and subsidiary rights for the period of one year from the date of the signing of this agreement. Big shall have the right to extend the initial option period for an additional year by sending notice to you before the expiration of the initial period, along with the payment of two thousand dollars ($2,000), which sum shall be applicable against the full purchase price.

2) Big promises to use its best efforts to produce a television program or feature film about your life story, and is acting in

reliance upon your promises in this agreement.

3) If the option is exercised, Big shall compensate you as full and final consideration for all rights conveyed as follows:

a) Television Movie-of-the-week or Mini-Series: A sum of fifty thousand dollars ($50,000) for a motion picture made for television based on the material.

b) Theatrical Motion Picture: A sum of ninty thousand dollars ($90,000) for a theatrical motion picture based on the material.

c) Television Series: A sum of three thousand five hundred dollars ($3,500) for the pilot episode and the sum of eight hundred dollars ($800) for each episode after that.

All of the consideration described in this paragraph shall be payable upon completion of principal photography.

4) Consulting Services: You agree to serve as a creative consultant concerning any production made under this agreement. You shall receive one thousand dollars ($1,000) per week for each week your services are required, not to exceed four weeks unless both parties agree otherwise. If you are required to travel more than fifty miles from your home, Big shall furnish you with first class roundtrip transportation and accommodations. Before the time that the option is exercised, at Big's request you shall disclose, without compensation, any information in your possession or under your control relating to your life story, including newspaper and magazine clippings, photographs, transcripts and notes, and you will consult with any writer hired by Big, and share with him your observations, recollections, opinions and experiences concerning events and activities in your life story.

5) If the option is exercised, Big will obtain the perpetual, exclusive and irrevocable right to depict you, whether wholly or partially factual or fictional, and to use your name or likeness and voice, and biography concerning the material and any production and the advertising and e ploitation of it in any and all media. While it is Big's intention to portray your

story as factually as possible, Big shall have the right to include such actual or fictional events, scenes, situations and dialogue as it may consider desirable or necessary in its sole discretion.

6) You agree to use your best efforts to obtain for Big at no additional cost those releases Big deems necessary from individuals who are a part of your life story or depicted in any information or materials you may supply Big. It is understood that you will not be expected to violate any confidences arising from any attorney-client relationship.

7) You understand that Big shall not be obligated under this agreement to exercise any of its right or to initiate production.

8) Big may sell, assign and/or license any of its rights under this agreement. You agree to execute any other assignments or other instruments necessary or expedient to carry out and effectuate the purposes and intent of this agreement. You agree to execute a complete long-form agreement with the customary language covering grants of biographical rights and a full release which will waive any claims or actions you may have against Big arising from the exercise of any of its rights under this agreement.

9) This agreement shall be governed and controlled by the laws of the State of California. This agreement constitutes the entire agreement between the parties and cannot be modified except in writing. Neither of the parties have made any promises or warranties other than those set forth herein.

Sincerely,

_____

on behalf of Very Big Prods.

AGREED TO AND ACCEPTED

_____

John Doe

DATE: _____

DEPICTION RELEASE
(Documentary Short-form)

MOTION PICTURE AND TELEVISION RELEASE

I hereby irrevocably agree and consent that you (Very Big Productions, Inc.), and your assigns, may use all or part of your videotaped or filmed interview of me for your documentary program about _____.

You have the right to use my picture, silhouette and other reproductions of my likeness and voice in connection with any motion picture or television program in which this interview may be incorporated, and in any advertising material promoting it.

You may edit my appearance as you see fit.

You shall have all right, title and interest in any and all results and proceeds from said use or appearance.

The rights granted you are perpetual and include the use of this interview in any medium all or part of the program may be shown, including broadcast and cable television, and videocassettes.

This consent is given as an inducement for you to interview me and I understand you will incur substantial expense in reliance thereof.

You are not obliged to make any use of this interview or exercise any of the rights granted you by this release.

I have read and understand the meaning of this release.

_____   _____

Signature   Date

_____   _____

Print Name   Phone

Question and Answer

1. I recently read a magazine article about a bank robbery. The story would make a wonderful movie. I tried to buy the rights from the author of the magazine article, but she declined to sell. Do I need to buy those rights? And do I need to buy the life story rights of the individuals portrayed in the article?

Answer: If you want to use the magazine writer's approach to the material, her expression, you will need to buy the rights from her. She owns the copyright to the story she wrote. She does not own, however, the rights to the underlying facts and incidents, and you are free to use them without her permission. So, if you don't base your movie on her article, but work off the underlying true story, using your own approach to the material, you don't need to buy the rights to her article.

You may need to buy life-story rights from the individuals involved, unless the entire story is deemed to be in the public domain. In determining whether a release is needed, one must consider whether without a release the subject would have a viable cause of action for defamation, invasion of privacy, copyright infringment and other causes of action. Alternatively, you could avoid buying a release if you fictionalize the story so that the actual individuals involved are not indentifiable to the public.

LOCATION RELEASE

Today filmmakers often shoot all or part of their motion pictures off the studio lot. They may travel widely in order to incorporate the flavor and realism of actual locations in their movies. Filmmakers who shoot on location without securing prior permission and the necessary releases risk legal liability. Filmmakers don't have an absolute First Amendment right to trespass on other people's property. In certain circumstances, property owners could also sue for an invasion of privacy/publicity and copyright and trademark infringement.

Even if a landowner doesn't bring suit, a filmmaker should secure releases for every location. Without such documents, it may be difficult to purchase Errors and Omissions (E&O) insurance and survive the scrutiny of the legal department of a potential distributor. Location agreements should be sought from landowners or land possessors when shooting on private property and from the appropriate government entity when shooting on public property.

Make sure that the person signing the release has the authority to grant the rights.

Location agreements don't necessarily cost much. In a small community where filmmakers rarely visit, the arrival of a movie crew can generate a lot of excitement. Residents may offer their homes for little or no money. On the other hand movie crews have worn out their welcome in many neighborhoods in Los Angeles. Residents are annoyed by the traffic congestion and noise that accompanies a shoot. Homeowners may have had their property damaged by film crews in the past. These homeowners also know what the major studios are willing to pay for locations. They will demand top dollar which can amount to several thousand dollars a day.

LOCATION AGREEMENT

Agreement entered into this _____ day of _____, 19__, by and between _____ ("Production Company") and _____ ("Grantor").

1. IDENTITY OF FILMING LOCATION: Grantor hereby agrees to permit Production Company to use the property located at

_____

("Property") in connection with the motion picture currently entitled _____ ("Picture") for rehearsing, photographing, filming and recording scenes and sounds for the Picture. Production Company and its licensees, sponsors, assigns and successors may exhibit, advertise and promote the Picture or any portion thereof, whether or not such uses contain audio and/or visual reproductions of the Property and whether or not the Property is identified, in any and all media which currently exist or which may exist in the future in all countries of the world and in perpetuity.

2. RIGHT OF ACCESS: Production Company shall have the right to bring personnel and equipment (including props and temporary sets) onto the Property and to remove same after completion of its use of the Property hereunder. Production Company shall have the right but not the obligation to photograph, film and use in the Picture the actual name, if any, connected with the Property or to use any other name for the Property. If Production Company depicts the interior(s) of any structures located on the Property, Grantor agrees that Production Company shall not be required to depict such interior(s) in any particular manner in the Picture.

3. TIME OF ACCESS: The permission granted hereunder shall be for the period commencing on or about _____ and continuing until _____. The period may be extended by Production Company if there are changes in the production schedule or delays due to weather conditions. The within permission shall also apply to future retakes and/ or added scenes.

4. PAYMENT: For each day the Production Company uses the location, it shall pay Grantor the sum of _____ in consideration for the foregoing.

5. ALTERATIONS TO LOCATION: Production Company agrees that (with Grantor's permission) if it becomes necessary to change, alter or rearrange any equipment on the Property belonging to Grantor, Production Company shall return and restore said equipment to its original place and condition, or repair it, if necessary. Production Company agrees to indemnify and hold harmless Grantor from and against any and all liabilities, damages and claims of third parties arising from Production Company's use hereunder of the Property (unless such liabilities, damages or claims arise from breach of Grantor's warranty as set forth in the immediately following sentence) (and from any physical damage to the Property proximately caused by Production Company, or any of its representatives, employees, or agents). Grantor warrants that it has the right and authority to enter this Agreement and to grant the rights granted by it herein. Grantor agrees to indemnify and hold harmless Production Company from and against any and all claims relating to breach of its aforesaid warranty.

6. NO KICKBACKS FOR USE: Grantor affirms that neither it nor anyone acting for it gave or agreed to give anything of value to any member of the production staff, anyone associated with the Picture, or any representative of Production Company, or any television station or network for mentioning or displaying the name of Grantor as a shooting location on the Property (except the use of the Property, which was furnished for use solely on or in connection with the Picture).

7. BILLING CREDIT: Grantor acknowledges that any identification of the Property which Production Company may furnish shall be at Production Company's sole discretion and in no event shall said identification be beyond that which is reasonably related to the content of the Picture.

8. RELEASE: Grantor releases and discharges Production Company, its employees, agents, licensees, successors and assigns from any and all claims, demands or causes of actions that Grantor may now have or may from now on have for libel, defamation, invasion of privacy or right of publicity, infringement of copyright or violation of any other right arising out of or relating to any utilization of the rights granted herein.

The undersigned represents that he/she is empowered to execute this Agreement for Grantor.

IN WITNESS WHEREOF, the parties have hereunto set their names and signatures:

_____

Production Company

By:_____

_____

Grantor (Name)

By:_____

Questions and Answers

1. What if I have permission to enter a location on which I am shooting and my camera captures the image of a nearby location that I do not have permission to use?

Answer: If the other location is not specifically identifiable, most producers would not bother obtaining a release. A non-identifiable building would be an ordinary non-descript one that cannot be distinguished from many others. Although architectural works are copyrightable, the copyright does not prevent filmmakers from filming a building that is ordinarily visible from a public place.

2. Will I be liable if I shoot a scene in an art gallery with permission of the owner, but without the permission of the artists whose work appears in the film?

Answer: If the art works are used in a distinctive way, a release should be obtained from each artist. Although the gallery owner may own a copy of an artist's work, that does not mean that he owns the underlying copyright to it.

CHAPTER 4

CLEARANCE OF RIGHTS

You wouldn't buy a car from someone unless you were sure he was the legitimate owner. Similarly, you wouldn't want to buy a literary property from someone who does not have clear title. How can you protect yourself?

COPYRIGHT SEARCH

First, you or your attorney should conduct a copyright search. If the literary property you desire is registered with the Copyright Office, a copyright report may reveal a transfer of the copyright, or the licensing of some rights. If the copyright report shows that the purported owner of the literary property is not the copyright holder, or if the copyright has been sold to another, you will not want to proceed with the purchase.

Private research companies can check additional sources of information for potential copyright, title and trademark conflicts. These companies may review catalogs and reference works that list publications, movies, sound recordings and products. Note that the reports supplied by the Copyright Office and from private research companies do not offer a conclusion as to ownership of a copyright. These reports merely supply the information needed to determine the status of a copyright. Often, the opinion of an experienced attorney should be sought. Also remember that copyright owners are not required to register their work, so a review of copyright records may prove inconclusive.

ERRORS AND OMISSIONS INSURANCE

Errors and Omissions Insurance (E&O Insurance) protects the policy holder from claims for defamation, invasion of privacy, trademark and copyright infringement. Let's say a studio (the policy holder) carelessly infringed on the copyrighted material of another when it produced a movie. The studio didn't intend to violate another's rights, but it is nevertheless liable for damages. E&O insurance will pay for any liability incurred as well as defense costs. Like other insurance policies, there is a deductible, typically $10,000 or more.

E&O insurance does not cover intentional wrongdoing. The insurance carrier will assume liability for negligent (careless) acts but not for intentional fraud. Producers typically have their attorney review a script before production to avoid any potential liability. The insurance carrier often requires that the applicant's attorney review and approve the script before a policy will be issued.

The insurer will want to review all necessary releases and permissions before issuing a policy. Also, a copyright report

CLEARANCE OF RIGHTS
CHECKLIST

1) OBTAIN A COPYRIGHT REPORT.

2) BUY ERRORS & OMISSIONS INSURANCE. (E&O INSURANCE) TO PROTECT AGAINST CLAIMS FOR DEFAMATION, INVASION OF PRIVACY, TRADEMARK AND COPYRIGHT INFRINGEMENT, ETC.

3) CLEARANCE OF TITLE.
   A) TITLES ARE NOT COPYRIGHTABLE
   B) OBTAIN TITLE REPORT
   C) CONSIDER MPAA REGISTRATION.

4) IDENTIFIABLE PRODUCTS, LOCATIONS, CHARACTERS & NAMES.
   A) OBTAIN RELEASE OR CHANGE NAME.

5) FILM CLIPS.
   A) PERMISSION FROM
      1) COPYRIGHT OWNER
      2) GUILDS AND UNIONS
      3) EVERY PERSON IN CLIP
      4) MUSICIANS AND RIGHTS TO UNDERLYING MUSICAL COMPOSITION.

and title report will be needed, and all employment agreements must be in writing. If music is going to be used, synchronization and performance licenses are necessary.

If the script is original, its origins must be determined to ensure that everything in it is original and none of it has been copied from another work. When the film is based on a true story, the screenplay should be derived from primary sources (e.g., court transcripts, interviews with witnesses), and not secondary sources (e.g., another author's work product), unless permission has been obtained to use such secondary sources.

CLEARANCE OF TITLE

Titles are not copyrightable: not today, not tomorrow, not under any circumstances. As discussed in chapter 12, you cannot copyright a title, idea, system, procedure or theme.

If you cannot copyright a title, how can you protect your title? Suppose there is a producer who made an awful low-budget science-fiction film that flopped at the box office. Now George Lucas comes along with his hit *Star Wars*. The low-budget producer has an inspiration, perhaps his one and only creative thought. He decides to retitle his picture *Star Wars II*. As a result, some moviegoers view his film and are greatly disappointed. Since the title *Star Wars* is not copyrightable, how can George Lucas protect himself?

While titles are not copyrightable, they may be protected under the laws of unfair competition and trademarks. As explained in Chapter 16, the gist of an unfair competition action is mislabeling or misdesignating a product (or service) in such a way as to cause confusion to consumers as to the origin of its manufacture. In other words, once the title *Star Wars* comes to be associated in the public mind with the work of George Lucas, it acquires what is known as a "secondary meaning." By titling his work *Star Wars II*, this producer is confusing the public as to the origin of his movie. That is because people associate *Star Wars* with the work of George Lucas, and Lucas had nothing to do with this picture.

The major limitation on an action for unfair competition is that you cannot bring a successful action until your film has acquired a secondary meaning. What if you spent three years working on a movie, invested thousands of dollars in prints and advertising, and the day before your film is released another producer releases a film with the same or similar title? Since your film hasn't been released, it has not yet acquired a secondary meaning.

You may be able to protect yourself against this danger by registering the title of your work for trademark protection. Because of recent changes in federal trademark law, one can now prospectively register a trademark before it is used in interstate commerce.[1] Thus once a producer has chosen a title, she may be able to register it as a trademark.[2] She could reserve that mark for a limited period.[3] If she does not use the mark, she will lose all rights to it. Otherwise, she can obtain a trademark for ten-years, renewable for ten year terms for as long as she is using the mark on her product.

A second way to pro-

SCREENPLAY *CHECKLIST*

1) IF THE SCREENPLAY IS BASED ON ANOTHER WORK, A COPYRIGHT REPORT WILL BE NEEDED TO ENSURE ALL REQUIRED RIGHTS HAVE BEEN OBTAINED.

2) THERE MUST BE A WRITTEN AGREEMENT BETWEEN THE CREATOR(S) OF ALL MATERIALS, INCLUDING QUOTATIONS FROM COPYRIGHTED WORK, GRANTING PERMISSION TO USE THE MATERIAL IN THE PRODUCTION.

3) WRITTEN RELEASES ARE REQUIRED FROM ALL PERSONS WHO ARE RECOGNIZABLE OR WHOSE NAME, IMAGE OR LIKENESS IS USED, AND IF SUCH A PERSON IS A MINOR, THE RELEASE MUST BE BINDING.

IF A SUBJECT IS DECEASED, A RELEASE MAY BE NEEDED IN SOME CIRCUMSTANCES.

RELEASES ARE NOT NEEDED IF THE PERSON IS PART OF A CROWD OR BACKGROUND SHOT AND IS NOT SHOWN FOR MORE THAN A FEW SECONDS OR GIVEN SPECIAL EMPHASIS.

CONTINUED

---

[1] Before the 1988 revisions to the trademark law, you could not register a federal trademark until you were actually using the mark on a product in interstate commerce. Thus, manufacturers would sometimes attach a mark to a product that they distributed in a token manner in order to try to protect themselves. Token use is no longer sufficient to obtain federal trademark protection.

[2] Titles of individual entertainment works have not been granted federal trademark registration on the ground that the title is merely descriptive of the work. However, titles of a series of works, such as a television series or magazine, may be registered.

[3] Extensions can be obtained.

tect a title is offered by the Motion Picture Association of America (MPAA). This trade group, which represents the major studios, has devised a scheme to protect its members from the danger of conflicting titles. You can imagine the confusion and problems that would arise if Fox and Paramount simultaneously released pictures with the same or similar titles. Both films would likely suffer.

The MPAA allows its members, and independent producers, to register a script with it. The first party to register a name has the right to use it. There is a $300 fee per year to be a subscriber to the service. There is a $200 charge to register ten titles. Registration is good for one year and can be renewed.[1]

The only shortcoming of the MPAA Title Registration Bureau is that it only protects producers against other producers who have signed the agreement. In other words, the MPAA protects titles by contract. All the major studios are parties to the deal, and some independents have choosen to join. But the MPAA scheme offers no protection against Joe Sleazoid, a producer who is not a signatory to the agreement.

SCREENPLAY *CHECKLIST*
(CONTINUED)

4) WHERE WORK IS FICTIONAL, NAMES OF ALL CHARACTERS MUST GENERALLY BE FICTIONAL. TAKE CARE TO ENSURE THAT THE NAMES OF FICTIONAL CHARACTERS DO NOT RESEMBLE THE NAMES OF IDENTIFIABLE LIVING INDIVIDUALS.

5) WHERE PARTICULAR BUSINESSES, PERSONAL PROPERTY OR IDENTIFIABLE PRODUCTS ARE DEPICTED, WRITTEN RELEASES MUST BE OBTAINED.

RELEASES ARE NOT NECESSARY IF PROPERTY IS NON-DISTINCTIVE BACKGROUND.

6) ALL RELEASES MUST:

A) GIVE RIGHT TO EDIT AND MODIFY MATERIAL.
B) RIGHT TO FICTIONALIZE PEOPLE PORTRAYED.
C) RIGHT TO MARKET PRODUCTION IN ALL MEDIA AND MARKETS.

7) TITLE REPORT FOR TITLE MUST BE OBTAINED SETTING FORTH PRIOR USES OF TITLE.

8) APPLICANT FOR INSURANCE MUST DISCLOSE RECEIPT OF SUBMISSIONS OF ANY SIMILAR MATERIAL.

9) MATERIAL MAY NOT CONTAIN ANY MATERIAL THAT CONSTITUTES DEFAMATION, INVASION OF PRIVACY OR INVASION OF THE RIGHT OF PUBLICITY.

---

[1] For more information, contact the MPAA, Director of Title Registration at (212) 840-6161.

One final method to protect oneself against title conflicts deserves mention. One can order a title report, which may disclose other products or services that have used the same or similar title. If someone has used the title you want on a similar product or service that is offered in the same geographical area, you should not use that title unless it has been abandoned or you have obtained a release.

In creating a title, a highly fanciful or original one is preferred because it will be least likely to infringe others. Such a title will also help the creator protect his title from subsequent infringers.

IDENTIFIABLE PRODUCTS, LOCATIONS & PERSONS

As mentioned in the discussion of merchandising deals in Chapter 2, producers should obtain releases for the depiction of any identifiable products shown in a film. Similarly, producers may need to obtain releases for identifiable locations and for any character names that resemble living individuals.[1]

You should not assume that a thinly disguised portrayal of a living person immunizes you from liability. If the person is recognizable from the circumstances, you could be liable. A disclaimer (e.g., "Any resemblance to people living or dead is purely coincidental. . .") does not provide absolute protection. What if you wrote a novel about supposedly fictional events in the life of a widow of an American President who was assassinated in Dallas. The widow later marries a Greek shipping tycoon. Call the character what you will, but readers may assume you are writing about Jackie Kennedy. She may be able to bring a successful suit if she is defamed or her privacy is invaded.

Depiction releases should allow the producer to edit, modify and embellish the story. If a minor has given consent, the consent must be legally binding.

---

[1] It may be easier to choose another name.

FILM CLIPS

Special problems arise if you want to incorporate film clips from other motion pictures into your production. Permission must be obtained from the copyright owner of the film, from various unions and guilds,[1] from every person who appears in the clip and, if music is used, from the musicians and the owners of the underlying musical composition. Usually, it is simpler and less expensive to shoot original footage than to incorporate existing footage.

Film footage can be purchased from stock footage suppliers. Additional releases may be required to use the footage. The National Archives has a library of public-domain footage available for the cost of duplication.

If film footage is bought from a studio or stock footage supplier, they will supply a release. Here is a sample release for a still photo:

PHOTO RELEASE
_____ Corporation

Owner :_____

Fee: $____

Subject hereby grants to _____ Corporation ("Company") the exclusive right to use the photograph(s) depicting subject listed in Exhibit A, attached hereto, for all merchandising purposes. Subject acknowledges that the depiction of him in the Photo may be duplicated and distributed in any and all manner and media throughout the world in perpetuity.

Subject grants Company the exclusive right, license and privilege to utilize the names, characters, artist's portrayal of characters, likeness, and visual representations in the Photo in connection with the manufacture, advertising, distribution and sale of any articles or products. Such granted rights include the unconditional and exclusive right throughout the world to use, simulate and portray subject's likeness, voice, personality, personal identification and

---

[1] WGA, SAG, DGA and AFofM

personal experiences, incidents, situations and events which here-tofore occurred or hereafter occur (in whole or in part) in any and all other media of any nature whatsoever, whether now known or hereafter devised. Subject agrees that Company may elect to refrain from using subject's real name and may use a pseudonym.

Subject hereby releases and discharges Company, its employees, agents, licensees, successors and assigns from any and all claims, demands or causes of actions that it may have or may hereafter have for libel, defamation, invasion of privacy or right of publicity, infringement of copyright or trademark, or violation of any other right arising out of or relating to any utilization of the rights granted under this agreement.

Subject warrants and represents that Subject possesses all rights necessary for the grant of this license and will indemnify and hold Company, its licensees and assigns harmless from and against any and all claims, damages, liabilities, costs and expenses arising out of a breach of the foregoing warranty.

Subject agrees that Company shall have the unlimited right to vary, change, alter, modify, add to and/or delete from his depiction in the Photo, and to rearrange and/or transpose his depiction, and to use a portion or portions of his depiction or character in conjunction with any other literary, dramatic or other material of any kind.

Subject has not committed or omitted to perform any act by which such rights could or will be encumbered, diminished or impaired; Subject further represents and warrants that no attempt shall be made hereafter to encumber, diminish or impair any of the rights granted herein and that all appropriate protection of such rights will continue to be maintained by Subject.

All rights, licenses and privileges herein granted to Company are irrevocable and not subject to rescission, restraint or injunction under any circumstances.

Nothing herein shall be construed to obligate Company to produce, distribute or utilize any of the rights granted herein.

This agreement shall be construed in accordance with the laws of the State of California applicable to agreements that are executed and fully performed within said State.

This agreement contains the entire understanding of the parties relating to the subject matter, and this agreement cannot be changed except by written agreement executed by the party to be bound.

IN WITNESS WHEREOF, the parties hereto have signed this Agreement as of _____, 19__.

_____
("Subject")

For _____ Corporation ("Company")

STATE OF   )
) ss.:
COUNTY OF   )

On the   ·day of   , 19__, before me personally came _____ to me known and known to be the individual described in and who executed the foregoing instrument, and he did duly acknowledge to me that he executed the same.

                    _____
                    Notary Public

CHAPTER 5

LITERARY ACQUISITION AGREEMENTS

A literary acquisition contract is an agreement to acquire all or some rights in a literary property such as a book. Producers typically use it to obtain screenplays or movie rights to other literary works.

Buyers (e.g., producers) will want owners (e.g., writers) to warrant that they own all the rights they are selling, free and clear of any other obligations (encumbrances). Sellers will disclose their copyright registration number so that buyers can check the copyright records and review the chain of title to be sure that they are getting all the rights they want.

Each agreement needs to define the extent of the rights being sold. Sometimes, all rights, the entire copyright, is sold. Other times, limited rights, on either an exclusive or non-exclusive basis, are licensed. As explained in Chapter 12, copyrights are bundles of rights which owners can divide any number of ways.

If movie rights are sold, the buyer typically will have the right to adapt the work into a motion picture and release it in ancillary markets such as home video. The buyer may also obtain sequel and remake rights, although an additional payment may be due when and if these rights are used.

The buyer is routinely granted the right to excerpt up to 7,500 words from the book for advertising and promotion purposes, although I can't recall an instance where a movie studio or network used such a large excerpt to promote a movie. Publicity is usually centered on stars and directors.

Writers will want to reserve certain rights. A writer who allows adaptation of his work into film might want to retain book rights, stage rights, radio rights and the right to use his characters in a new plot.[1]

Sometimes the buyer will agree to let the writer retain certain rights, provided the writer gives the buyer first shot at purchasing the rights should he later decide to sell them.

For example, let's say that Writer A has sold the movie rights to his book to Warner Bros. (WB). The writer has retained all dramatic (play) rights. WB obtains a "Right of First Negotiation," giving it first opportunity to purchase the play rights if the Writer should choose to sell them. WB thinks it is only fair for it to have such a right. It is investing millions of dollars in turning the writer's book into a movie, making the underlying property and all its derivative forms more valuable. The Right of First Negotiation only requires that the writer negotiate in good faith with WB first. If no agreement is reached within a set time (e.g. thirty days), the Writer could negotiate and sell the play rights to a third party.

Another provision that may be used with, or as an alternative to the Right of First Negotiation, is the Right of Last Refusal. Here the buyer has the right to acquire the reserved right under the same terms and conditions as any offer made by a third party. If WB had a Right of Last Refusal, then the Writer would be free to offer the play rights to another buyer. Before closing the deal, however, the writer would have to offer to sell WB the rights on the same terms as the best offer received by the Writer.

As a practical matter, when a writer has given a studio a Right of Last Refusal, it can be difficult to interest third parties in buying a reserved right. Why should Universal Pictures spend time negotiating the terms of a sale with the writer, only to have

---

[1] This should be distinguished from sequel rights which provide the buyer with the right to use the characters in sequel motion pictures. What the writer is reserving is the right to use his characters in another book.

the deal supplanted at the last moment by WB? Thus, the Right of Last Refusal discourages third-party offers.

Another point important to the buyer will be the unlimited right to make changes to the work when adapting it. Paramount Pictures is not going to invest large sums of money to develop a screenplay only to find itself in a vulnerable position, unable to change a line of dialogue without the author's permission. Suppose the movie is in the midst of production and the author cannot be located? What if the author unreasonably withholds consent? No studio is going to let a writer hold a gun to its head by withholding permission to make changes.

On the other hand, authors frequently complain that studios and directors ruin their work. They are embarrassed when a studio releases a movie inferior to the original work. Some countries, such as France, grant artists so-called moral rights ("droit moral"), which may prevent buyers from desecrating or changing an artist's work without their permission.[1] The United States does not expressly recognize the doctrine of moral rights.[2] Moreover, the buyer is going to ask the seller to waive these rights.

Writers who can't stand to see their work changed should write books and plays where they have a larger measure of control over their work. A stage director, for example, cannot change a word of a Neil Simon play without the writer's permission. Screenwriters, however, must accept the possibility that their work will be significantly changed. Indeed, you may not even recognize your work when all the rewrites and revisions are complete. You wrote a novel about a farmer in Iowa, and now the story is set on a U-Boat in the North Atlantic.

One consolation is the money earned from the sale of movie rights and for screenwriting. Movie rights to bestselling novels can fetch a million dollars or more. Accomplished screenwriters often earn six-figure fees for their services. The Writers Guild minimum for screenwriters is about $50,000, which is much more than many beginning novelists receive in book royalties.

In a literary acquisition agreement buyers will also want

---

[1] Moral rights in France, however, are limited for collaborative works.

[2] Various state and federal laws, however, accomplish much the same result through other doctrines, such as the law of unfair competition and defamation.

sellers to make certain warranties, or promises. For example, the writer will often warrant that the work does not defame or invade anyone's privacy, or infringe on another's copyright. Buyers usually want the warranties to be absolute, while writers want the warranties based on the best of the writer's knowledge and belief. The difference is this: if the writer unknowingly defames another, he would be liable under an absolute warranty but not necessarily under one to the best of his knowledge and belief. In other words, if the writer in good faith believed he had not defamed anyone, he wouldn't be liable.

Buyers also want writers to stand behind their warranties and indemnify buyers in the event a warranty is breached. When a writer indemnifies the buyer, the writer agrees to reimburse the buyer for any litigation costs and judgment that may be rendered.

Let's say a novelist invents a character named John West who lives in Ann Arbor, Michigan, where he is a bartender who moonlights as a criminal. The novel becomes a bestseller and a studio makes a movie based on it. One day a person by the name of John West who lives in Ann Arbor and tends bar sees the movie. He is shocked to see a character with his name portrayed as a criminal. He brings suit against the studio for defamation. The studio seeks indemnification (i.e., reimbursement) from the writer. The writer may be liable, even though he didn't intend to defame anyone.

Of course, an indemnity is only worth as much as the person standing behind it. It would be a waste of time for a studio to seek reimbursement from an impoverished writer. To protect themselves from potential liability, producers and studios can purchase Errors and Omissions (E&O) insurance. The studio's lawyers, as well as the insurance company's lawyers, may review proposed scripts before production to try to avoid any liability. In this example, a studio lawyer might telephone directory information for Ann Arbor and see if there is anyone by the name of John West living there. If so, it might make sense to change the name of the character or the location of the story.

Attorneys and agents representing writers often ask that the writer be added as a named insured on the E&O policy. This may add a few hundred dollars to the premium but will ensure that the insurance company defends the writer as well as the studio and bears any litigation expenses. It would cost the writer much more to buy an insurance policy on his own.

Another provision found in literary purchase agreements requires that the seller not let the property fall into the public domain. Under the old copyright law (effective before 1978), a copyright lasted for twenty-eight years and could be renewed for an additional twenty-eight year term. Consequently, the buyer wanted to make sure the writer would renew the copyright when it came up for renewal at the end of the first term. For works created since 1978, authors are given a copyright for their lifetimes plus fifty years. There are no renewal terms for these works.

Credit is another topic that needs to be addressed. The buyer wants the right to use the name and likeness of the author to promote the picture, although the writer is rarely featured in advertising. As for billing credit, the Writers Guild agreement will usually determine who receives writing credit (assuming the Writer is in the guild and the production company is a guild signatory). The producer cannot arbitrarily assign credit. In case of a dispute over credits, the Writers Guild will impanel a group of impartial writers to arbitrate. They will read drafts of the script and allocate credit. The rules used to determine credit allocation are available from the Writers Guild.

The literary purchase agreement will also contain an explicit provision stating that the producer is under no obligation to actually produce a movie. The producer wants the right to make a movie but not the obligation to do so. This prevents the writer from forcing the producer into production.

If the writer has a reversion clause, all rights to the script can revert to him if production is not commenced within a set time (e.g., five years from the date the movie rights were bought). Thus the writer will regain rights to the property and has a chance to set it up elsewhere.

Another provision found in literary purchase agreements is the assignment clause. This permits the buyer to assign his rights to another. A producer will want the ability to assign rights because a distributor or financier may insist upon an assignment as a condition of participating in the project. If the writer is concerned where the project may end up, he may try to limit the assignment to major studios and networks. He could also ask that no assignments be permitted unless he gives his approval, which he may agree will not be unreasonably withheld. The writer may want the assignment to state that any assignee must assume all the obligations owed the writer, and perhaps the assignor will remain liable as well.

Finally, the literary purchase agreement will often require the writer to refrain from engaging in any publicity activities unless they are with the consent of the buyer. The studio wants to make sure it can orchestrate a publicity campaign without worrying about the writer giving interviews on his own.

The following case illustrates the kind of problems that can arise from a poorly worded acquisition agreement.

WARNER BROS. V. COLUMBIA BROADCASTING (1954)[1]

FACTS: Warner Bros., P, acquired the movie rights in Dashiell Hammett's book *The Maltese Falcon*, which featured the character, detective Sam Spade. Later Hammett wrote additional stories featuring Spade and granted the television, radio and movie rights in those stories to Columbia Broadcasting (CBS). CBS began a series of radio programs featuring Sam Spade, and Warner Bros. brought suit claiming that Hammett could not sell these additional stories to CBS because Warners owned characters in them.

ISSUE: Does the sale of movie rights to a book include the rights to characters in the book?

HOLDING: Not necessarily. Decision for Hammett and CBS.

RATIONALE: The contract did not specifically say that Hammett was granting Warners exclusive rights to the character. Warner's drew up the contract and any ambiguity should be construed against it. Although Warners owns the copyright to the *Maltese Falcon*, that does not prevent the author from using the characters in other stories. "The characters were vehicles for the story told, and the vehicles did not go with the sale of the story."

Hammett sold *The Maltese Falcon* to buyer One (Warners), then invented new stories with the same characters and sold them to

[1] 216 F.2d 945 (1954).

buyer Two (CBS). The contract never addressed the issue of whether Warners obtained all rights to the characters when it bought *The Maltese Falcon*. Since the contract was ambiguous, and since Warner's drafted the contract, the ambiguity was construed against it. Consequently, Hammett and CBS won.

As a general principal of contract law, ambiguous contracts are construed against the drafter. This type of problem rarely arises today because attorneys are careful to delineate precisely which rights the writer is granting and which are retained. The writer typically retains the right to use characters in a new plot.

Readers should note that in the New York case of *Burnett v. Warner Bros. Pictures*,[1] the court came to a different conclusion on facts similar to the Sam Spade case. In *Burnett*, plaintiffs wrote the play *Everyone Comes to Rick's*, which was sold to Warner Bros. for $20,000 and became the basis for the film *Casablanca*. The agreement gave Warner Bros. "all now or hereafter existing rights of every kind and character whatsoever pertaining to said work, whether or not such rights are now known, recognized or contemplated..."

Warner Bros. subsequently produced a television series based on the play and movie. Plaintiffs sued, claiming that Warners had no right to use the characters in the television series. The court concluded that the language of the contract should be interpreted to mean that plaintiffs gave up all their rights to the work, although the language didn't specifically

MAJOR PROVISIONS
LITERARY ACQUISITION AGREEMENT

1) WARRANTY OF OWNERSHIP

2) EXTENT OF RIGHTS CONVEYED

3) RIGHTS RESERVED
   A) RIGHT OF FIRST NEGOTIATION
   B) RIGHT OF LAST REFUSAL

4) RIGHT TO MAKE CHANGES ("DROIT MORAL")

5) CONSIDERATION

6) INDEMNIFICATION

7) PROTECTION OF COPYRIGHT

8) CREDIT
   A) RIGHT TO USE NAME TO PROMOTE
   B) BILLING CREDIT

9) NO OBLIGATION TO PRODUCE

10) ASSIGNMENT

11) RESTRICT PUBLICITY

---

[1] *Burnett v. Warner Bros. Pictures*, 493 N.Y.S.2d (App. Div., 1985).

mention character rights. Once again, this illustrates the importance of a carefully worded contract.

Questions and Answers

1. I'm interested in acquiring the movie rights to a screenplay. Do the "movie rights" typically include the right to make sequels?

Answer: Often the rights acquired by the purchaser include the right to make one or more sequels and/or remakes. Sellers may reserve such rights, however. If the purchaser obtains sequel or remake rights, the agreement usually provides that, in the event a sequel or remake is made, the author of the screenplay is entitled to additional compensation.

2. Can a novelist who sells the movie rights to a book write a sequel novel?

Answer: It depends on the terms of the agreement. Often the purchaser (producer/studio) has the right to make sequel films, but the author reserves the right to write sequel books. The buyer may want to obtain a right of first negotiation or last refusal on the movie rights to a sequel novel.

3. What is a reversion clause?

Answer: A reversion clause states that certain rights revert at some future time or under some condition. In the movie industry, the author of a book who sells movie rights might ask for a reversion clause that provides that if the buyer of the rights doesn't make a movie within five years from the date of purchase, then all rights revert to the author. Thus, if the buyer (producer) is unable to make a film, the author regains those rights eventually and can try to set up the project elsewhere.

OPTION & LITERARY PURCHASE AGREEMENT

THIS AGREEMENT, made and entered into as of
_____ (date), by and between _____ (name and address
of seller) ("Seller") and _____ (name and address of
buyer) ("Buyer").

1.   SELLER'S REPRESENTATIONS AND WARRANTIES:

(a) Sole Proprietor: Seller represents and warrants to
Buyer that Seller is the sole and exclusive proprietor, throughout
the world of that certain original literary material written by
_____ entitled _____ ("the Literary Material"
or "Literary Property").

(b) Facts: Seller represents and warrants to Buyer that
the following statements are true and correct in all respects
with respect to said literary material:

(i) Seller is the sole author of the Literary Material.

(ii) The Literary Material was first published on (date) by
_____, under the title _____, and was registered
for copyright in the name of _____, under copyright
registration number _____, in the Office of the United
States Register of Copyrights, Washington, D.C.

No Motion Picture or dramatic version of the Literary Property, or any part of it, has been manufactured, produced,
presented or authorized; no radio or television development,
presentation or program based on the Literary Property, or
any part of it, has been manufactured, produced, presented,
broadcast or authorized; and no written or oral agreements or
commitments at all with respect to the Literary Property or
with respect to any right therein, have previously been made
or entered by or on behalf of Seller (except with respect to
the publication of the Literary Material as set forth above).

(c) No Infringement or Violation of Third Party Rights:
Seller represents and warrants to Buyer that Seller has not
adapted the Literary Property from any other literary, dramatic
or other material of any kind, nature or description, nor,
excepting for material which is in the public domain, has Seller
copied or used in the Literary Property the plot, scenes, sequence or story of any other literary, dramatic or other material;
that the Literary Property does not infringe upon any common

law or statutory rights in any other literary, dramatic, or other material; that as far as Seller has knowledge, no material in the Literary Property is libelous or violative of the right of privacy of any person and the full use of the rights in the Literary Property which are covered by the within option would not violate any rights of any person, firm or corporation; and that the Literary Property is not in the public domain in any country in the world where copyright protection is available.

(d) No Impairment of Rights: Seller represents and warrants to Buyer that Seller is the exclusive proprietor, throughout the world, of the rights in the Literary Property which are covered by the within option; that Seller has not assigned, licensed nor in any manner encumbered, diminished or impaired these rights; that Seller has not committed nor omitted to perform any act by which these rights could or will be encumbered, diminished or impaired; and that there is no outstanding claim or litigation pending against or involving the title, ownership and/or copyright in the Literary Property, or in any part of it, or in the rights which are covered by the within option. Seller further represents and warrants that no attempt hereafter will be made to encumber, diminish or impair any of the rights herein granted and that all appropriate protections of such rights will continue to be maintained by Seller.

Without limiting any other rights Buyer may have in the Literary Property, Seller agrees that if there is any claim and/or litigation involving any breach or alleged breach of any such representations and warranties of Seller, the option period granted hereunder and any periods within which Buyer may, pursuant to the provisions of Clause 3 hereof, extend the option, shall automatically be extended until no claim and/or litigation involving any breach or alleged breach of any such representation and warranties of seller is outstanding, but in any event not for a period more than one (1) additional year. Any time after the occurrence of such a claim and/or litigation until the expiration of the option period, as extended, Buyer may, besides any other rights and remedies Buyer may have in the Literary Property, rescind this agreement and in such event, despite anything else to the contrary contained herein, Seller agrees to repay Buyer any monies paid by Buyer to Seller hereunder concerning the Property and any reasonable amounts expended by Buyer in developing or exploiting the Property. Without limiting the generality of the foregoing, Seller agrees that Seller will not, any time during the option period, exercise or authorize or permit the exercise by others of any of the rights covered by the option or any of the rights reserved by Seller under the provisions of Exhibit A which are not to be exercised or licensed to others during any period therein specified.

2. CONSIDERATION FOR OPTION: In consideration of the payment to Seller of the sum of $_____, receipt of which is hereby acknowledged, Seller agrees to and does hereby give and grant to Buyer the exclusive and irrevocable option to purchase from Seller the rights in the Property as described in Exhibit A for the total purchase price specified and payable as provided in Exhibit A, provided that any sums paid under this Clause 2 or any other provision of this agreement with respect to the option shall be credited against the first sums payable on account of such purchase price. If Buyer shall fail to exercise this option, then the sums paid to Seller hereunder with respect to the option shall be and remain the sole property of Seller.

3. OPTION PERIOD: The within option shall be effective during the period commencing on the date hereof and ending _____ ("the Initial Option Period"). The Initial Option Period may be extended for an additional _____ months by the payment of $_____ on or before the expiration date specified above ("the Second Option Period").

4. EXERCISE OF OPTION:

(a) Notice of Exercise: If Buyer elects to exercise the within option, Buyer (any time during the Option Period) shall serve upon Seller written notice of the exercise of it by addressing such notice to seller at his address as specified in Exhibit A and by depositing such notice, so addressed by certified mail, return receipt requested with postage prepaid, in the United States mail. The deposit of such notice in the United States mail as herein specified shall constitute service of it, and the date of such deposit shall be deemed to be the date of service of such notice.

(b) The purchase price shall be paid to Seller according to Exhibit A.

(c) The option may be exercised only by notice in writing as aforesaid; no conduct or oral statement by Buyer or his agents, representatives or employees shall constitute an exercise of the option.

(d) Additional Documents: If Buyer exercises the within option, Seller, without cost to Buyer (other than the consideration provided for herein or in Exhibit A) shall execute, acknowledge and deliver to Buyer, or shall cause the execution, acknowledgement and delivery to Buyer of such further instruments as Buyer may reasonably require to confirm unto Buyer the rights, licenses, privileges and property which are the subject of the within option. If Seller shall fail to execute and deliver or to cause the execution and delivery to Buyer of any such instruments, Buyer is hereby irrevocably granted the power coupled with an interest to execute such instruments and to take such other steps and proceedings as may be necessary concerning it in the name and on behalf of Seller and as Seller's attorney-in-fact. Seller shall supply all supporting agreements and documentation requested by Buyer.

(e) Failure to Execute Documents: If Seller shall fail to execute, acknowledge or deliver to Buyer any agreements, assignments or other instruments to be executed, acknowledged and delivered by Seller hereunder, then Buyer is hereby irrevocably appointed Seller's attorney-in-fact with full right, power and authority to execute, acknowledge and deliver the same in the name of and on behalf of Seller, Seller acknowledging that the authority and agency given Buyer is a power coupled with an interest. If the property has not been published or registered for copyright in the United States Copyright Office, and as a result thereof Exhibits "A," "B" and "C," attached hereto, have not been completed with respect to the publication and copyright data and other data, then Buyer is authorized and instructed by Seller to insert the correct publication and copyright data in the appropriate blanks in Exhibits "A," "B" and "C" or after the property has been published and registered for copyright, and in this connection Seller agrees to notify Buyer promptly in writing of the publication and registration of the Property for copyright, specifying in such notice the name of the publisher, the date and place of publication, the name of the copyright proprietor and the date and entry number of the copyright registration in the United States Copyright Office, all of which information may be inserted by Buyer in the appropriate blanks in such documents.

5. EFFECTIVENESS OF EXHIBITS "A," "B" AND "C": Concurrently with the execution of this agreement, Seller has executed Exhibits A (Literary Purchase Agreement), B (Short Form Option Agreement for Recordation) and C (Assignment of the Copyright), which are undated, and it is agreed that if Buyer shall exercise the option (but not otherwise), then the signature of Seller to Exhibits A, B and C shall be deemed to be effective, and these Exhibits shall constitute valid and binding agreements and assignment effective as of the date of exercise of such option, and Buyer is hereby authorized and empowered to date such instruments accordingly. If Buyer shall fail to exercise the option, then the signature of Seller to Exhibits A, B and C shall be void and of no further force or effect whatever, and Buyer shall not be deemed to have acquired any rights in or to the Property other than the option hereinabove provided for. If Buyer exercises the option, Buyer will execute and deliver to Seller copies of Exhibit A, dated as of the date of the exercise of the option, and Seller will, if so requested by Buyer, execute and de er to Buyer additional copies of Exhibits A, B and C. Jot thstanding the failure or omission of either party to exe ute and/or deliver such additional documents, it is agreec that upon the exercise of the option by Buyer, all rights in and to the Property agreed to be transferred to Buyer pursuant to the provisions of Exhibit A shall be deemed vested in Buyer, effective as of the date of exercise of the option, which rights shall be irrevocable.

6. RIGHT TO ENGAGE IN PRE-PRODUCTION: Seller acknowledges that Buyer may, at its own expense, during the option period, undertake pre-production activities in connection with any of the rights to be acquired hereunder including, without limitation, the preparation and submission of treatments and/or screenplays based on the Property.

7. RESTRICTIONS: During the Option Period, Seller shall not exercise or otherwise use any of the rights herein granted to Buyer and as more particularly described in Exhibit A hereof nor the rights reserved to Seller pursuant to Clause 2 (Rights Reserved) of Exhibit A, nor shall Seller permit the use of nor shall Seller use any other right Seller has reserved in a way that would in any manner or for any purpose unfairly com-

pete with, interfere with or conflict with the full and unrestricted use of the rights herein granted to Buyer and as described in Exhibit A.

8. ASSIGNMENT: This Option Agreement and the rights granted hereunder may be assigned by Buyer to any other person, firm or corporation.

9. OPTION REVERSION AND TURNAROUND RIGHT:

(a) If the Buyer does not timely exercise the option during its original or extended term and timely pay the purchase price, the option shall end and all rights in the Literary Property shall immediately revert to the seller. The seller shall retain all sums therefore paid. Buyer shall immediately execute and deliver to seller any assignments and documents required to effectuate the Reversion. If Buyer shall fail or be unable to do so, Buyer hereby grants seller a power coupled with an interest to execute and deliver such documents as Buyer's attorney-in-fact.

(b) If the option is timely exercised and the purchase price paid and if a motion picture company does not produce a motion picture based on the Literary Property within _____ years from purchase of the Literary Property, seller shall have a turnaround right to reacquire and set up the Literary Property elsewhere, and upon obtaining such other commitment, to reimburse the Buyer or Motion Picture company for its actual direct out-of-pocket development costs in connection with the Literary Property, such as fees to scriptwriters, but excluding payments to seller and any payments to Buyer not directly related to scripting services.

(c) In addition, if Buyer decides not to exercise the option in Clause 1, above, any time before the expiration of the Option Period, or decides not to extend such option for _____ , Buyer agrees to notify Seller of such decision as soon as reasonably possible, but in no event later than the applicable option or extension deadline. When such notice is given, the option granted hereunder to Buyer shall automatically revert to Seller.

10. FORCE MAJEURE: "Force Majeure" means any fire, flood, earthquake, or public disaster; strike, labor dispute or unrest; embargo, riot, war, insurrection or civil unrest; any act of God, any act of legally constituted authority; or any other

cause beyond the buyer's control which would excuse buyer's performance as a matter of law. If because of force majeure, buyer's performance hereunder is delayed or prevented then the option period provided herein and any performance by purchase shall be extended for the time of such delay or prevention.

11. SECTION HEADINGS: The headings of paragraphs, sections and other subdivisions of this agreement are for convenient reference only. They shall not be used in any way to govern, limit, modify, construe this agreement or any part or provision of it.

12. ARBITRATION: Any controversy or claim arising out of or relating to this agreement or any breach thereof shall be settled by arbitration in accordance with the Rules of the American Arbitration Association; and judgment upon the award rendered by the arbitrators may be entered in any court having jurisdiction thereof. The prevailing party shall be entitled to reimbursement for costs and reasonable attorneys' fees. The determination of the arbitrator in such proceeding shall be final, binding and non-appealable.

13. ENTIRE AGREEMENT: This agreement, including the Exhibits attached hereto, contains the complete understanding and agreement between the parties with respect to the within subject matter, and supersedes all other agreements between the parties whether written or oral relating thereto, and may not be modified or amended except by written instrument executed by both of the parties hereto. This agreement shall in all respects be subject to the laws of the State of _____ applicable to agreements executed and wholly performed within such State. All the rights, licenses, privileges and property herein granted to Buyer are irrevocable and not subject to rescission, restraint, or injunction under any or all circumstances.

    IN WITNESS WHEREOF, the parties hereto have signed this Option Agreement as of the day and year first hereinabove written.

SELLER:_____

BUYER:_____

Exhibit A

This Agreement made on _____ (date) by and between
_____ (after this called "Seller") and _____
(after this called "BUYER").

W I T N E S S E T H

WHEREAS, Seller is the sole and exclusive seller throughout the world of all rights in and to the literary work entitled:
_____, Written by _____, which work has been
filed in the United States Copyright Office under Copyright
Registration Number _____; this work including all adaptations and/or versions, the titles, characters, plots, themes and
storyline is collectively called the "Property"; and

WHEREAS, Buyer wants to acquire certain rights of the
Seller in consideration for the purchase price provided herein
and in reliance upon the Seller's representations and warranties;

NOW, THEREFORE, the parties agree to as follows:

1. RIGHTS GRANTED: Seller hereby sells, grants, conveys
and assigns to Buyer, its successors, licensees and assigns
exclusively and forever, all motion picture rights (including
all silent, sound dialogue and musical motion picture rights),
all television motion-picture and other television rights, with
limited radio broadcasting rights and 7,500-word publication
rights for advertisement, publicity and exploitation purposes,
and certain incidental and allied rights, throughout the world,
in and to the Property and in and to the copyright of it and all
renewals and extensions of copyright. Included among the
rights granted to Buyer hereunder (without in any way limiting the grant of rights hereinabove made) are the following
sole and exclusive rights throughout the world:

(a) To make, produce, adapt and copyright one or more
motion picture adaptations or versions, whether fixed on film,
tape, disc, wire, audio-visual cartridge, cassette or through
any other technical process whether now known or from now
on devised, based in whole or in part on the Property, of
every size, gauge, color or type, including, but not limited to,

musical motion pictures and remakes of and sequels to any motion picture produced hereunder and motion pictures in series or serial form, and for such purposes to record and reproduce and license others to record and reproduce, in synchronization with such motion pictures, spoken words taken from or based upon the text or theme of the Property and any kinds of music, musical accompaniments and/or lyrics to be performed or sung by the performers in any such motion picture and any other kinds of sound and sound effects.

(b) To exhibit, perform, rent, lease and generally deal in and with any motion picture produced hereunder:

(i) by all means or technical processes whatsoever, whether now known or from now on devised including, by way of example only, film, tape, disc, wire, audio-visual cartridge, cassette or television (including commercially sponsored, sustaining and subscription or pay-per-view television, or any derivative of it); and

(ii) anywhere whatsoever, including homes, theaters and elsewhere, and whether a fee is charged, directly or indirectly, for viewing any such motion picture.

(c) To broadcast, transmit or reproduce the Property or any adaptation or version of it (including without limitations to, any motion picture produced hereunder and/or any script or other material based on or using the Property or any of the characters, themes or plots of it), by means of television or any process analogous thereto whether now known or from now on devised (including commercially sponsored, sustaining and subscription or pay-per-view television), by motion pictures produced on films or by means of magnetic tape, wire, disc, audio-visual cartridge or any other device now known or from now on devised and including such television productions presented in series or serial form, and the exclusive right generally to exercise for television purposes all the rights granted to Buyer hereunder for motion picture purposes.

(d) Without limiting any other rights granted Buyer, to broadcast and/or transmit by television or radio or any process analogous thereto whether now known or from now on devised, all or any part of the Property or any adaptation or version of it, including any motion picture or any other version or versions of it, and announcements about said motion picture or other version or versions, for advertising, publicizing or exploiting such motion picture or other version or versions, which broadcasts or transmissions may be accomplished with living actors performing simultaneously with such broadcast or transmission or by any other method or means including the use of motion pictures (including trailers) reproduced on film or by means of magnetic tape or wire or through other recordings or transcriptions.

(e) To publish and copyright or cause to be published and copyrighted in the name of Buyer or its nominee in any languages throughout the world, in any form or media, synopses, novelizations, serializations, dramatizations, abridged and/or revised versions of the Property, not exceeding 7,500 words each, adapted from the Property or from any motion picture and/or other version of the Property for advertising, publicizing and/or exploiting any such motion picture and/or other version.

(f) For the foregoing purposes to use all or any part of the Property and any of the characters, plots, themes and/or ideas contained therein, and the title of the Property and any title or subtitle of any component of the Property, and to use said titles or subtitles for any motion picture or other version of adaptation whether the same is based on or adapted from the Property and/or as the title of any musical composition contained in any such motion picture or other version or adaptation.

(g) To use and exploit commercial or merchandise tie-ups and recordings of any sort and nature arising out of or connected with the Property and/or its motion picture or other versions and/or the title or titles of it and/or the characters of it and/or their names or characteristics.

All rights, licenses, privileges and property herein granted Buyer shall be cumulative and Buyer may exercise or use any or all said rights, licenses, privileges or property simultaneously with or in connection with or separately and apart from the exercise of any other of said rights, licenses, privileges and property. If Seller from now on makes or publishes or permits to be made or published any revision, adaptation, sequel, translation or dramatization or other versions of the Property, then Buyer shall have and Seller hereby grants to Buyer without payment therefore all of the same rights therein as are herein granted Buyer. The terms "Picture" and "Pictures" as used herein shall be deemed to mean or include any present or future kind of motion picture production based upon the Property, with or without sound recorded and reproduced synchronously with it, whether the same is produced on film or by any other method or means now or from now on used for the production, exhibition and/or transmission of any kind of motion picture productions.

2. RIGHTS RESERVED: The following rights are reserved to Seller for Seller's use and disposition, subject, however, to the provisions of this agreement:

(a) Publication Rights: The right to publish and distribute printed versions of the Property owned or controlled by Seller in book form, whether hardcover or softcover, and in magazine or other periodicals, whether in installments or otherwise subject to Buyer's rights as provided for in Clause 1 supra.

(b) Stage Rights: The right to perform the Property or adaptations of it on the spoken stage with actors appearing in person in the immediate presence of the audience, provided no broadcast, telecast, recording, photography or other reproduction of such performance is made. Seller agrees not to exercise, or permit any other person to exercise, said stage rights earlier than _____ years after the first general release or telecast, if earlier, of the first Picture produced hereunder, or _____ years after the date of exercise of the buyer's option to acquire the property, whichever is earlier.

(c) Radio Rights: The right to broadcast the Property by sound (as distinguished from visually) by radio, subject however to Buyer's right always to: (i) exercise its radio rights provided in Clause 1 supra for advertising and exploitation purposes by living actors or otherwise, by using excerpts from or condensations of the Property or any Picture produced hereunder; and (ii) in any event to broadcast any Picture produced hereunder by radio. Seller agrees not to exercise, or permit any other person to exercise, Seller's radio rights earlier than _____ years after the first general release or initial telecast, if earlier, of the first Picture produced hereunder or _____ years after the date of exercise of buyer's option to acquire the property, whichever is earlier.

(d) Author-Written Sequel: A literary property (story, novel, drama or otherwise), whether written before or after the Property and whether written by Seller or by a successor in interest of Seller, using one or more of the characters appearing in the Property, participating in different events from those found in the Property, and whose plot is substantially different from that of the Property. Seller shall have the right to exercise publication rights (i.e., in book or magazine form) any time. Seller agrees not to exercise, or permit any other person to exercise, any other rights (including but not limited to motion picture or allied rights) of any kind in or to any author-written sequel earlier than _____ years after the first general release of the first Picture produced hereunder, or _____ years after the date of exercise of buyer's option to acquire the property, whichever is earlier, provided such restriction on Seller's exercise of said author-written sequel rights shall be extended to any period during which there is in effect, in any particular country or territory, a network television broadcasting agreement for a television motion picture, (i) based upon the Property, or (ii) based upon any Picture produced in the exercise of rights assigned herein, or (iii) using a character or characters of the Property, plus one (1) year, which shall also be a restricted period in such country or territory, whether such period occurs wholly or partly during or entirely after the _____ year period first referred to in this clause. Any disposition of motion picture or allied rights in an author-written sequel made to any person or company other than Buyer shall be made subject to the following limitations and restrictions:

(e) Since the characters of the Property are included in the exclusive grant of motion picture rights to Buyer, no sequel rights or television series rights may be granted to such other person or company, but such characters from the Property which are contained in the author-written sequel may be used in a motion picture and remakes of it whose plot is based substantially on the plot of the respective author-written sequel.

It is expressly agreed that Seller's reserved rights under this subclause relate only to material written or authorized by

Seller and not to any revision, adaptation, sequel, translation or dramatization written or authorized by Buyer, although the same may contain characters or other elements contained in the Property.

3. RIGHT TO MAKE CHANGES: Seller agrees that Buyer shall have the unlimited right to vary, change, alter, modify, add to and/or delete from the Property, and to rearrange and/or transpose the Property and change the sequence of it and the characters and descriptions of the characters contained in the Property, and to use a portion or portions of the property or the characters, plots, or theme of it with any other literary, dramatic or other material of any kind. Seller hereby waives the benefits of any provisions of law known as the "droit moral" or any similar law in any country of the world and agrees not to permit or prosecute any action or lawsuit on the ground that any Picture or other version of the Property produced or exhibited by Buyer, its assignees or licensees, in any way constitutes an infringement of any of the Seller's droit moral or is in any way a defamation or mutilation of the Property or any part of it or contains unauthorized variations, alterations, modifications, changes or translations.

4. DURATION AND EXTENT OF RIGHTS GRANTED: Buyer shall enjoy, solely and exclusively, all the rights, licenses, privileges and property granted hereunder throughout the world, in perpetuity, as long as any rights in the Property are recognized in law or equity, except as far as such period of perpetuity may be shortened due to any now existing or future copyright by Seller of the Property and/or any adaptations of it, in which case Buyer shall enjoy its sole and exclusive rights, licenses, privileges and property hereunder to the fullest extent permissible under and for the full duration of such copyright or copyrights, whether common law or statutory, and any renewals and/or extensions of it, and shall after that enjoy all such rights, licenses, privileges and property non-exclusively in perpetuity throughout the world. The rights granted herein are in addition to and shall not be construed in derogation of any rights which Buyer may have as a member of the public or pursuant to any other agreement. All rights, licenses, privileges and property granted herein to Buyer are irrevocable and not subject to rescission, restraint or injunction under any circumstances.

5. CONSIDERATION: As consideration for all rights granted

and assigned to Buyer and for seller's representations and warranties, Buyer agrees to pay to Seller, and Seller agrees to accept:

(a) For a theatrical or television motion picture $_____ besides any sums paid in connection with the option periods so payable upon exercise of the option to acquire the Property.

(b) For any mini-series, $_____ per hour, pro-rated for part hours.

(c) For any sequel or remake of a theatrical or television motion picture based on the Property, one-half ($\frac{1}{2}$) and one-third ($\frac{1}{3}$), respectively, of the amount paid for the initial motion picture, payable upon commencement of principal photography of the subsequent production.

(d) For any television series produced, based on the Property, Buyer will pay the following royalties per initial production upon completion of production of each program: up to 30 minutes $_____; over 30, but not more than 60, minutes $_____; over 60 minutes $_____; and in addition to the foregoing, as a buy-out of all royalty obligations, one-hundred percent (100%) of the applicable initial royalty amount, in equal installments over five (5) reruns, payable within thirty (30) days after each such rerun.

As and for contingent compensation _____ percent of one-hundred percent (100%) of the net profits (including allied and ancillary rights) of each motion picture and television program or series based on the Property, in whole or in part, with profits defined according to the same definition obtained by Buyer; provided, however, that Seller's percentage shall not be subject to any reductions or preconditions whatsoever.

6. REPRESENTATIONS AND WARRANTIES:

(a) Sole Proprietor: Seller represents and warrants to Buyer that Seller is the sole and exclusive proprietor, throughout the universe, of that certain original literary material written by Seller entitled "_____."

(b) Facts: Seller represents and warrants to Buyer as follows:

(i) Seller is the sole author and creator of the Property.

(ii) The Property was first published in 19__ by _____ (publisher) under the title _____, and was registered for copyright in the name of _____, under copyright registration number _____, in the Office of the United States Register of Copyrights, Washington, D.C.

(iii) No motion picture or dramatic version of the Property, or any part of it, has been manufactured, produced, presented or authorized; no radio or television development, presentation, or program based on the Property, or any part of it, has been manufactured, produced, presented, broadcast or authorized; and no written or oral agreements or commitments at all with respect to the Property, or with respect to any rights therein, have been made or entered by or on behalf of Seller (except with respect to the Publication of the Property as set forth above).

(iv) None of the rights herein granted and assigned to Buyer have been granted and/or assigned to any person, firm or corporation other than Buyer.

(c) No Infringement or Violation of Third-Party Rights: Seller represents and warrants to Buyer that Seller has not adapted the Property from any other literary, dramatic or other material of any kind, nature or description, nor, except material which is in the public domain, has Seller copied or used in the Property the plot, scenes, sequence or story of any other literary, dramatic or other material; that the Property does not infringe upon any common law or statutory rights in any other literary, dramatic or other material; that no material contained in the Property is libelous or violative of the right of privacy of any person; that the full utilization of any and all rights in and to the Property granted by Seller pursuant to this Agreement will not violate the rights of any person, firm or corporation; and that the Property is not in the public domain in any country in the world where copyright protection is available.

(d) No Impairment of Rights: Seller represents and warrants to Buyer that Seller is the exclusive proprietor, throughout the universe, of all rights in and to the Property granted herein to Buyer; that Seller has not assigned, licensed or in any manner encumbered, diminished or impaired any such rights; that Seller has not committed or omitted to perform any act by which such rights could or will be encumbered, diminished or impaired; and that there is no outstanding claim or litigation pending against or involving the title, ownership and/or copyright in the Property, or in any part thereof, or in any rights granted herein to Buyer. Seller further represents and warrants that no attempt shall be made hereafter to encumber, diminish or impair any of the rights granted herein and that all appropriate protection of such rights will continue to be maintained by Seller.

7. INDEMNIFICATION:

(a) Seller agrees to indemnify Buyer against all judgments, liability, damages, penalties, losses and expense (including reasonable attorneys' fees) which may be suffered or assumed by or obtained against Buyer by reason of any breach or failure of any warranty or agreement herein made by Seller.

(b) Buyer shall not be liable to Seller for damages of any kind in connection with any Picture it may produce, distribute or exhibit, or for damages for any breach of this agreement (except failure to pay the money consideration herein specified) occurring or accruing before Buyer has had reasonable notice and opportunity to adjust or correct such matters.

(c) All rights, licenses and privileges herein granted to Buyer are irrevocable and not subject to rescission, restraint or injunction under any circumstances.

8. PROTECTION OF RIGHTS GRANTED: Seller hereby grants to Buyer the free and unrestricted right, but at Buyer's own cost and expense, to institute in the name and on behalf of Seller, or Seller and Buyer jointly, any and all suits and proceedings at law or in equity, to enjoin and restrain any infringements of the rights herein granted, and hereby assigns and sets over to Buyer any and all causes of action relative to or based upon any such infringement, as well as any and all recoveries obtained thereon. Seller will not compromise, settle or in any manner interfere with such litigation if brought; and Buyer agrees to indemnify and hold Seller harmless from any costs, expenses, or damages which Seller may suffer as a result of any such suit or proceeding.

9. COPYRIGHT: Regarding the copyright in and to the Property, Seller agrees that:

(a) Seller will prevent the Property and any arrangements, revisions, translations, novelizations, dramatizations or new versions thereof, whether published or unpublished and whether copyrighted or not copyrighted, from vesting in the public domain, and will take or cause to be taken any and all steps and proceedings required for copyright or similar protection in any and all countries in which the same may be published or offered for sale, insofar as such countries now or hereafter provide for copyright or similar protection. Any contract or agreement entered into by Seller authorizing or permitting the publication of the Property or any arrangements, revisions, translations, novelizations, dramatizations or new versions thereof in any country will contain appropriate provisions requiring such publisher to comply with all the provisions of this clause.

(b) Without limiting the generality of the foregoing, if the Property or any arrangement, revision, translation, novelization, dramatization or new version thereof is published in the United States or in any other country in which registration is required for copyright or similar protection in accordance with the laws and regulations of such country, and Seller further agrees to affix or cause to be affixed to each copy of the Property or any arrangement, revision, translation, novelization, dramatization or new version thereof which is published or offered for sale such notice or notices as may be required for copyright or similar protection in any country in which such publication or sale occurs.

(c) At least _____ months prior to the expiration of any copyright required by this provision for the protection of the Property, Seller will renew (or cause to be renewed) such copyright, as permitted by applicable law, and any and all rights granted Buyer hereunder shall be deemed granted to Buyer throughout the full period of such renewed copyright, without the payment of any additional consideration, it being agreed that the consideration payable to Seller under this agreement shall be deemed to include full consideration for the grant of such rights to Buyer throughout the period of such renewed copyright.

(d) If the Property, or any arrangement, revision, translation, novelization, dramatization or new version thereof, shall ever enter the public domain, then nothing contained in this agreement shall impair any rights or privileges that the Buyer might be entitled to as a member of the public; thus, the Buyer may exercise any and all such rights and privileges as though this agreement were not in existence. The rights granted herein by Seller to Buyer, and the representations, warranties, undertakings and agreements made hereunder by Seller, shall endure in perpetuity and shall be in addition to any rights, licenses, privileges or property of Buyer referred to in this subclause (d).

10. CREDIT OBLIGATIONS: Buyer shall have the right to publish, advertise, announce and use in any manner or medium, the name, biography and photographs or likenesses of Seller in connection with any exercise by Buyer of its rights hereunder, provided such use shall not constitute an endorsement of any product or service.

During the term of the Writers Guild of America Minimum Basic Agreement ("WGA Agreement"), as it may be amended, the credit provisions of the WGA Agreement shall govern the determination of credits, if any, which the Buyer shall accord the Seller hereunder in connection with photoplays.

Subject to the foregoing, Seller shall be accorded the following credit on a single card on screen and in paid ads controlled by Buyer and in which any other writer is accorded credit, and in size of type (as to height, width, thickness and boldness) equal to the largest size of type in which any other writer is accorded credit:

(a) If the title of the Picture is the same as the title of the Property "_____"; or

(b) If the title of the Picture differs from the title of the Work, "_____."

Additionally, if Buyer shall exploit any other rights in and to the Property, then Buyer agrees to give appropriate source material credit to the Property, to the extent that such source material credits are customarily given in connection with the exploitation of such rights.

No casual or inadvertent failure to comply with any of

the provisions of this clause shall be deemed a breach of this agreement by the Buyer. Seller hereby expressly acknowledges that in the event of a failure or omission constituting a breach of the provisions of this paragraph, the damage (if any) caused Seller thereby is not irreparable or sufficient to entitle Seller to injunctive or other equitable relief. Consequently, Seller's rights and remedies in the event of such breach shall be limited to the right to recover damages in an action at law. Buyer agrees to provide in its contracts with distributors of the Picture that such distributors shall honor Buyer's contractual credit commitments and agrees to inform such distributors of the credit provisions herein.

11. RIGHT OF FIRST NEGOTIATION: The term "Right of First Negotiation" means that if, after the expiration of an applicable time limitation, Seller desires to dispose of or exercise a particular right reserved to Seller herein ("Reserved Right"), whether directly or indirectly, then Seller shall notify Buyer in writing and immediately negotiate with Buyer regarding such Reserved Right. If, after the expiration of _____ days following the receipt of such notice, no agreement has been reached, then Seller may negotiate with third parties regarding such Reserved Right subject to Clause 12 infra.

12. RIGHT OF LAST REFUSAL: The term "Right of Last Refusal" means that if Buyer and Seller fail to reach an agreement pursuant to Buyer's right of first negotiation, and Seller makes and/or receives any bona fide offer to license, lease and/or purchase the particular Reserved Right or any interest therein ("Third-Party Offer"), and if the proposed purchase price and other material terms of a Third Party Offer are no more favorable to Seller than the terms which were acceptable to Buyer during the first negotiation period, Seller shall notify Buyer, by registered mail or telegram, if Seller proposes to accept such Third-Party Offer, the name of the offerer, the proposed purchase price, and other terms of such Third-Party Offer. During the period of _____ days after Buyer's receipt of such notice, Buyer shall have the exclusive option to license, lease and/or purchase, as the case may be, the particular Reserved Right or interest referred to in such Third-Party Offer, at the same purchase price and upon the same terms and conditions as set forth in such notice. If Buyer elects to exercise thereof by registered mail or telegram within such _____ day period, failing which Seller shall

be free to accept such Third-Party Offer; provided that if any such proposed license, lease and/or sale is not consummated with a third party within _____ days following the expiration of the aforesaid _____ day period, Buyer's Right of Last Refusal shall revive and shall apply to each and every further offer or offers at any time received by Seller relating to the particular Reserved Right or any interest therein; provided, further, that Buyer's option shall continue in full force and effect, upon all of the terms and conditions of this paragraph, so long as Seller retains any rights, title or interests in or to the particular Reserved Right. Buyer's Right of Last Refusal shall inure to the benefit of Buyer, its successors and assigns, and shall bind Seller and Seller's heirs, successors and assigns.

13. NO OBLIGATION TO PRODUCE: Nothing herein shall be construed to obligate Buyer to produce, distribute, release, perform or exhibit any motion picture, television, theatrical or other production based upon, adapted from or suggested by the Property, in whole or in part, or otherwise to exercise, exploit or make any use of any rights, licenses, privileges or property granted herein to Buyer.

14. ASSIGNMENT: Buyer may assign and transfer this agreement or all or any part of its rights hereunder to any person, firm or corporation without limitation, and this agreement shall be binding upon and inure to the benefit of the parties hereto and their successors, representatives and assigns forever.

15. NO PUBLICITY: Seller will not, without Buyer's prior written consent in each instance, issue or authorize the issuance or publication of any news story or publicity relating to (i) this Agreement, (ii) the subject matter or terms hereof, or to any use by Buyer, its successors, licensees and assigns, and (iii) any of the rights granted Buyer hereunder.

16. AGENT COMMISSIONS: Buyer shall not be liable for any compensation or fee to any agent of Seller in connection with this Agreement.

17. ADDITIONAL DOCUMENTATION: Seller agrees to execute and procure any other and further instruments necessary to transfer, convey, assign and copyright all rights in the Property granted herein by Seller to Buyer in any country throughout the world. If it shall be necessary under the laws

or any country that copyright registration be acquired in the name of Seller, Buyer is hereby authorized by Seller to apply for said copyright registration thereof; and, in such event, Seller shall and does hereby assign and transfer the same unto Buyer, subject to the rights in the Property reserved hereunder by Seller. Seller further agrees, upon request, to duly execute, acknowledge, procure and deliver to Buyer such short form assignments as may be requested by Buyer for the purpose of copyright recordation in any country, or otherwise. If Seller shall fail to so execute and deliver, or cause to be executed and delivered, the assignments or other instruments herein referred to, Buyer is hereby irrevocably granted the power coupled with an interest to execute such assignments and instruments in the name of Seller and as Seller's attorney-in-fact.

18. NOTICES: All notices to Buyer under this agreement shall be sent by United States registered mail, postage prepaid, or by telegram addressed to Buyer at _____ _____(address) with a courtesy copy to _____ (Buyer's attorney), and all notices to Seller under this agreement shall be sent by United States registered mail, postage prepaid, or by telegram addressed to at _____ (address) seller with a courtesy copy to _____ (Seller's attorney). The deposit of such notice in the United States mail or the delivery of the telegram message to the telegraph office shall constitute service thereof, and the date of such deposit shall be deemed to be the date of service of such notice.

19. ARBITRATION: Any controversy or claim arising out of or relating to this agreement or any breach thereof shall be settled by arbitration in accordance with the Rules of the American Arbitration Association; and judgment upon the award rendered by the arbitrator may be entered in any court having jurisdiction thereof. The prevailing party shall be entitled to reimbursement for costs and reasonable attorneys' fees. The determination of the arbitrator in such proceeding shall be final, binding and non-appealable.

20. MISCELLANEOUS:

(a) Relationship: This agreement between the parties does not constitute a joint venture or partnership of any kind.

(b) Cumulative Rights and Remedies: All rights, remedies, licenses, undertakings, obligations, covenants, privileges and other property granted herein shall be cumulative, and Buyer may exercise or use any of them separately or in conjunction with any one or more of the others.

(c) Waiver: A waiver by either party of any term or condition of this agreement in any instance shall not be deemed or construed to be a waiver of such term or condition for the future, or any subsequent breach thereof.

(d) Severability: If any provision of this agreement as applied to either party or any circumstances shall be adjudged by a court to be void and unenforceable, such shall in no way affect any other provision of this agreement, the application of such provision in any other circumstance, or the validity or enforceability of this agreement.

(e) Governing Law: This agreement shall be construed in accordance with the laws of the State of _____ applicable to agreements which are executed and fully performed within said State.

(f) Captions: Captions are inserted for reference and convenience only and in no way define, limit or describe the scope of this agreement or intent of any provision.

(g) Entire Understanding: This agreement contains the entire understanding of the parties relating to the subject matter, and this agreement cannot be changed except by written agreement executed by the party to be bound.

IN WITNESS WHEREOF, the parties hereto have signed this Agreement as of the day and year first above written.

_____
("Seller")

_____
("Buyer")

Exhibit B

OPTION AGREEMENT
(Short Form for Recordation at U.S. Copyright Office)

For good and valuable consideration, receipt of which is hereby acknowledged, the undersigned hereby grants to _____ (the "BUYER"), its successors and assigns, the sole and exclusive option to purchase all motion picture and certain allied rights, in the original literary and/or dramatic work (the "Work") described as follows:

> Title:
> Author:
> Publisher:
> Date of Publication:
> Copyright Registration:

The Work includes but is not limited to: (i) all contents; (ii) all present and future adaptations and versions; (iii) the title, characters and theme; and (iv) the copyright and all renewals and extensions of copyright.

This instrument is executed in accordance with and is subject to the agreement (the "Option Agreement") between the undersigned and the Buyer dated as of _____(date) relating to the option granted to the Buyer to purchase the above-mentioned rights in the Work, which rights are more fully described in the Purchase Agreement, attached to the Option Agreement.

Date: _____

Attest _____ _____
(name of witness)   (name of seller)

Exhibit C
(Short Form Copyright Assignment)

KNOW ALL MEN BY THESE PRESENTS that, in consideration of One Dollar ($1.00) and other good and valuable consideration, receipt of which is hereby acknowledged, the undersigned _____ ("Assignor") do(es) hereby sell, grant, convey and assign unto _____ ("Assignee"), its successors, assigns and licensees forever, all right, title and interest including but not limited to the exclusive worldwide Motion Picture and allied rights of Assignor in and to that certain literary work to wit: that certain original screenplay written by _____ entitled _____ ("Literary Property"), and all drafts, revisions, arrangements, adaptations, dramatizations, translations, sequels and other versions of the Literary Property which may heretofore have been written or which may hereafter be written with the sanction of Assignor.

Dated this _____ day of _____, 19__.

_____
("Assignor")

AGREED TO:

_____
("Assignee")

Acknowledgment

STATE OF   )
) ss.:
COUNTY OF   )

On the   day of   , 19__, before me personally came _____ to me known and known to be the individual described in and who executed the foregoing instrument, and he did duly acknowledge to me that he executed the same.

_____
Notary Public

CHAPTER 6

EMPLOYMENT CONTRACTS

LOAN-OUT COMPANIES

Writers, directors and actors often incorporate themselves by setting up loan-out companies. At one time there were significant tax advantages to setting up such companies. Most of these benefits have now been abolished, although some pension and health-plan benefits remain. Also, a loan-out corporation on a fiscal year basis could spread out income to its owner over two personal calendar tax years, placing income in lower tax brackets.[1]

In a loan-out deal, the studio (employer) does not contract directly with the talent (e.g., the writer). The employer contracts with the talent's company, a company that is typically owned 100% by the talent or his family.

The company is called a "loan-out" company because it loans out the talent's services first to studio A, then to studio B, and so on. All the money earned from the talent's services are paid to

---

[1] That is, by timing the payouts of salary, and having a corporate tax year that runs from June to May, for example (instead of the usual calender year of January to December), the corporation can spread income over two personal tax years. This may keep more of an individual's income in lower tax brackets.

the company. The loan-out company pays the talent's business expenses and a salary.

Studios don't object to paying talent through their loan-out companies if the studio's interests are protected. The studio usually wants the talent to sign an "Inducement Agreement." This is a contract between the studio and the talent guaranteeing that the talent will abide by the agreement between the studio and the loan-out company. Otherwise, if the loan-out company breaches the contract, the studio can only sue the company. The company may not have any assets and cannot perform itself (i.e., corporations cannot act, write, direct—only people can).

Therefore, when talent requests that the deal be structured as a loan-out deal, three agreements are made. First is the employment contract between the studio and the loan-out company. Second is the agreement between the studio and the talent, the inducement agreement. And third is the employment agreement between the loan-out company and the talent.

Employing talent through a loan-out agreement is not much different than employing talent directly. You can immediately spot a loan-out deal because it refers to one party as the "Lender." The "Lender" is the loan-out company, not a bank.

WRITERS

Writers can create screenplays on their own and sell them to a studio (or a producer). As discussed in Chapter 12 on Copyright, the screenplay is a form of intellectual property and it can be sold by the owner like any other property. We have already reviewed option agreements and literary purchase agreements which are contracts for the sale of a writer's rights in a literary property.

Another method studios use to acquire screenplays entails hiring someone to write one for them. The idea for the screenplay may be proposed by the writer in a pitch meeting, or it may be suggested by the studio. [1]

The advantage to the writer of being employed is that the

---

[1] The idea could be an original one or one based on another work, such as play, magazine article or book, that the studio wants to adapt as a movie.

employer takes the risk of the project not turning out well. A writer who spends six months creating a screenplay that he cannot sell does not earn any income for his efforts. The writer working as an employee, however, receives a guaranteed payment for his labor, even if the script never gets produced. And if the script is produced, the writer may receive additional compensation in the form of a bonus or percentage of profits.

Producers use employment contracts to hire writers. As a "work for hire," the employer owns the copyright. The writer gets the money; the studio gets the script. Since the studio owns the work, it can shelve the project or hire someone else to rewrite it at any time.

As you will see, many provisions found in a writer's employment agreement are also present in actor and director employment agreements. The methods of structuring compensation, force-majeure conditions and credit provisions are similar.

A producer can hire a writer on a step deal or flat deal basis. In a step deal, the employer has the right to end the writer's services after each step. Step deals are often used when an employer is hiring a novice writer or a writer whose ability is uncertain. The employer reduces his financial risk by proceeding in a series of steps instead of hiring the writer to write an entire script.

Let's say you are a producer interested in hiring writer A to create a romantic comedy for you, based on your own idea. Writer A has never written a romantic comedy before. You are uncertain whether he has the ability to write what you want. You don't want to risk $50,000 (approximately WGA scale for a feature) to hire him. So you propose a step deal.

The steps could be:

   a) treatment/outline

   b) first-draft screenplay

   c) second draft

   d) rewrite

   e) polish

After each step, you will have the option of whether to

proceed to the next step. After any step you can decide to shelve the project or bring in another writer. As the employer, you own all the writer's work. The writer gets to keep the money for the work he completes, even if he does not complete all steps.

The Writers Guild sets minimums for each step, and the total compensation paid for the steps will be no less than the minimum scale payment for a flat deal for a complete screenplay.

A step deal will set forth "reading periods." These are periods, usually a couple of weeks, in which the producer has the opportunity to decide whether he wants to go to the next step. If the producer does not exercise his right to proceed within the reading period, he risks losing the writer. During the reading period the writer cannot accept other assignments that might prevent him from completing the remaining steps.

The writer's employment agreement will also set out the time requirements when various items are due. Usually the writer gets one to three months to complete a first draft.

There are different ways that writers receive compensation. Fixed compensation is a guaranteed payment. Typically, producers pay half up front and half when the work is delivered. If the writer doesn't do the work in a craftsman-like manner, the producer is not obliged to pay for it. But the producer is obliged to pay fixed compensation regardless of whether the producer likes the writer's work or whether the script gets produced. Thus, the employer takes the risk of the script turning out poorly.

The Writers Guild prohibits its members from working on speculation without a guarantee of fixed compensation. The amount of fixed compensation is often minimum WGA scale for a first-time writer. For more experienced writers, the amount is often a modest increase over their last deal. Of course, if the writer wins an Academy Award or a movie of his becomes a blockbuster hit, his price will multiply.

Bonus compensation is another form of payment. Let's say you are a producer and a writer asks to be paid $90,000. You can't afford that amount up front, so you counter by offering $60,000 fixed compensation and another $30,000 as bonus compensation. Bonus compensation is not guaranteed. Payment is contingent on a certain event, such as the script going into production. So if the script doesn't get produced, the bonus need not be paid. Thus, bonus compensation is more iffy than fixed compensation.

Deferred compensation is more iffy than bonus compensation. Deferments are often used in low-budget films when the producer can't afford to pay his cast and crew their usual wages. Perhaps he offers to hire everyone at $250 a week and to defer the rest of the salary they would normally earn. Deferments are usually not payable unless the script gets produced, the movie is released and revenue is received. Deferments can be payable before or after investors recoup their investment. The employment agreement may provide that some deferment holders be paid first or everyone share in revenues equally (in pari passu).

The most iffy kind of payment is contingent compensation, or net profits (points). Here the employee will receive payment only if the script is produced, released and it generates revenue. And the revenue must be substantial enough that after recoupment of all costs and expenses, including distribution fees and marketing costs, there is something left. It is rare that net profit participants receive anything. Artists often complain that studios use creative accounting to deny them their share of profits. This topic is addressed in Chapter 11.

Writers typically receive between 1% and 5% of 100% of net profits. Why do we state the writer's share in terms of a percent of 100%? So that there won't be any ambiguity as to the size of the writer's portion of net profits. If we simply said the writer gets 5% of net profits, it would be unclear whether she gets 5% of all the net profits or 5% of the producer's share of net profits.

Typically, the studio and the producer split net profits 50/50. The producer, however, often must give a writer, director and star a piece of his net profits. These profit participants take from the producer's half of net profits. Nevertheless, the custom in the industry is to express net profits in terms of the whole (all profits) so that there is no ambiguity. Instead of saying a writer gets 5% of 100% of net profits, one could say he gets 10%t of 50%. It would be the same size slice of the pie.

Another form of payment is known as "additional" compensation. Producers make these payments if they make a sequel, remake or television spin-off series based on the original work. Writers often receive 50% of what they were paid for the original movie for a sequel and 33% for a remake. For a television spin-off series the writer usually gets a royalty for every episode. An example of a successful spin-off series would be "M.A.S.H." The television series was based upon a successful movie written by Richard Hooker and Ring Lardner, Jr. Since the series was so successful, the writers may have earned more in royalties from the series than they were paid for writing the film.

The series royalty is a passive one. That means the writer is not obliged to do any work on the series. The payment is due him because of his work on the original. The writer is entitled to the royalty even if he is not involved in the series. Of course, if the writer works on the series, he would be entitled to additional payment.

The writer's employment agreement will also contain a credit clause. For a WGA writer and a signatory company, the WGA credit determination rules apply. Consequently, the producer does not have the discretion to allocate writing credits anyway he may choose. After the "Notice of Tentative Credits" is given, all writers on the project have an opportunity to object and request credit arbitration.

Credit is important for reasons besides ego and professional stature. The determination of credit can have financial repercussions. Often the amount of points a writer receives will vary depending on whether he receives sole, shared or no credit.

Writers sometimes complain about directors who have their writer friends needlessly rewrite a script, thereby forcing the first writer to share credit and profits with another. The Writers Guild credit guidelines give a strong preference to the first writer. The second writer will only obtain credit if his contribution is 50% or more of the completed script. Of course, this encourages the second writer to extensively revise the first and may induce him to revise good material.

Performance standards will also be addressed in the employment agreement. The writer is required to perform diligently and efficiently, to follow the suggestions and instructions of the company, and to devote all time exclusively to the project during the term of the agreement.

A force majeure clause is another common provision. Force majeure means superior force, and it refers to certain events beyond control of the production company that may force suspension of the contract. Such forces could be a fire, earthquake, strike, act of God, war, new law, closing of most theaters in the country, and death or illness of a principal member of the cast or director.

In the event one of these events causes a suspension of work, the company does not have to pay the writer any compensation during the suspension. Usually, if the suspension lasts more than five weeks, for example, the production company and the writer each have the right to terminate the contract.

Finally, contracts with WGA writers will provide that, should anything in the agreement conflict with the WGA's collective- bargaining agreement, the terms of the latter agreement will prevail. This is to prevent the employer from negotiating a deal with a writer that is more favorable than the minimums set forth in the agreement reached through collective bargaining.

MAJOR PROVISIONS
WRITER EMPLOYMENT
AGREEMENT

1) TYPE OF DEAL

    FLAT DEAL OR STEP DEAL

2) TIME DEADLINE

3) READING PERIODS

4) COMPENSATION

    FIXED

    BONUS

    DEFERRED

    CONTINGENT

    ADDITIONAL

5) CREDIT

6) PERFORMANCE STANDARDS

7) FORCE MAJEURE

8) SUPERSEDING EFFECT OF WGA

DEALMAKING
IN THE
FILM AND
TELEVISION
INDUSTRY

100

Here is a sample writer employment agreement. It was used to employ a writer who worked as part of a writing team and it is structured as a loan out-agreement.

WRITER EMPLOYMENT AGREEMENT

Agreement dated _____ 19 , between The Writer's Co., a New York Corporation ("Lender") Federal I.D. # _____, regarding the services of Jim Writer ("Writer") and Big Films ("Production Company").

1. EMPLOYMENT: Production Company agrees to borrow from Lender and Lender agrees to lend to Production Company the writing services of writer's, upon the terms and conditions herein specified, for the proposed Theatrical Motion Picture currently entitled "_____" ("Picture"), based upon a screenplay of the same name supplied by Production Company ("Basic Property"). Lender represents and warrants that it is a New York Corporation, that Lender has entered into a written contract with Writer which is now in full force and effect, and that pursuant to such contract Lender has the right and authority to lend to Production Company the services of Writer upon the terms and conditions herein specified. Lender and Writer shall perform such writing services in collaboration with _____ pursuant to the Employment Agreement dated _____ 19__, between _____ and Production Company ("Agreement"). Writer and _____ are hereinafter collectively referred to as the "Writer's Team."

2. THE PRODUCT AGREEMENT WITH OPTIONS: The completed results of Writer's services hereunder shall be deemed collectively the "Product" and individually the "Product Form," and shall be created as follows:

First-Draft screenplay with option for one Revision/Draft thereof and dependent option for one polish.

3. COMMENCEMENT OF SERVICES: Lender shall cause Writer to commence services in writing the first draft of the screenplay upon execution of this agreement and Production Company becoming a signatory of the Writers Guild of America. Lender shall cause Writer to commence writing each subsequent Product Form on a date to be designated by Production Company, which date may be earlier, but shall not be later than the first business day after expiration of the then current Reading Period or Option Period, as the case may be, described in Clause 4.

4. TIME REQUIREMENTS — Writer's services shall be rendered pursuant to the following time requirements:

(a) Delivery Periods: Lender shall cause Writer to deliver each Product Form within the period ("Delivery Period") which commences on the date Writer is obligated to commence writing each designated Product Form and which ends upon expiration of the applicable time period listed in Clause 4(e).

(b) Reading Periods: Each time Writer delivers any Product Form, if Writer's engagement herein requires additional writing services, Production Company shall have a period ("Reading Period"), which commences on the first business day following the delivery of such Product Form and which continues for the length of time listed in Clause 4(e) opposite the description of the Product Form delivered within which to read such Product Form and advise Lender to cause Writer to commence writing the next Product Form.

(c) Postponement of Services: If Production Company does not exercise within the applicable Reading Period its right to require Lender to cause Writer to commence writing either the first set of revisions or the polish, Production Company may nonetheless require Lender to cause Writer to render such services at any time within the one (1) year period commencing upon delivery of the immediately preceding Product Form, subject to Writer's availability and provided: 1) Writer's services are to be rendered during the one year period, and 2) Production Company shall furnish Lender with thirty (30) days prior written notice of the date designated for the commencement of such services, and 3) that Production Company has paid Lender in a timely manner for the postponed product forms as those services were timely rendered.

(d) Option Periods: Each Option, if any, under Clause 4(e), shall be exercised if at all in writing within the period ("Option Period") which commences on the first business day following the delivery of the Product Form immediately preceding that for which an Option may be exercised, or upon the expiration of the Delivery Period applicable to such Product Form, whichever is later, and which continues for the length of time listed in Clause 4(e) opposite the description of the Product Form delivered.

(e) Length of Periods—Delivery, Reading and Option Periods shall be the following lengths:

DEALMAKING
IN THE
FILM AND
TELEVISION
INDUSTRY

102

Product Form	Delivery Period	Reading/Option Period
First-Draft Screenplay	8 weeks	2 weeks
First Revision/ Second-Draft Screenplay	4 weeks	2 weeks
Polish of Screenplay	2 weeks	2 weeks

5. DELIVERY: TIME OF THE ESSENCE:

(a) Effective Delivery: Delivery of Product Form to any person other than _____ shall not constitute delivery of such Product Form as required by this Agreement.

(b) Time of the Essence: Lender shall cause Writer to write and deliver each Product Form for which Writer is engaged as soon as reasonably possible after commencement of Writer's services thereon, but not later than the date upon which the applicable Delivery Period expires. Time of delivery is of the essence.

(c) Revisions: For each Product Form which is in the nature of a Revision, Writer's services shall include the writing and delivery of such changes as may be required by Production Company within a reasonable time prior to the expiration of the Delivery Period applicable to such Product Form.

6. COMPENSATION:

(a) Fixed Compensation—Production Company shall pay Lender as set forth below for Writer's services and all rights granted by Lender:

(1) For First Draft Screenplay: $_____, payable half upon commencement, half upon delivery.

(2) For First Revision/Second Draft Screenplay: $_____, payable half upon commencement, half upon delivery.

(3) For Polish of Screenplay: $_____, payable half upon commencement, half upon delivery.

(b) Payment: Production Company shall have no obligation to pay Lender any compensation with respect to any Product Form for which Production Company has failed to exercise its Option under Clause 4.

(c) Bonus Compensation: Subject to the production and release of the Picture, and to the Lender and Writer not being in material default hereunder, in addition to the Fixed Compensation set forth above, Lender shall be entitled to be paid the following:

(i) If Writer receives sole or shared screenplay credit pursuant to final Writers Guild of America ("WGA") credit determination with respect to the Picture, Lender shall be entitled to receive as Bonus Compensation the sum of $25,000 over the compensation provided by Clause 6(a), less the aggregate of all sums paid to Lender pursuant to Clause 6(a) above, and shall be payable upon commencement of principal photography.

(ii) If the production budget is above $700,000, the bonus payment shall escalate $2,500 per $100,000 increase. If the production budget exceeds $1 million, the production bonus will be $50,000. The sums payable under this section shall be less the aggregate of all sums (not already deducted) paid to Lender pursuant to Clause 6 (a) and 6 (c) above and shall be payable 60 days after completion of principal photography.

(iii) Repayment: If Bonus Compensation set forth in Clause 6(c) above is paid to Lender as set forth hereinabove, and if Writer receives neither sole screenplay credit nor shared screenplay credit pursuant to final WGA credit determination for the Picture, Lender shall repay to Production Company such sum so paid to Writer within five (5) days of such determination.

(d) Contingent Compensation: Subject to the production and release of the Picture and subject to Lender and Writer not being in default of their obligations hereunder, in addition to the Fixed Compensation and Bonus Compensation set forth above, Lender shall be entitled to be paid the following:

(i) Sole Screenplay Credit: If the Writer's writing Team receives sole screenplay credit pursuant to final WGA credit determination for the Picture, Lender shall be entitled to receive as Contingent Compensation an amount equal to two and one-half percent (2½%) of one hundred percent (100%) of the Net Profits of the Picture.

(ii) Shared Screenplay Credit: If the Writer's writing team receives shared screenplay credit pursuant to final WGA credit determination for the Picture, Lender shall be entitled to receive as Contingent Compensation an amount equal to one and one-quarter percent (1¼%) of one-hundred percent (100%) of the Net Profits of the Picture.

(e) For purposes of this Agreement, "Net Profits" shall be computed, determined and paid in accordance with definition of net-profits defined in the production/distribution agreement between production company and the distributor of the Picture,

DEALMAKING
IN THE
FILM AND
TELEVISION
INDUSTRY

104

provided that Lender's definition shall be as favorable as any other net profit participant.

(f) Additional payments to Lender for Sequel, Remake and Television Use of the Work; Right of First Negotiation: Subject to the provisions of Clauses 6(g) and 6(h) below, and subject to the production and release of the Picture and the performance of all obligations of Lender and Writer hereunder:

(i) Sequel Theatrical Motion Picture: If the Writer's Writing Team receives sole/shared screenplay credit or is accorded separation of rights pursuant to applicable WGA determination with respect to the Picture, then for each Sequel Theatrical Motion Picture based on the Picture produced and released, Lender shall be entitled to be paid an amount equal to fifty percent (50%) of one-hundred percent (100%) of the sum paid to Lender as Compensation pursuant to Clause 6(a) and 6(c) supra, and a percentage participation in the Net Profits of such Sequel Theatrical Motion Picture in an amount equal to fifty percent (50%) of one hundred percent (100%) of the rate of percentage participation in Net Profits of the Picture payable to Lender as Contingent Compensation pursuant to Clauses 6(d)(i) or 6(d)(ii) above, if any.

(ii) Theatrical Remakes: If the Writer's Writing Team receives sole/shared screenplay credit or is accorded separation of rights pursuant to applicable WGA determination for the Picture, then for each Theatrical Remake of the Picture produced and released, Lender shall be entitled to be paid an amount equal to thirty-three percent (33%) of one-hundred percent (100%) of the sum paid to Writer as Compensation pursuant to Clause 6(a) and 6(c) supra, and thirty-three percent (33%) of one-hundred percent (100%) of the percentage participation in Net Profits of the Picture payable to Lender as Contingent Compensation pursuant to Clauses 6(d)(i) or 6(d)(ii) above, if any.

(iii) Sequel Television Motion Pictures and Television Remakes:

(A) Pilot and Series: If Writer is accorded separation of rights pursuant to applicable WGA determination with respect to the Picture, then for each Studio Sequel Television Motion Picture based upon the Picture and/or Television Remake of the Picture which is produced and licensed for exhibition by Production Company and which is a Pilot or an episode of an episodic or anthology television series (collectively "TV Program"), Lender shall be entitled to receive the following royalties:

(1) $_____ for each TV Program of not more than thirty (30) minutes in length.

(2) $_____ for each TV Program in excess of thirty (30) minutes but not more than sixty (60) minutes in length.

(3) $_____ for each TV Program in excess of sixty (60) minutes in length.

(4) If any TV Program is rerun, Lender shall be paid twenty percent (20%) of the applicable sum initially paid Lender pursuant to Subclauses (1), (2) or (3) above for the second run, third run, fourth run, fifth run, and sixth run respectively. No further rerun payments shall be due or payable for any rerun after the sixth run.

(B) Movies-of-the-Week and Mini-Series: If Writer is accorded separation of rights pursuant to applicable WGA determination for the Picture, then for each Sequel Television Motion Picture or Television Remake of the Picture which is produced and licensed for exhibition by Production Company and which is a so-called "Movie-of-the-Week" or so-called "Mini-Series," Lender shall be entitled to receive the following royalties which sum shall constitute full payment for all rerun use and/or other exploitation thereof:

(1) $_____ for the first two (2) hours of running time of each such Movie-of-the-Week and/or each such Mini-Series.

(2) $_____ for every hour of running time, if any, exceeding the first two (2) hours of running time of such Movie of the Week and/or such Mini-Series up to a maximum of $_____.

(iv) Definitions—The following terms as utilized in connection with this Agreement, shall be defined as set forth below:

(A) "Television Remake": A remake primarily intended to be initially distributed for free-television exhibition.

(B) "Television Studio Sequel Motion Picture": A studio sequel motion picture primarily intended to be initially distributed for free-television exhibition.

(C) "Theatrical Remake": A remake primarily intended to be initially distributed for theatrical exhibition.

(D) "Theatrical Studio Sequel Motion Picture": A studio sequel motion picture primarily intended to be initially distributed for theatrical exhibition.

(E) WGA Agreement: All sums payable to Lender pursuant to this Agreement shall be in lieu of, and not in addition to, any similar payment to which Lender may be entitled pursuant to the current Writers Guild of America Theatrical and Television Agreement ("WGA Agreement").

7. CONDITIONS AFFECTING OR RELATED TO COMPENSATION:

(a) Method of Payment: All compensation which shall become due to Lender hereunder shall be sent to Lender at the address provided in Clause 26. Such address may be changed to

DEALMAKING
IN THE
FILM AND
TELEVISION
INDUSTRY

106

such other address as Lender may hereafter notify Production Company in accordance with Clause 26.

(b) Performance: Production Company's obligation to pay compensation or otherwise perform hereunder shall be conditioned upon Lender and Writer not being in default of their obligations under the Agreement. No compensation shall accrue to Lender during Lender or Writer's inability, failure or refusal to perform, according to the terms and conditions of this Agreement, the services contracted for herein, nor shall compensation accrue during any period of Force Majeure, Suspension or upon Termination except as otherwise herein provided.

(c) Governmental Limitation: No withholding, deduction, reduction or limitation of compensation by Production Company which is required or authorized by law ("Governmental Limitation") shall be a breach of this Agreement by Production Company or relieve Lender and Writer from Lender's and Writer's obligations hereunder. Payment of compensation as permitted pursuant to the Governmental Limitation shall continue while such Governmental Limitation is in effect and shall be deemed to constitute full performance by Production Company of its obligation to pay compensation hereunder.

(d) Garnishment/Attachment: If Production Company is required, because of the service of any garnishment, writ of execution or lien, or by the terms of any contract or assignment executed by Lender to withhold, or to pay all or any portion of the compensation due Lender hereunder to any other person, firm or corporation, the withholding or payment of such compensation or portion thereof, pursuant to the requirements of any such garnishment, writ of execution, lien, contract or assignment, shall not be construed as a breach by Production Company of this Agreement.

(e) Overpayment/Offset: If Production Company makes any overpayment to Lender hereunder for any reason or if Lender and/or Writer is indebted to Production Company for any reason, Lender or Writer shall pay Production Company such overpayment or indebtedness on demand, or at the election of Production Company may deduct and retain for its own account an amount equal to all or any part of such overpayment or indebtedness from any sums that may be due or become due or payable by Production Company to Lender or for the account of Lender and such deduction or retention shall not be deemed a breach of this Agreement.

(f) Pay or Play: Production Company shall not be obligated to use Writer's services for the Picture, nor shall Production Company be obligated to produce, release, distribute, advertise, exploit or otherwise make use of the results and proceeds of Writer's services if such services are used. Production Company may elect to terminate Writer's services at any time without legal justification or excuse provided that the Fixed Compensation provided in Clause 6(a), which shall have been earned and accrued prior to such termination shall be paid to Lender. In the event of such termination, all other rights of Lender and Writer herein shall be deemed void ab initio except such rights as may have accrued to Lender/Writer in accordance with the terms of Clauses 21 (relating to Guilds and Unions), 22 (relating to Credits) and 6(c) (relating to bonus compensation).

8. PERFORMANCE STANDARDS: Writer's services hereunder shall be rendered promptly and in collaboration with _____
in a diligent, conscientious, artistic and efficient manner to Writer's best ability. Writer shall devote all of Writer's time and shall render Writer's services exclusively (during writing periods only) to Production Company in performing the writing services contemplated hereunder, and shall not render services for any other party during the period of Writer's engagement. Writer's services shall be rendered in such manner as Production Company may direct pursuant to the instructions, suggestions and ideas of and under the control of and at the times and places required by Production Company's authorized representatives. Lender shall cause Writer, as and when requested by Production Company, to consult with Production Company's daily authorized representatives and shall be available for conferences in person or by telephone with such representatives for such purposes at such times during Writer's engagement as may be required by such representatives.

9. RESULTS AND PROCEEDS OF SERVICES:

(a) Ownership: Production Company shall solely and exclusively own the Product, each Product Form and all of the results and proceeds thereof, in whatever stage of completion as may exist from time to time (including but not limited to all rights of whatever kind and character, throughout the world, in perpetuity, in any and all languages of copyright, trademark, patent, production, manufacture, recordation, reproduction, transcription, performance, broadcast and exhibition by any art, method or device, now known or hereafter devised, including without limitation radio broadcast, theatrical and non-theatrical exhibition, and television exhibition or otherwise) whether such results and proceeds consist of literary, dramatic, musical, motion picture, mechanical or any other form or works, themes, ideas, compositions, creations or products. Production Company's acquisition hereunder shall also include all rights generally known in the field of literary and musical endeavor as the "moral rights

DEALMAKING
IN THE
FILM AND
TELEVISION
INDUSTRY

108

of authors" in and/or to the Product, each Product Form, and any musical and literary proceeds of Writer's services. Production Company shall have the right but not the obligation, with respect to the Product, each Product Form, the results and proceeds thereof, to add to, subtract from, change, arrange, revise, adapt, rearrange, make variations, and to translate the same into any and all languages, change the sequence, change the characters and the descriptions thereof contained therein, change the title of the same, record and photograph the same with or without sound (including spoken words, dialogue and music synchronously recorded), use said title or any of its components in connection with works or motion pictures wholly or partially independent thereof, to sell, copy and publish the same as Production Company may desire and to use all or any part thereof in new versions, adaptations and sequels in any and all languages and to obtain copyright therein throughout the world. Lender/Writer hereby expressly waives any and all rights which Lender or Writer may have, either in law, in equity, or otherwise, which Writer may have or claim to have as a result of any alleged infringements of Lender's or Writer's so-called "moral rights of authors." Lender acknowledges that the results and proceeds of Writer's services are works specially ordered by Production Company for use as part of a motion picture and the results and proceeds of Writer's services shall be considered to be works made for hire for Production Company, and, therefore, Production Company shall be the author and copyright owner of the results and proceeds of Writer's services.

(b) Assignment and Vesting of Rights: All rights granted or agreed to be granted to Production Company hereunder shall vest in Production Company immediately and shall remain vested whether this Agreement expires in normal course or is terminated for any cause or reason, or whether Writer executes the Certificate of Authorship required infra. All material created, composed, submitted, added or interpolated by Writer hereunder shall automatically become Production Company's property, and Production Company, for this purpose, shall be deemed author thereof with Writer acting entirely as Production Company's employee. Lender and Writer do hereby assign and transfer to Production Company all of the foregoing without reservation, condition or limitation, and no right of any kind, nature or description is reserved by Lender or Writer. The said assignment and transfer to Production Company by Lender and Writer are subject to the limitations contained in the current Writers Guild of America Theatrical and Television Film Basic Agreement ("WGA Agreement").

(c) Execution of Other Documents:

(i) Certificate of Authorship: Lender further agrees, if Production Company requests Lender to do so, to cause Writer to execute and deliver to Production Company, in connection with all material written by writer hereunder, a Certificate of Authorship in substantially the following form:

I hereby certify that I wrote the manuscript hereto attached, entitled "The Big Story" based upon a screenplay of the same name written by Jane Doe, as an employee of Big Films which furnished my services pursuant to an employment Agreement between The Writer's Co., a New York Corporation, and Big Films dated _____, in performance of my duties thereunder and in the regular course of my employment, and that Big Films is the author thereof and entitled to the copyright therein and thereto, with the right to make such changes therein and such uses thereof as it may from time to time determine as such author.

IN WITNESS WHEREOF, I have hereto set my hand this _____ (date). If Production Company desires to secure separate assignments or Certificates of Authorship of or for any of the foregoing, Lender agrees to have Writer execute such certificate upon Production Company's request therefore. Lender and Writer irrevocably grant(s) Production Company the power coupled with an interest to execute such separate assignments or Certificates of Authorship in Lender's/Writer's name and as Lender's/Writer's attorney-in-fact.

(ii) Lender recognizes that the provisions in Clause 9(c)(iii) dealing with any other documents to be signed by Lender are not to be construed in derogation of Production Company's rights arising from the employer-employee relationship but are included because in certain jurisdictions and in special circumstances the rights in and to the material which flow from the employer-employee relationship may not be sufficient in and of themselves to vest ownership in Production Company.

(iii) If Production Company desires to secure further documents covering, quitclaiming or assigning all or any of the results and proceeds of Writer's services; or all or any rights in and to the same, then Lender/Writer agrees to execute and deliver to Production Company any such documents at any time and from time to time upon Production Company's request, and in such form as may be prescribed by Production Company; without limiting the generality of the foregoing Lender/Writer agrees to execute and deliver to Production Company upon Production Company's request therefore an assignment of all rights, it being agreed that all of the representations, warranties and agreements

DEALMAKING
IN THE
FILM AND
TELEVISION
INDUSTRY

110

made and to be made by Lender/Writer under this Exhibit shall be deemed made by Lender/Writer as part of this agreement. If Lender/Writer shall fail or refuse to execute and deliver the certificate above described and/or any such documents within ten business days of a written request, Lender/Writer hereby irrevocably grants Production Company the power coupled with an interest to execute this certificate and/or documents in Lender's/Writer's name and as Lender's/Writer's attorney-in-fact. Lender's/Writer's failure to execute this certificate and/or documents shall not affect or limit any of Production Company's rights in and to the results and proceeds of Writer's services.

(iv) Separation of Rights: Since Writer has been assigned material, he is not entitled to separation of rights under the WGA Agreement. Notwithstanding anything to the contrary contained herein, Production Company shall have the right to publish and copyright, or cause to be published and copyrighted, screenplays, teleplays and scripts adapted from or based upon the Product and the novelization of screenplays, teleplays and scripts adapted from or based upon the Product or any Product Form created hereunder.

10. LENDER'S/WRITER'S WARRANTIES:

Subject to Article 28 of the WGA Basic Agreement, Lender/Writer warrants:

(a) that, except as provided in the next sentence hereof, all material composed and/or submitted by Writer for or to Production Company shall be wholly original with Writer and shall not infringe upon or violate the right of privacy of, nor constitute a libel or slander against, nor violate any common-law rights or any other rights of any person, firm or corporation. The same agreements and warranties are made by Lender and Writer regarding any and all material, incidents, treatments, characters and action which Writer may add to or interpolate in any material assigned by Production Company to Writer for preparation, but are not made regarding violations or infringements contained in the material so assigned by Production Company to Writer. The said agreements and warranties on Lender's/Writer's part are subject to the limitations contained in the WGA Agreement.

(b) Further Warranties: Lender and Writer hereby warrant that Writer is under no obligation or disability, created by law or otherwise, which would in any manner or to any extent prevent or restrict Lender and Writer from entering into and fully performing this Agreement, and Lender and Writer hereby accept the obligations hereunder. Lender and Writer warrant that Lender/Writer has not entered into any agreement or commitment that would prevent their fulfilling its commitments with Production Company hereunder and that Lender and Writer will not enter into any such agreement or commitment without Production Company's specific approval. Lender and Writer hereby agree that Writer shall devote his entire time and attention and best talents and ability exclusively to Production Company as specified herein and observe and be governed by the rules of conduct established by Production Company for the conduct of its employees.

(c) Indemnification: Lender and Writer agree to indemnify Production Company, its successors, assigns, licensees, officers, directors and employees, and hold them harmless from and against any and all claims, liability, losses, damages, costs, expenses (including but not limited to attorneys' fees), judgments and penalties arising out of Lender's and Writer's breach of warranties under this Agreement. Production Company agrees to indemnify Lender, its successors, assigns, licensees, and employees, and hold them harmless from and against any and all claims, liability, losses, damages, costs, expenses (including but not limited to attorneys' fees), judgments and penalties arising out of any suit against Lender/Writer (arising from Lender's employment under this agreement) not based on Lender's/Writer's breach of his warranties under this Agreement.

11. NAME AND LIKENESS: Production Company shall always have the right to use and display Writer's name and likeness for advertising, publicizing and exploiting the Picture or the Product. However, such advertising may not include the direct endorsement of any product (other than the Picture) without Writer's prior written consent. Exhibition, advertising, publicizing or exploiting the Picture by any media, even through a part of or in connection with a product or a commercially-sponsored program, shall not be deemed an endorsement of any nature.

12. PUBLICITY RESTRICTIONS: Lender or Writer shall not, individually or jointly, or by any means of press agents or publicity or advertising agencies or others, employed or paid by Lender or Writer or otherwise, circulate, publish or otherwise disseminate any news stories or articles, books or other publicity, containing Writer's name relating directly or indirectly to Lender's/Writer's employment by Production Company, the subject matter of this Agreement, the Picture, or the services to be rendered by Lender or Writer or others for the Picture, unless first approved by Production Company. Lender/Writer shall not transfer or attempt to transfer any right, privilege, title or interest in or to any of the aforestated things, nor shall Lender/Writer willingly permit any infringement upon the exclusive rights granted to Production Company. Lender and Writer authorizes Production Company, at Production Company's expense, in Lender's or Writer's name or otherwise, to institute any proper legal

DEALMAKING
IN THE
FILM AND
TELEVISION
INDUSTRY

112

proceedings to prevent such infringement.

13. REMEDIES:

(a) Remedies Cumulative: All remedies of Production Company or Lender shall be cumulative, and no one such remedy shall be exclusive of any other. Without waiving any rights or remedies under this Agreement or otherwise, Production Company may from time to time recover, by action, any damages arising out of any breach of this Agreement by Lender and/or Writer and may institute and maintain subsequent actions for additional damages which may arise from the same or other breaches. The commencement or maintaining of any such action or actions by Production Company shall not constitute or result in the termination of Lender's/Writer's engagement hereunder unless Production Company shall expressly so elect by written notice to Lender. The pursuit by Production Company or Lender of any remedy under this Agreement or otherwise shall not be deemed to waive any other or different remedy which may be available under this Agreement or otherwise.

(b) Services Unique: Lender and Writer acknowledge that Writer's services to be furnished hereunder and the rights herein granted are of a special, unique, unusual, extraordinary and intellectual character which gives them a peculiar value, the loss of which cannot be reasonably or adequately compensated in damages in an action at law, and that Lender's or Writer's Default will cause Production Company irreparable injury and damage. Lender and Writer agrees that Production Company shall be entitled to injunctive and other equitable relief to prevent default by Lender or Writer. In addition to such equitable relief, Production Company shall be entitled to such other remedies as may be available at law, including damages.

14. FORCE MAJEURE:

(a) Suspension: If, (i) by reason of fire, earthquake, labor dispute or strike, act of God or public enemy, any municipal ordinance, any state or federal law, governmental order or regulation, or other cause beyond Production Company's control, Production Company is prevented from or hampered in the production of the Picture, or if, (ii) by reason of the closing of substantially all the theaters in the United States for any of the aforesaid or other causes which would excuse Production Company's performance as a matter of law, Production Company's production of the Picture is postponed or suspended, or if, (iii) by reason of any of the aforesaid contingencies or any other cause or occurrence not within Production Company's control, including but not limited to the death, illness or incapacity of any principal member of the cast

of the Picture or the director or individual producer, the preparation, commencement, production or completion of the Picture is
hampered, interrupted or interfered with, and/or if, (iv) Production
Company's normal business operations are hampered or otherwise
interfered with by virtue of any disruptive events which are beyond
Production Company's control ("Production Company Disability"),
then Production Company may postpone the commencement of or
suspend the rendition of Writer's services and the running of time
hereunder for such time as the Production Company Disability
continues; and no compensation shall accrue or become payable to
Lender hereunder during such suspension. Such suspension shall
end upon the cessation of the cause thereof.

(b) Termination:

(i) Production Company Termination Right: If a Production
Company Disability continues for a period of eight (8) weeks,
Production Company may terminate this Agreement upon writ-
ten notice to Lender.

(ii) Lender's Termination Right: If a Production Company
Disability results in the payment of compensation being sus-
pended hereunder for a period exceeding eight (8) weeks,
Lender may terminate this Agreement upon written notice to
Production Company.

(iii) Production Company Re-Establishment Right: Despite
Lender's election to terminate this Agreement, within five (5)
business days after Production Company's actual receipt of such
written notice from Lender, Production Company may elect to re-
establish the operation of this Agreement.

15. WRITER'S INCAPACITY: If, by reason of mental or physical
disability, Writer shall be incapacitated from performing or complying with any of the terms or conditions hereof ("Writer's
Incapacity") for a consecutive period exceeding fifteen days
during the performance of Writer's services, then:

(a) Suspension: Production Company may suspend the
rendition of services by Writer and the running of time hereunder so long as Writer's Incapacity shall continue.

(b) Termination: Production Company may terminate this
Agreement and all of Production Company's obligations and
liabilities hereunder upon written notice to Lender.

(c) Right of Examination: If any claim of mental or physical
disability is made by Writer or on Writer's behalf, the Production
Company may have Writer examined by such physicians as
Production Company may designate. Writer's physician may be
present at such examination, and shall not interfere therewith.
Any tests performed on Writer shall be related to and be custom-

DEALMAKING
IN THE
FILM AND
TELEVISION
INDUSTRY

114

ary for the treatment, diagnosis or examination to be performed in connection with Writer's claim.

16. LENDER/WRITER DEFAULT: If Lender or Writer fails or refuses to write, complete and deliver to Production Company the Product Form provided for herein within the respective periods specified or if Lender or Writer otherwise fails or refuses to perform or comply with any of the terms or conditions hereof (other than by reason of Writer's Incapacity) ("Lender/Writer Default"), then:

(a) Suspension: Production Company may suspend the rendition of services by Writer and the running of time hereunder as long as the Lender/Writer Default shall continue.

(b) Termination: Production Company may terminate this Agreement and all of Production Company's obligations and liabilities hereunder upon written notice to Lender.

(c) Lender/Writer Default shall not include any failure or refusal of Writer to perform or comply with the material terms of this Agreement by reason of a breach or action by Production Company which makes the performance by Writer of his services impossible.

(d) Prior to termination of this Agreement by Production Company based upon Lender/Writer Default, Production Company shall notify Lender and Writer specifying the nature of the Lender/Writer Default and Lender/Writer shall have a period of 72 hours after giving of such notice to cure the Default. If the Lender/Writer Default is not cured within said period, Production Company may terminate this Agreement forthwith.

17. EFFECT OF TERMINATION: Termination of this Agreement, whether by lapse of time, mutual consent, operation of law, exercise of right of termination or otherwise shall:

(a) Compensation: Terminate Production Company's obligation to pay Lender any further compensation. Nevertheless, if the termination is not for Lender/Writer Default, Production Company shall pay Lender any compensation due and unpaid prior to termination.

(b) Refund/Delivery: If termination occurs pursuant to Clauses 14, 15, or 16, prior to Writer's delivery to Production Company of the Product Form on which Writer is then currently working, then Lender or Writer (or in the event of Writer's death, Writer's estate) shall, as Production Company requests, either forthwith refund to Production Company the compensation which may have been paid to Lender as of that time for such Product Form, or immediately deliver to Production Company all of the Product then completed or in progress, in whatever stage of completion it may be.

18. EFFECT OF SUSPENSION: No compensation shall accrue to Lender during any suspension. During any period of suspension hereunder, Lender shall not permit Writer to render services for any party other than Production Company. However, Writer shall have the right to render services to third parties during any period of suspension based upon a Production Company Disability subject, however, to Production Company's right to require Writer to resume the rendition of services hereunder upon three (3) days prior notice. Production Company shall have the right (exercisable at any time) to extend the period of services of Writer hereunder for a period equal to the period of such suspension. If Production Company shall have paid compensation to Lender during any period of Writer's Incapacity or Lender/Writer Default, then Production Company shall have the right (exercisable at any time) to require Writer to render services hereunder without compensation for a period equal to that period of Writer's Incapacity or Lender/Writer Default.

19. LENDER'S RIGHT TO CURE: Any Writer's Incapacity or Lender/Writer Default shall be deemed to continue until Production Company's receipt of written notice from Lender specifying that Writer is ready, willing and able to perform the services required hereunder; provided that any such notice from Lender to Production Company shall not preclude Production Company from exercising any rights or remedies Production Company may have hereunder or at law or in equity by reason of Writer's Incapacity or Lender/Writer Default.

20. TEAM OF WRITERS: The obligations of the Writer's Team of Writers under this Agreement shall be joint and several, and references in this Agreement to Writer shall be deemed to refer to the Team of Writers jointly and severally. Should any right of termination arise as a result of the Incapacity or Default of any one of the Team of Writers, the remedies of the Production Company may be exercised either as to such Writer or as to the Team of Writers or as to Lender, at Production Company's election. Should Production Company elect to exercise its remedies only as to the Writer affected, the engagement of the other Writer or Lender shall continue and such remaining Lender/Writer shall receive only his share of the compensation provided herein.

21. GUILDS AND UNIONS:

(a) Membership: During Writer's engagement hereunder, as Production Company may lawfully require, Lender at Lender's sole cost and expense (and at Production Company's request) shall remain or become and remain a member in good standing of the then properly designated labor organization or organizations (as defined and determined under the then applicable law)

DEALMAKING
IN THE
FILM AND
TELEVISION
INDUSTRY

116

representing persons performing services of the type and character required to be performed by Writer hereunder.

(b) Superseding Effect of Guild Arrangements: Nothing contained in this Agreement shall be construed so as to require the violation of the applicable WGA Agreement, which by its terms is controlling with respect to this Agreement; and whenever there is any conflict between any provision of this Agreement and any such WGA Agreement, the latter shall prevail. In such event the provisions of this Agreement shall be curtailed and limited only to the extent necessary to permit compliance with such WGA Agreement.

22. CREDITS:

(a) Billing: Provided that Lender and Writer fully perform all of Lender's/Writer's obligations hereunder and the Picture is completed and distributed, Production Company agrees that credits for authorship by Writer shall be determined and accorded pursuant to the provisions of the WGA Agreement in effect at the time of such determination.

(b) Inadvertent Non-Compliance: Subject to the foregoing provisions, Production Company shall determine, in Production Company's discretion, the manner of presenting such credits. No casual or inadvertent failure to comply with the provisions of this clause, nor any failure of any other person, firm or corporation to comply with its agreements with Production Company relating to such credits, shall constitute a breach by Production Company of Production Company's obligations under this clause. Lender and Writer hereby agree that, if through inadvertence Production Company breaches its obligations pursuant to this Paragraph, the damages (if any) caused Lender or Writer by Production Company are not irreparable or sufficient to entitle Lender/Writer to injunctive or other equitable relief. Consequently, Lender's and/or Writer's rights and remedies in such event shall be limited to Lender's/ Writer's rights, if any, to recover damages in an action at law, and Lender and Writer shall not be entitled to rescind this Agreement or any of the rights granted to Production Company hereunder, or to enjoin or restrain the distribution or exhibition of the Picture or any other rights granted to Production Company. Production Company agrees, upon receipt of notice from Writer of Production Company's failure to comply with the provisions of this Paragraph, to take such steps as are reasonably practicable to cure such failure on future prints and advertisements.

23. INSURANCE: Production Company may secure life, health, accident, cast or other insurance covering Writer, the cost of which shall be included as a direct charge of the Picture. Such insurance shall be for Production Company's sole benefit and

Production Company shall be the beneficiary thereof, and Lender/ Writer shall have no interest in the proceeds thereof. Lender and Writer shall assist in procuring such insurance by submitting to required examinations and tests and by preparing, signing and delivering such applications and other documents as may be reasonably required. Lender and Writer shall, to the best of their ability, observe all terms and conditions of such insurance of which Production Company notifies Lender as necessary for continuing such insurance in effect.

24. EMPLOYMENT OF OTHERS: Lender and Writer agree not to employ any person to serve in any capacity, nor contract for the purchase or renting of any article or material, nor make any agreement committing Production Company to pay any sum of money for any reason whatsoever in connection with the Picture or services to be rendered by Writer or provided by Lender hereunder, or otherwise, without written approval first being had and obtained from Production Company.

25. ASSIGNMENT AND LENDING:

(a) Assignability: This Agreement is non-assignable by Lender and Writer. Production Company and any subsequent assignee may freely assign this Agreement and grant its rights hereunder, in whole or in part to any person, firm, or corporation provided that such party assumes and agrees in writing to keep and perform all of the executory obligations of Production Company hereunder. Upon such assumption, Production Company is hereby released from all further obligations to Lender and Writer hereunder, except that unless the assignee or borrower is a so-called major motion picture company, or minimajor, Production Company shall remain secondarily liable under this agreement.

(b) Right to Lend to Others: Lender understands and acknowledges that the actual production entity of a motion picture to be made from the Product may be a party other than Production Company. In such event, Writer's services shall be rendered hereunder for the actual production entity but without releasing Production Company from its obligations hereunder.

26. NOTICES:

(a) Lender's Address: All notices from Production Company to Writer, in connection with this Agreement, may be given in writing by addressing the same to Lender c/o _____. Production Company may deliver such notice to Lender or Writer personally, either orally or in writing. A courtesy copy shall be given to _____ at the address above. If such notice is sent by mail, the date of mailing shall be deemed to be the date of service of such notice.

DEALMAKING
IN THE
FILM AND
TELEVISION
INDUSTRY

118

(b) Writing Requirement: Any oral notice given in respect to any right of termination, suspension or extension under this Agreement shall be confirmed in writing. If any notice is delivered to Lender personally, a copy of such notice shall be sent to Lender at the above address.

(c) Producer's Address: All notices from Lender to Production Company hereunder shall be given in writing addressed to Production Company as follows: _____ and by depositing the same, so addressed, postage prepaid, in the mail. A courtesy copy shall be given to _____, Attorney at Law _____. Unless otherwise expressly provided, the date of mailing shall be deemed to be the date of service of such notice.

27. TRANSPORTATION AND EXPENSES: When Writer's services are required by Production Company to be rendered hereunder at a place more than fifty (50) miles from Writer's domicile, Production Company shall furnish Writer transportation to and from such places and meals and lodging accommodations while Writer is on location to render Writer's services.

28. GOVERNING LAW: This Agreement shall be construed in accordance with the laws of the State of California applicable to agreements which are executed and fully performed within said State.

29. CAPTIONS: The captions used in connection with the clauses and subclauses of this Agreement are inserted only for the purpose of reference. Such captions shall not be deemed to govern, limit, modify, or in any other manner affect the scope, meaning or intent of the provisions of this Agreement or any part thereof; nor shall such captions otherwise be given any legal effect.

30. SERVICE OF PROCESS: In any action or proceeding commenced in any court in the State of California for the purpose of enforcing this Agreement or any right granted herein or growing out hereof, or any order or decree predicated thereon, any summons, order to show cause, writ, judgment, decree, or other process, issued by such court, may be delivered to Lender or Writer personally without the State of California; and when so delivered, Lender and Writer shall be subject to the jurisdiction of such court as though the same had been served within the State of California, but outside the county in which such action or proceeding is pending.

31. ILLEGALITY: Nothing contained herein shall require the commission of any act or the payment of any compensation which is contrary to an express provision of law or contrary to

the policy of express law. If there shall exist any conflict between any provision contained herein and any such law or policy, the latter shall prevail; and the provision or provisions herein affected shall be curtailed, limited or eliminated to the extent (but only to the extent) necessary to remove such conflict; and as so modified the remaining provisions of this Agreement shall continue in full force and effect.

32. EMPLOYMENT ELIGIBILITY: All of Production Company's obligations herein are expressly conditioned upon Writer's completion, to Production Company's satisfaction, of the I-9 form (Employee Eligibility Verification Form) and upon Writer's submission to Production Company of original documents satisfactory to demonstrate to Production Company Writer's employment eligibility.

33. ENTIRE AGREEMENT: This Agreement contains the entire agreement of the parties and all previous agreements, warranties and representations, if any, are merged herein.

By signing in the spaces provided below, Lender and Production Company accept and agree to all of the terms and conditions of this Agreement.

_____

The Writer's Co. ("Lender")   Date:

Big Films
("Production Company")

By: _____   Date:

_____, its President.

DEALMAKING
IN THE
FILM AND
TELEVISION
INDUSTRY

120

CERTIFICATE OF AUTHORSHIP

Each of the undersigned does hereby certify that pursuant to a loan-out agreement between _____ (loan-out co.) ("Lender") f/s/o _____ (name of writer) ("Writer") and _____ (name of production company), Lender, for good and valuable consideration, loaned Production Company the services of Writer and that pursuant to said loan-out agreement, all literary material (the "Material") submitted and to be submitted by Writer, other than the "Assigned Material" (as defined in the Agreement between Lender and Production Company), in connection with a motion picture tentatively entitled _____ (name of picture) was written and will be written by Writer as a work-made-for-hire specially ordered or commissioned by Production Company for use as part of a motion picture, with Production Company being deemed the author of the Material and entitled to the copyrights (and all extensions and renewals of copyrights) therein and thereto, with the right to make such changes therein and such uses thereof as Production Company may from time to time determine as such author. Subject only to Article 28 of the applicable Writers Guild of America, West, Inc. Theatrical and Television Basic Agreement, each of the undersigned hereby warrants that other than Assigned Material, the Material is original with Writer, does not to the best of Writer's knowledge defame, infringe upon or violate the rights of privacy or other rights of any person, firm or corporation and is not the subject of any litigation or claim that might give rise to litigation and the undersigned does hereby agree to indemnify Production Company, its assignees and licensees against any breach of any of the aforesaid warranties and undertake to execute such documents and do such other acts and deeds as may be required by Production Company or its assignees or licensees to further evidence or effectuate its rights hereunder. Production Company's rights in the Material may be freely assigned and licensed and its rights shall be binding upon the undersigned and inure to the benefit of such assignees and licensees.

IN WITNESS WHEREOF the parties hereto have caused this document to be executed this _____ day of _____, 19 .

Name of lender

_____
(Lender)

By_____

Its:_____

INDUCEMENT AGREEMENT

Big Films
22 Fantasy Lane
Hollywood, CA

Re: "The Big Story"

Reference is made to the Agreement dated _____,
("Lending Agreement"), being executed concurrently herewith,
between (The Writer's Co.), a New York Corporation ("Lender")
and Big Films ("Borrower"), covering the loan of the services of
the undersigned The Writer's Co. ("Artist").

1. CONCURRENT EMPLOYMENT AGREEMENT: Artist has heretofore entered into an agreement ("Employment Agreement")
with Lender covering the rendition of Artist's services for Lender
for a period not less than the period Lender provides Artist's
services under the Lending Agreement and Lender has the right
to enter into the Lending Agreement and to furnish the Artist's
services and to grant the rights granted pursuant to the terms and
conditions therein specified.

2. RATIFICATION OF LENDING AGREEMENT: Artist is familiar
with the terms and conditions of the Lending Agreement and
consents to the signing thereof; Artist shall perform and comply
with all of the terms and conditions of the Lending Agreement
requiring performance or compliance by Artist even if the Employment Agreement should hereafter be terminated, suspended
or become ineffective; Artist shall render to Borrower all of the
services provided to be rendered by Artist under the Lending
Agreement; all notices served upon Lender in accordance with
the Lending Agreement shall be deemed notices to Artist of the
contents thereof with the same effect as if served upon Artist
personally. Artist hereby expressly agrees that all of the results
and product of all services to be performed by Artist pursuant to
the Lending Agreement are results considered a work made for
hire for Borrower and that Borrower shall be the author and
copyright owner of such results and product.

3. NO RESTRICTIONS: Artist is under no obligation or disability,
by law or otherwise, which would interfere with Artist's full
performance and compliance with all of the terms and conditions
of the Lending Agreement which require performance or compliance by Artist.

4. REMUNERATION SOLE RESPONSIBILITY OF LENDER: Except
as may otherwise be provided in the Lending Agreement, Artist
shall look solely to Lender for all compensation and other

DEALMAKING
IN THE
FILM AND
TELEVISION
INDUSTRY

122

remuneration for any and all rights and services which Artist and/or Lender may grant and render to Borrower under the Lending Agreement.

5. BREACH: Artist's services are unique and extraordinary and the breach of this Inducement Agreement and/or of any of the terms of the Lending Agreement which require performance or compliance by Artist will cause irreparable damage to Borrower. Therefore, in the event of breach or threatened breach by Artist of this Inducement Agreement, Borrower shall be entitled to legal or equitable relief by way of injunction or otherwise, against Artist or against Lender or against both, at the discretion of Borrower, to restrain, enjoin and/or prevent such breach by Artist, Lender, or both. All of the foregoing shall be to the same extent and with the same force and effect as if Artist was a direct party to the Lending Agreement in the first instance, and as if in the Lending Agreement, Artist had personally agreed to render the services therein provided to be rendered by Artist and to perform and observe each and all of the terms and conditions of the Lending Agreement requiring performance or compliance on the part of Artist, Lender, or both.

6. SUBSTITUTION FOR LENDER: If Lender should be dissolved or should otherwise cease to exist or for any reason whatsoever should fail, neglect, refuse or be unable to perform and observe each and all of the terms or conditions of the Lending Agreement requiring performance or compliance by Lender, Artist shall, at the election of Borrower, be deemed substituted as a direct party to said Lending Agreement in the place and stead of Lender.

7. GOVERNING LAW: This Inducement Agreement shall be governed and construed by the laws of the State of _____.

Very truly yours,

_____

Artist

WGA CREDIT ARBITRATION

Producers do not have the unfettered power to award writing credits in their sole discretion. The Writers Guild contract provides that a production company must send each writer a copy of the final shooting script and a "Notice of Tentative Credits." If a writer agrees with the tentative credits, he does nothing. If he disagrees, he must protest within the time specified in the notice. Writers may meet on their own and try to agree how credit should be allocated. If they cannot agree the matter will be resolved through arbitation.

Writers have the right to challenge a reasonable number of arbiters. Three arbiters are selected from those remaining on the list. Identities remain confidential. At the request of any participating writer, the identities of the writers are not revealed to the arbitrators. Each writer may submit a written statement of his position to the arbiters.

As a writer, you should protect your rights by saving copies of every draft. Each draft should be dated and have your name on it. If you make suggestions in story conferences which do not appear in the script, document your contribution by sending a dated memorandum to the producer. If scripts are similar, arbiters will assume that a subsequent writer had access to prior drafts.

If you are collaborating with another writer, the Guild assumes the collaboration is a 50/50 partnership unless there is evidence to the contrary. If that is not your understanding, you should document your agreement in writing.

According to WGA credit rules, a writer whose work represents 33% of a screenplay is entitled to a screenplay credit. However, for original screenplays, subsequent writers must contribute 50% to the final screenplay to receive a credit. The Guild guarantees the writer of an original screenplay a minimum credit ("irreducible story minimum") of a shared story credit.

DIRECTORS

The director is the person primarily responsible for supervising the creation of a film or television program. She must be

DEALMAKING
IN THE
FILM AND
TELEVISION
INDUSTRY

124

enough of an artist to satisfy critics and viewers and enough of a businessperson to satisfy the financiers. From the studio's point of view, hiring a director is critical because she is the person charged with keeping the production on budget and on schedule.

Director employment agreements have many provisions also found in writer employment agreements. The agreement may be structured as direct employment or through a loan-out arrangement. In the latter case, the director's company is called the "Lender."

Directors are hired for the period of principal photography as well as the time needed beforehand to prepare for filming (pre-production) and time after to supervise editing (post-production). The director may also work with the writer during development.

Often the director is hired on a flat fee basis that covers all these phases. Payments are made in installments with most of the fee paid during principal photography. A director is typically hired on an exclusive basis, preventing her from accepting outside employment and working on more than one film at a time.

The agreement is frequently a "pay or play" deal, which means that if the studio does not use the director's services, or replaces her, the director is still entitled to her fixed compensation. The director may also receive bonus, deferred, contingent and additional compensation, although these payments may not vest until and unless the person is entitled to a director credit.

Usually the director does not have the right of "final cut," which is the power to determine the composition of the final edited version of the picture. Studios may insist on reserving this right to protect their investment and make sure that the director does not create an artistic masterpiece that is a commercial flop. Also, the agreement will specify that the film be a certain length (e.g., within 90 to 120 minutes). Directors may be required to produce two versions of the film: one for theatrical release and another for television broadcast.

The director may have the right to select key personnel such as the Director of Photography, Production Manager and Editor. A veteran director with clout could have the power to hire certain cast and crew members without studio approval.

DIRECTOR EMPLOYMENT AGREEMENT

Agreement

Agreement dated _____ between _____ ("Director")
and _____ ("Production Company").

1. EMPLOYMENT: Production Company agrees to employ Director to perform and Director agrees to perform, upon the terms
and conditions herein specified, directing services in connection
with the Theatrical Motion Picture currently entitled _____
("Picture").

2. TERM: The Term of this agreement shall commence on
_____ and shall continue until the completion of all of
Director's required services on the Picture.

3. SERVICES:

(a) Pre-Production: Director shall be available and undertake a location search on or about _____.

(b) Photography: Director's exclusive services for the Picture shall commence _____ weeks prior to the start of principal
photography and shall be rendered exclusively after that until
completion of all photography. The start date of principal photography shall be mutually approved by Production Company
and Director. The scheduled start date of principal photography
is _____.

(c) Post-Production: Director's post-production services shall
be rendered on a non-exclusive but first-call basis, if Production
Company so requires in order to work during the post-production period with the editor until completion of the final corrected
answer print. Director's other undertakings shall not interfere
with director's post-production services hereunder.

(1) Cooperation with Editor: Director hereby warrants and
agrees that Director will do nothing to hinder or delay the
assemblage of film by the editor during the photography of the
Picture so that the assembled sequences will be completed
immediately following the completion of principal photography.

(2) Post-Production Schedule: Attached hereto marked Exhibit "S" and by this reference incorporated herein is a schedule
for the post-production work on the Picture which has been
agreed to by Director and Production Company. Director agrees
that this schedule will be followed by Director.

(3) Final Cutting Authority: _____ is designated as the
Production Company Executive with final cutting authority over
the Picture. The foregoing shall be subject to applicable guild
and union requirements, if any.

DEALMAKING
IN THE
FILM AND
TELEVISION
INDUSTRY

126

(d) Dailies: Production Company shall have the right to view the dailies during the production of the Picture, the rough cut and all subsequent cuts of the Picture.

(e) Television Cover Shots: Director shall furnish Production Company with protective cover shots necessary for the release of the Picture on television, based on network continuity standards in existence at the time of commencement of principal photography.

(f) Additional Post-Production Services: If after the completion of principal photography, Production Company requires retakes, changes, dubbing, transparencies, added scenes, further photography, trailers, sound track, process shots or other language versions (herein collectively called "retakes, etc.") for the Picture, Director shall report to Production Company for such retakes, etc., at such place or places and on such consecutive or non-consecutive days as Production Company may designate. Subject to Director's professional availability, Director shall cooperate to make such services available to Production Company at the earliest possible date.

4. COMPENSATION: As full and complete consideration for Director's services and Director's undertakings hereunder and for all rights granted to Production Company hereunder, and subject to Director's full compliance with the terms and conditions of this Agreement, Production Company agrees to pay Director as follows:

(a) Fixed Compensation:

(1) The total sum of _____ payable:

(A) $_____ upon approval of the Budgeted Negative Cost for production of the Picture.

(B) $_____ pro rated commencing ____ weeks prior to the start of principal photography of the Picture.

(C) $_____ payable in equal weekly installments over the scheduled period of principal photography.

(D) $_____ upon delivery of the director's cut.

(E) $_____ upon the completion of the final answer print of the Picture.

(2) Flat-Fee Basis: Production Company and Director hereby mutually acknowledge that the Fixed Compensation as hereinabove specified is a "flat fee" and Director shall not be entitled to any additional and/or so-called "overage" compensation for any services rendered by Director during the development, pre-production, production or post-production phases, or for addi-

tional post-production services rendered by Director. Without limiting the generality of the foregoing, no additional compensation shall be payable to Director under Clause 4(a)(i)(C) above if the actual principal photography period for the Picture exceeds the scheduled principal photography period, nor for any services rendered pursuant to Clause 3(f).

(b) Deferred Compensation: In addition to the Fixed Compensation payable under Clause 4(a), subject to the production and release of the Picture and subject to the performance of all obligations of Director hereunder, Director shall be entitled to receive the sum of _____ which shall be deferred and paid pro rata with all similar deferments of compensation payable _____ at the point just preceding the payment of percentage participations in the Net Profits of the Picture.

(c) Contingent Compensation: In addition to the Fixed Compensation payable under Clause 4(a), and any Deferred Compensation payable under Clause 4(b), subject to the production and release of the Picture and subject to the performance of Director's obligations hereunder Director shall be entitled to receive as Contingent Compensation an amount equal to _____ percent of the Net Profits of the Picture, if any.

(d) Net Profits Definition: Net Profits shall be computed, determined and paid in accordance with Exhibit ___ attached hereto and by this reference incorporated herein.

(e) Conditions Related to Compensation: Notwithstanding anything to the contrary contained in any of the above compensation provisions:

(1) Performance: No compensation shall accrue or become payable to Director during Director's inability, failure or refusal to perform the services contracted for herein according to the terms and conditions of this Agreement.

(2) Pay or Play: Production Company shall not be obligated to use Director's services on the Picture, nor shall Production Company be obligated to produce, release, distribute, advertise, exploit or otherwise make use of the Picture; provided, however, that the full amount of the Fixed Compensation hereinabove specified shall be paid to Director should Production Company without legal justification or excuse (as provided elsewhere in this Agreement or by operation of law), elect not to utilize Director's services.

(f) Vesting: The Fixed Compensation and Contingent Compensation hereinabove specified shall be deemed fully vested if, notwithstanding the termination of Director's services due to Producer Disability or Director's incapacity or Director default,

DEALMAKING
IN THE
FILM AND
TELEVISION
INDUSTRY

128

Director shall be entitled to receive "Directed by" credit pursuant to the Director's Guild of America Basic Agreement of 1973, as same may be amended from time to time ("Basic Agreement").

If the services of Director are terminated by Production Company due to Production Disability or Director's Incapacity or Director Default, as defined below, and Director is not entitled to receive credit pursuant to the Basic Agreement, then the Fixed Compensation shall vest and accrue in the same manner as set forth herein and the Contingent Compensation shall accrue and vest in the same ratio that the number of linear feet in the completed Picture as released, which was directed by Director, bears to the total number of linear feet in the completed Picture as released. Notwithstanding the foregoing, if principal photography has not commenced on the scheduled start date as set forth in Clause 3(b) hereof, then the total Fixed Compensation shall vest and accrue on the aforesaid scheduled start date and production of the Picture is thereafter terminated prior to completion of principal photography and/or delivery of the final answer print to Production Company, then that portion of the Fixed Compensation not theretofore accrued shall fully vest and accrue on the date of such termination. If Production Company terminates this Agreement by reason of a Director Default, notwithstanding any vesting of Fixed Compensation and/or Contingent Compensation as set forth above, such vesting shall be subject to any and all the rights accorded to Production Company at law and in equity.

(g) Mitigation: If Production Company elects to exercise its pay or play right as set forth above and/or fails to produce the Picture, Director shall have no obligation to mitigate damages.

5. CREDITS:

(a) Credit: Subject to the production and release of the Picture and provided Director performs his material obligations hereunder, then Production Company shall accord Director credit in connection with the Picture in accordance with the requirements of the Director's Guild of America, Inc., Basic Agreement of 1973 immediately after the main title, which shall be 50% of the size of the title on a separate card.

(b) Artwork Title Exception: If both a regular (or repeat) title and an artwork title are used, the position and percentage requirements above, as they relate to the title of the Picture, shall relate to the regular (or repeat) title. If only an artwork title is used, the percentage requirements above, as they relate to the title, shall be not less than 15 percent (15%) of the average size of the letters used in the artwork title.

(c) Credit Limitation: Production Company agrees that no other individual and/or entity (other than members of the cast receiving "starring" billing before or after the title of the Picture or the company distributing and/or financing the Picture) shall receive credit larger than that used to display the credit accorded to Director.

(d) Inadvertent Non-Compliance: No casual or inadvertent failure to comply with the provisions of this Paragraph shall be deemed to be a breach of this Agreement by Production Company. Director hereby recognizes and confirms that in the event of a failure or omission by Production Company constituting a breach of Production Company obligations under this Paragraph, the damages, if any, caused Director by Production Company are not irreparable or sufficient to entitle Director to injunctive or other equitable relief. Consequently, Director's rights and remedies hereunder shall be limited to the right, if any, to obtain damages at law and Director shall have no right in such event to rescind this Agreement or any of the rights assigned to Production Company hereunder or to enjoin or restrain the distribution or exhibition of the Picture. Production Company agrees to advise its assignees and licensees of the credit requirements herein. If Production Company shall learn of such failure of a third party to give such credit, Production Company shall notify such party of such failure and Production Company may, but shall not be obligated to, take action to cause such party to prospectively cure such failure.

6. TRANSPORTATION AND EXPENSES: If Director's services are required at Production Company's request to be rendered on location more than (e.g., fifty (50)) miles from the City of Los Angeles, Production Company shall furnish Director first-class round-trip transportation for one (1), and Production Company shall reimburse Director for Director's living expenses in the amount of $_____ per week. If Director can demonstrate to Production Company's satisfaction that said living expense allowance is insufficient for any particular location, Production Company shall, at such time, give good-faith consideration to an increase. For any period week which is less than one (1) week, said reimbursement shall be upon the pro rata basis that one (1) day is equal to one-seventh ($1/7$) of one (1) week. Director shall furnish Production Company with itemized detailed accountings of such living expenses, including vouchers, bills, receipts and statements satisfactory to meet the requirements and regulations of the Internal Revenue Service.

7. PERFORMANCE STANDARDS: Except as specifically provided to the contrary herein, during the Term of this Agreement, Director shall render his directive services exclusively to Production Company and, to such extent as Production Company may require, in otherwise assisting in the production of the Picture.

DEALMAKING
IN THE
FILM AND
TELEVISION
INDUSTRY

130

Said services shall be rendered either alone or in collaboration with another or other artists in such manner as Production Company may direct, pursuant to the instructions, controls and schedules established by Production Company, and at the times, places and in the manner required by Production Company. Such manners, instructions, directions, and controls shall be exercised by Production Company in accordance with standards of reasonableness and also with what is customary practice in the Motion Picture industry. Such services shall be rendered in an artistic, conscientious, efficient and punctual manner, to the best of Director's ability and with full regard to the careful, efficient, economical and expeditious production of the Picture within the budget and shooting schedule established by Production Company immediately prior to the commencement of principal photography. It is further understood that the production of motion pictures by Production Company involves matters of discretion to be exercised by Production Company with respect to art and taste, and Director's services and the manner of rendition thereof is to be governed entirely by Production Company.

8. UNIQUE SERVICES: Except as specifically provided to the contrary hereinabove, Director's services shall be rendered exclusively to Production Company until expiration of the Term of this Agreement, it being mutually understood that said services are extraordinary, unique and not replaceable, and that there is no adequate remedy at law for breach of this contract by Director, and that Production Company, in the event of such breach by Director, shall be entitled to equitable relief by way of injunction or otherwise to prevent default by Director.

9. RESULTS AND PROCEEDS OF SERVICES: Production Company shall be entitled to and shall solely and exclusively own, in addition to Director's services hereunder, all results and proceeds thereof (including but not limited to all rights, throughout the world, of copyright, trademark, patent, production, manufacture, recordation, reproduction, transcription, performance, broadcast and exhibition of any art or method now known or hereafter devised, including radio broadcasting, theatrical and nontheatrical exhibition, and exhibition by the medium of television or otherwise), whether such results and proceeds consist of literary, dramatic, musical, motion picture, mechanical or any other forms of works, themes, ideas, compositions, creations or production, together with the rights generally known in the field of literary and musical endeavor as the "moral rights of authors" in and any musical and/or literary proceeds of Director's services, including but not limited to the right to add to, subtract from, arrange, revise, adapt, rearrange, make variations of the property, and to translate the same into any and all languages, change the se-

quence, change the characters and the descriptions thereof contained in the property, change the title of the same, record and photocopy the same with or without sound (including spoken words, dialogue and music synchronously recorded), use this title or any of its components in connection with works or motion pictures wholly or partially independent of said property, and to use all or any part of the property in new versions, adaptations and sequels in any and all languages, and to obtain copyright therein throughout the world. Director does assign and transfer to Production Company all the foregoing without reservation, condition, or limitations, and no right of any kind, nature, or description is reserved by Director. If Production Company shall desire separate assignments or other documents to implement the foregoing, Director shall execute the same upon Production Company's request, and if Director fails or refuses to execute and deliver any such separate assignments or other documents, Production Company shall have and is granted the right and authority to execute the same in Director's name and as Director's attorney-in-fact. Production Company shall supply Director with a copy of any document so executed.

10. WARRANTIES RELATED TO CREATED MATERIAL: Director hereby warrants and agrees that all material, works, writings, idea, "gags" or dialogue written, composed, prepared, submitted or interpolated by Director in connection with the Picture or its preparation or production shall be wholly original with Director and shall not be copied in whole or in part from any other work, except that submitted to Director by Production Company as a basis for such material. Director further warrants that neither the said material nor any part thereof will to the best of Director's knowledge violate the rights of privacy or constitute a libel or slander against any person, firm, or corporation, and that the material will not infringe upon the copyright, literary, dramatic or photoplay rights of any person. Director further warrants and agrees to hold Production Company and its successors, licensees, and assigns harmless against all liability or loss which they or any of them may suffer by reason of the breach of any of the terms or warranties of this Clause.

11. VESTING OF PRODUCTION COMPANY'S RIGHTS: All rights granted or agreed to be granted to Production Company hereunder shall vest in Production Company immediately and shall remain so vested whether this Agreement expires in normal course or is terminated for any cause or reason.

12. NAME AND LIKENESS: Production Company shall always have the right to use and display Director's name and likeness for advertising, publicizing, and exploiting the picture. However, such advertising may not include the direct endorsement of any

DEALMAKING
IN THE
FILM AND
TELEVISION
INDUSTRY

132

product (other than the Picture) without Directors's consent. Exhibition, advertising, publicizing or exploiting the Picture by any media, even though a part of or in connection with a product or a commercially sponsored program, shall not be deemed an endorsement of any nature.

13. PUBLICITY RESTRICTIONS: Director shall not individually or by means of press agents or publicity or advertising agencies or others, employed or paid by Director or otherwise, circulate, publish or otherwise disseminate any news stories or articles, books or other publicity, containing Director's name relating to Director's employment by Production Company, the subject matter of this contract, the Picture or the services to be rendered by Director or others in connection with the Picture unless first approved by Production Company. Director shall not transfer any right, privilege, title, or interest in or to any of the things above specified, nor shall Director authorize or willingly permit infringement upon the exclusive rights granted to Production Company, and Director authorizes Production Company, at Production Company's expense, in Director's name or otherwise, to institute any proper legal proceedings to prevent any infringement.

14. FORCE MAJEURE:

(a) Suspension: If, by reason of fire, earthquake, labor dispute or strike, act of God or public enemy, any municipal ordinance, any state or federal law, governmental order or regulation, or other cause beyond Production Company's control which would excuse Production Company's performance as a matter of law, Production Company is prevented from or hampered in the production of the Picture, or if, by reason of the closing of substantially all theaters in the United States, which would excuse Production Company's performance as a matter of law, Production Company's production of the Picture is postponed or suspended, or if, by reason of any of the aforesaid contingencies or any other cause or occurrence not within Production Company's control, including but not limited to the death, illness or incapability of any principal member of the cast of the Picture, the preparation or production of the Picture is interrupted or delayed and/or, if Production Company's normal business operations are interrupted or otherwise interfered with by virtue of any disruptive events that are beyond Production Company's control ("Production Company Disability"), then Production Company may postpone the commencement of or suspend the rendition of services by Director and the running of time hereunder for such time as the Production Company Disability shall continue; and no compensation shall accrue or become payable to Director hereunder during the period of such suspension. Such suspension shall end upon the cessation of the cause thereof.

(b) Termination:

(1) Production Company Termination Right: If a Production Company Disability continues for a period in excess of six (6) weeks, Production Company shall have the right to terminate this Agreement upon written notice to Director.

(2) Director's Termination Right: If a Production Company Disability results in compensation being suspended hereunder for a period in excess of six (6) weeks, Director shall have the right to terminate this Agreement upon written notice to Production Company.

(3) Production Company Re-Establishment Right: Despite Director's election to terminate this Agreement, within _____ days after Production Company's actual receipt of such written notice from Director, Production Company shall have the right to elect to re-establish the operation of this Agreement.

15. DIRECTOR'S INCAPACITY:

(a) Effect of Director's Incapacity: If, by reason of mental or physical disability, Director is incapacitated from performing or complying with any of the terms of conditions hereof ("Director's Incapacity") for a consecutive period in excess of seven (7) days or aggregate period in excess of ten (10) days, then Production Company shall have the right to terminate this Agreement upon written notice to Director.

(b) Right of Examination: If any claim of mental or physical disability is made by Director or on Director's behalf, Production Company shall have the right to have Director examined by such physicians as Production Company may designate. Director's physician may be present at such examination but shall not interfere therewith. Any tests performed on Director shall be related to and customary for the treatment, diagnosis or examination to be performed in connection with Director's claim.

16. DIRECTOR'S DEFAULT: If Director fails or refuses to perform or comply with any of the material terms or conditions hereof (other than by reason of Director's Incapacity) ("Director's Default"), then Production Company may terminate this Agreement upon written notice to Director. Director Default shall not include any failure or refusal of Director to perform or comply with the material terms of this Agreement due to a breach or action by Production Company which makes the performance by Director of his services impossible. Prior to termination of this Agreement by Production Company based upon Director Default, Production Company shall notify Director specifying the nature of the Director Default and Director shall have a period of 48 hours to cure the Director Default. If the Director Default is not cured

DEALMAKING
IN THE
FILM AND
TELEVISION
INDUSTRY

134

within said 48 hour period, Production Company may terminate this Agreement forthwith.

17. EFFECT OF TERMINATION: Termination of this Agreement, whether by lapse of time, mutual consent, operation of law, exercise of a right of termination or otherwise shall:

(a) Terminate Production Company's obligation to pay Director any further compensation. Nevertheless, if the termination is not for Director's Default, Production Company shall pay Director any compensation due and unpaid prior to the termination, and;

(b) Production Company shall not be deemed to have waived any other rights it may have or alter Production Company's rights or any of Director's agreements or warranties relating to the rendition of Director's services prior to termination.

18. PRODUCTION COMPANY RIGHT TO SUSPEND: In the event of Director's Incapacity or Director's Default, Production Company may postpone upon written notice the commencement of or suspend the rendition of services by Director and the running of time hereunder so long as any Director's Disability or Director's Default shall continue; and no compensation shall accrue or become payable to Director during the period of such suspension.

(a) Director's Right to Cure: Any Director's Incapacity or Director's Default shall be deemed to continue until Production Company's receipt of written notice from Director specifying that Director is ready, willing and able to perform the services required hereunder; provided that any such notice from Director to Production Company shall not preclude Production Company from exercising any rights or remedies Production Company may have hereunder or at law or in equity by reason of Director's Incapacity or Director's Default.

(b) Alternative Services Restricted: During any period of suspension hereunder, Director shall not render services for any person, firm or corporation other than Production Company. However, Director shall have the right to render services to third parties during any period of suspension based upon a Production Company Disability, subject, however, to Production Company's right to require Director to resume the rendition of services hereunder upon 24 hours prior notice.

(c) Production Company Right to Extend: If Production Company elects to suspend the rendition of services by Director as herein specified, then Production Company shall have the right (exercisable at any time) to extend the period of services of Director hereunder for a period equal to the period of such suspension.

(d) Additional Services: If Production Company shall have paid compensation to Director during any period of Director's Incapacity or Director's Default, then Production Company shall have the right (exercisable at any time) to require Director to render services hereunder without compensation for a period equal to the period for which Production Company shall have paid compensation to Director during such Director's Incapacity or Director's Default.

19. FURTHER WARRANTIES: Director hereby warrants that Director is not under any obligation or disability, created by law or otherwise, which would in any manner or to any extent prevent or restrict Director from entering into and fully performing this Agreement; Director warrants that Director has not entered into any agreement or commitment that would prevent Director from fulfilling Director's commitments with Production Company hereunder and that Director will not enter into any such agreement or commitment without Production Company's specific approval; and Director hereby accepts the obligation hereunder and agrees to devote Director's entire time and attention and best talents and abilities exclusively to Production Company as specified herein, and to observe and to be governed by the rules of conduct established by Production Company for the conduct of its employees.

(a) Indemnity: Director shall at all times indemnify Production Company, its successors, assignees and licensees, from and against any and all costs, expenses, losses, damages, judgments and attorneys' fees arising out of or connected with or resulting from any claims, demands or causes of action by any person or entity which is inconsistent with any of Director's representations, warranties or agreements hereunder. Director will reimburse Production Company on demand for any payment made by Production Company at any time after the date hereof in respect of any liability, loss, damage, cost or expense to which the foregoing indemnity relates.

20. REMEDIES: All remedies accorded herein or otherwise available to either Production Company or Director shall be cumulative, and no one such remedy shall be exclusive of any other. Without waiving any rights or remedies under this Agreement or otherwise, Production Company may from time to time recover, by action, any damages arising out of any breach of this Agreement by Director, and may institute and maintain subsequent actions for additional damages which may arise from the same or other breaches. The commencement or maintenance of any such action or actions by Production Company shall not constitute an election on Production Company's part to terminate this Agreement nor constitute or result in termination of Director's services

DEALMAKING
IN THE
FILM AND
TELEVISION
INDUSTRY

136

hereunder unless Production Company shall expressly so elect by written notice to Director. The pursuit by either Production Company or Director of any remedy under this Agreement or otherwise shall not be deemed to waive any other or different remedy which may be available under this Agreement or otherwise, either at law or in equity.

21. INSURANCE: Production Company may secure life, health, accident, cast, or other insurance covering Director, the cost of which shall be included as a Direct Charge of the Picture. Such insurance shall be for Production Company's sole benefit and Production Company shall be the beneficiary thereof, and Director shall have no interest in the proceeds thereof. Director shall assist in procuring such insurance by submitting to required examinations and tests and by preparing, signing, and delivering such applications and other documents as may be reasonably required. Director shall, to the best of Director's ability, observe all terms and conditions of such insurance of which Production Company notifies Director as necessary for continuing such insurance in effect.

If Production Company is unable to obtain pre-production or cast insurance covering Director at prevailing standard rates and without any exclusions, restrictions, conditions, or exceptions of any kind, Director shall have the right to pay any premium in excess of the prevailing standard rate in order for Production Company to obtain such insurance. If Director fails or refuses to pay such excess premium, or if Production Company having obtained such insurance, Director fails to observe all terms and conditions necessary to maintain such insurance in effect, Production Company shall have the right to terminate this Agreement without any obligation to Director by giving Director written notice of termination.

22. EMPLOYMENT OF OTHERS: Director agrees not to employ any person to serve in any capacity, nor contract for the purchase or renting of any article or material, nor make any agreement committing Production Company to pay any sum of money for any reason whatsoever in connection with the Picture or services to be rendered by Director hereunder or otherwise, without written approval first being had and obtained from Production Company.

23. ASSIGNMENT: This Agreement, at the election of Production Company, shall inure to the benefit of Production Company's administrators, successors, assigns, licensees, grantees, and associated, affiliated and subsidiary companies, and Director agrees that Production Company and any subsequent assignee may freely assign this Agreement and grant its rights hereunder, in

whole or in part, to any person, firm or corporation, provided that such person, firm or corporation assumes and agrees in writing to keep and perform all of the executory obligations of Production Company hereunder.

24. ARBITRATION: Any controversy or claim arising out of or relating to this agreement or any breach thereof shall be settled by arbitration in accordance with the Rules of the American Arbitration Association; and judgment upon the award rendered by the arbitrators may be entered in any court having jurisdiction thereof. The prevailing party shall be entitled to reimbursement for costs and reasonable attorneys' fees.

Signed and agreed to by the undersigned as of _____1993.

_____
John Doe on behalf of
Big Productions Inc.
("Production Company")

_____
Henry Smith
("Director")

DEALMAKING
IN THE
FILM AND
TELEVISION
INDUSTRY

138

ACTORS

Actor employment agreements contain many provisions also found in writer and director agreements. Agreements often refer to the employer as the "Producer" and the employee as the "Player."

The actor's employment agreement will grant the producer the right to use the name and likeness of the actor in the film. The producer may also obtain the right to use the actor's name and likeness for merchandising, in which case the actor will be entitled to a percentage participation of the revenues received by the producer.

Typically, the producer will supply any costumes required for a role. However, if a contemporary story is being filmed, the producer may ask the player to provide his own clothing. In this case, the actor should receive a cleaning allowance.

Employment of child actors raises special concerns because minors can disaffirm contracts.[1] A producer cannot enforce a disaffirmed contract. However, the law provides that when a minor is employed as an entertainer, he cannot disaffirm a contract if that contract has been approved by the Superior Court beforehand. The minor or the employer must petition the Superior Court to determine if the contract is fair to the minor. The court may require that part of the minor's earnings be set aside in a trust fund for him.

In hiring a minor, the employer must also comply with provisions of the California Labor Code and regulations of the Labor Commission. For example, an employer must obtain a work permit from the Division of Labor Standards Enforcement.[2] Minors cannot perform work that is hazardous or detrimental to their health, safety, morals or education.[3] Working hours are limited, and minors of school age must attend three hours of schooling per day during the school year.[4] Minors under 16 years of age must have a parent or guardian present on the set.[5]

---

[1] See California Civil Code § 35.

[2] California Administrative Code Title 8, §11753.

[3] California Administrative Code, Title 8, §11751.

[4] California Administrative Code Title 8, §§11760 & 11755.1.

[5] California Administrative Code, Title 8 §11757.

Actor employment agreements may contain a "morals" clause that requires the actor to conduct himself so as not to violate public conventions or subject himself to public hatred, contempt or ridicule. If the actor violates this clause, the employer has the right to terminate the agreement.

The employer may want to purchase life, accident or health insurance covering the actor. The actor is typically required to submit to a medical examination to obtain this coverage. If the employer is unable to obtain insurance at standard rates, the employer may have the right to terminate the employment agreement. If the actor fails the medical exam or insurance coverage is denied, the employer may be required to give prompt notice to the actor.

A producer who hires an actor for a television series will want to have an option on that actor's services for five to seven years. The actor may have to refuse attractive offers that conflict with this commitment. Before an actor enters an exclusive agreement he also needs to consider whether it will restrict him from performing in such related fields as theatrical motion pictures, the legitimate stage and commercials.

Negotiators sometimes try to resolve issues quickly by agreeing to a "favored-nations" clause. Such a provision guarantees that no other actor on the picture will obtain more advantageous terms. If another actor negotiates better terms, the terms of the deal for the actor with a favored-nations clause must be upgraded to the same extent. It makes sense for a fledgling actor to accept a favored-nations clause because, if an actor with more clout gets better terms, the fledgling actor will benefit.

When a novice signs a series deal, he has little bargaining power. The agreement will set the amount of compensation due in future years. If the series becomes a hit, the actor may become a star, and he may chafe under the terms of an agreement that he now thinks does not compensate him fairly. With his newfound clout, he might try to renegotiate the deal and achieve more favorable terms. Sometimes the star will refuse to work or become uncooperative or "sick" to pressure the employer to sweeten the deal. The employer may threaten to sue, but often a compromise is reached as neither party wants to kill the golden goose.

DEALMAKING
IN THE
FILM AND
TELEVISION
INDUSTRY

140

ACTOR EMPLOYMENT AGREEMENT
(Theatrical Release)

Continuous Employment
Weekly Basis
Weekly Salary

One Week
Minimum Employment

THIS AGREEMENT, made this _____ day of _____, 199___, between _____, hereafter called "Producer," and _____, hereafter called "Player."

1. PHOTOPLAY, ROLE, SALARY AND GUARANTEE: Producer hereby engages Player to render services as such in the role of _____, in a photoplay, the working title of which is now _____, at the salary of $_____ per "studio week." (Schedule B Players must receive an additional overtime payment of four (4) hours at straight-time rate for each overnight location Saturday.) Player accepts such engagement upon the terms herein specified. Producer guarantees that it will furnish Player not less than _____ weeks' employment (if this blank is not filled in, the guarantee shall be one week). Player shall be paid pro rata for each additional day beyond guarantee until dismissal.

2. TERM: The term of employment hereunder shall begin on or about _____ and shall continue thereafter until the completion of the photography and recordation of said role.

3. BASIC CONTRACT: All provisions of the collective bargaining agreement between Screen Actors Guild, Inc. and Producer, relating to theatrical motion pictures, which are applicable to the employment of the Player hereunder, shall be deemed incorporated herein.

4. PLAYER'S ADDRESS: All notices which the Producer is required or may desire to give to the Player may be given either by mailing the same addressed to the Player at _____, or such notice may be given to the Player personally, either orally or in writing.

5. PLAYER'S TELEPHONE: The Player must keep the Producer's casting office or the assistant director of said photoplay advised as to where the Player may be reached by telephone without unreasonable delay. The current telephone number of the Player is _____.

6. MOTION PICTURE RELIEF FUND: The Player does hereby authorize the Producer to deduct from the compensation

hereinabove specified an amount equal to _____ percent of each installment of compensation due the Player hereunder, and to pay the amount so deducted to the Motion Picture and Television Relief Fund of America, Inc.

7. FURNISHING OF WARDROBE: The Player agrees to furnish all modern wardrobe and wearing apparel reasonably necessary for the portrayal of said role; it being agreed, however, that should so-called "character" or "period" costumes be required, the Producer shall supply the same. When Player furnishes any wardrobe, Player shall receive the cleaning allowance and reimbursement, if any, specified in the basic contract.

Number of outfits furnished by Player:

_____ @ $_____

(formal)   _____ @ $_____

8. ARBITRATION OF DISPUTES: Should any dispute or controversy arise between the parties hereto with reference to this contract, or the employment herein provided for, such dispute or controversy shall be settled and determined by conciliation and arbitration in accordance with the conciliation and arbitration provisions of the collective bargaining agreement between the Producer and Screen Actors Guild relating to theatrical motion pictures, and such provisions are hereby referred to and by such reference incorporated herein and made a part of this Agreement with the same effect as though the same were set forth herein in detail.

9. NEXT STARTING DATE: The starting date of Player's next engagement is:_____.

10. The Player may not waive any provision of this contract without the written consent of the Screen Actors Guild, Inc.

11. Producer makes the material representation that either it is presently a signatory to the Screen Actors Guild collective-bargaining agreement covering the employment contracted for herein, or that the above-referred-to photoplay is covered by such collective-bargaining agreement under the Independent Production provisions of the General Provisions of the Producer-Screen Actors Guild Codified Basic Agreement of 1983 as the same may be supplemented and/or amended.

12. Producer shall have the exclusive right to make one or more promotional films of thirty (30) minutes or less and to utilize the results and proceeds of Player's services therein upon all of the terms and provisions set forth in the SAG Agreement. Player

DEALMAKING
IN THE
FILM AND
TELEVISION
INDUSTRY

142

agrees to render such services for said promotional films during the term of his employment hereunder as Producer may request and Player further agrees to use by Producer of film clips and behind-the-scenes shots in which Player appears in such promotional films. Provided Player appears therein, Producer shall pay to Player the sum specified by the SAG Agreement of _____ within ten (10) days after the first use of each such promotional film on television or before a paying audience.

13. Producer shall have the exclusive right to use and to license the use of Player's name, sobriquet, photograph, likeness, voice and/or caricature and shall have the right to simulate Player's voice, signature and appearance by any means in and in connection with the film and the advertising, publicizing, exhibition, and/or other exploitation thereof in any manner and by any means and in connection with commercial advertising and publicity tie-ups.

14. Producer is also granted the further exclusive right and license, but only in connection with the role portrayed by Player in the film, to use and to license the use of Player's name, sobriquet, photograph, likeness, caricature and/or signature (collectively referred to herein as "name and likeness") in and in connection with any merchandising and/or publishing undertakings. In consideration therefore, Producer shall pay Player a pro rata share (payable among all players whose name, etc. is used) of 2 1/2% of the gross monies actually derived by Producer after deducting therefrom a distribution fee of fifty percent (50%) and a sum equal to all Producer's actual out-of-pocket expenses in connection therewith, for the use of such name or likeness on merchandising and publishing items which utilize Player's name and likeness, other than in a listing of cast credits.

15. Producer is also granted the further and exclusive right to use and to license the use of and to advertise and publicize the use of Player's voice from the soundtrack of the film on commercial phonograph records and albums and the exclusive right to use Player's name and likeness on jackets and labels of such commercial phonograph records and albums. If Producer issues or authorizes the issuance of such record or album using Player's voice, Producer shall pay to Player a sum equal to applicable AFTRA scale.

16. EMPLOYMENT ELIGIBILITY: All of Production Company's obligation herein are expressly conditioned upon Performer's completion, to Production Company's satisfaction, of the I-9 form (Employee Eligibility Verification Form), and upon Performer's submission to Production Company of original documents satisfac-

tory to demonstrate to Production Company Performer's employment eligibility.

IN WITNESS WHEREOF, the parties have executed this agreement on the day and year first above written.

Producer_____

By_____

Player_____

Social Security No._____

DEALMAKING
IN THE
FILM AND
TELEVISION
INDUSTRY

144

LOW-BUDGET NON-UNION DAY PLAYER AGREEMENT

THIS AGREEMENT is made and entered into as of the _____ day of _____, 1993, by and between Big Deal Entertainment, Inc., a California corporation (hereinafter "Producer"), and _____ (hereinafter "Player").

A. Producer intends to produce a theatrical motion picture (hereinafter the "Picture") based upon that certain screenplay tentatively entitled "_____" (hereinafter the "Screenplay") which Picture is intended for initial theatrical exhibition.

B. Producer wishes to utilize the services of Player in connection with the Picture upon the terms and conditions herein contained.

ACCORDINGLY, IT IS AGREED AS FOLLOWS:

1. PHOTOPLAY, ROLE, SALARY AND GUARANTEE: Producer hereby engages Player to render services as such in the role of _____, in the screenplay, at the salary of $_____ per day. Player accepts such engagement upon the terms herein specified. Producer guarantees that it will furnish Player not less than _____ days' employment.

2. TERM: The term of employment hereunder shall begin on or about _____, 19__ (the "Start Date"), and continue until _____, 19__, or until the completion of the photography and recordation of said role.

3. PLAYER'S ADDRESS: All notices which the Producer is required or may desire to give to the Player may be given either by mailing the same addressed to the Player at the address listed at the end of this agreement, or such notice may be given to the Player personally, either orally or in writing.

4. PLAYER'S TELEPHONE: The Player must keep the Producer's casting office or the assistant director of said photoplay advised as to where the Player may be reached by telephone without unreasonable delay. The current telephone number of the Player is listed at the end of this agreement.

5. FURNISHING OF WARDROBE: The Player agrees to furnish all modern wardrobe and wearing apparel reasonably necessary for the portrayal of said role; it being agreed, however, that should so-called "character" or "period" costumes be required, the Producer shall supply the same. When Player furnishes any wardrobe, Player shall receive a reasonable cleaning allowance and reimbursement for any soiled or damaged clothes.

Number of outfits furnished by Player:

_____ @ $_____

_____ @ $_____

6. NEXT STARTING DATE: The starting date of Player's next engagement is:_____.

7. NON-UNION PICTURE: Producer makes the material representation that it is not a signatory to the Screen Actors Guild collective bargaining agreement or any other union or guild agreement. Player warrants that Player is not a member of any union or guild, memberships in which would prevent Player from working in this picture.

8. PROMOTIONAL FILM: Producer shall have the exclusive right to make one or more promotional films of thirty (30) minutes or less and to utilize the results and proceeds of Player's services therein. Player agrees to render such services for said promotional films during the term of his employment hereunder as Producer may request and Player further agrees to use by Producer of film clips and behind-the-scenes shots in which Player appears in such promotional films. Provided Player appears therein, Producer shall pay to Player the sum of one hundred dollars ($100) within ten (10) days after the first use of each such promotional film on television or before a paying audience.

9. NAME AND LIKENESS: Producer shall have the exclusive right to use and to license the use of Player's name, sobriquet, photograph, likeness, voice and/or caricature and shall have the right to simulate Player's voice, signature and appearance by any means in and in connection with the film and the advertising, publicizing, exhibition, and/or other exploitation thereof in any manner and by any means and in connection with commercial advertising and publicity tie-ups.

10. MERCHANDISING: Producer is also granted the further exclusive right and license, but only in connection with the role portrayed by Player in the film to use and to license the use of Player's name, sobriquet, photograph, likeness, caricature and/ or signature (collectively referred to herein as "name and likeness") in and in connection with any merchandising and/or publishing undertakings. In consideration therefore, Producer shall pay Player a pro rata share (payable among all players whose name, etc. is used) of 2½% of the gross monies actually

DEALMAKING
IN THE
FILM AND
TELEVISION
INDUSTRY

146

derived by Producer after deducting therefrom a distribution fee of fifty percent (50%) thereof and a sum equal to all Producer's actual out-of-pocket expenses in connection therewith, for the use of such name or likeness on merchandising and publishing items which utilize Player's name and likeness, other than in a listing of cast credits.

11. TRAVEL EXPENSES: Any right of Player to transportation and expenses pursuant to this Agreement shall be effective when and only when Player is required by Producer to render services more than seventy-five (75) miles from Player's principal place of residence. Any weekly expense allowance provided Employee under this Agreement shall be prorated at one-seventh ($^1/_7$) thereof per day. Player shall be reimbursed at the rate of _____ per mile for use of Player's car to travel to distant locations.

12. INCLUSIVE PAYMENTS: All payments to Player hereunder shall be deemed to be equitable and inclusive remuneration for all services rendered by Player in connection with the Picture and to be paid by way of a complete buy-out of all rights granted to Producer hereunder and no further sums shall be payable to Player by Producer by reason of the exploitation of the Picture and all results and proceeds of Player's services hereunder in any and all media throughout the universe pursuant to any collective bargaining agreement, if any, or otherwise, by way of residuals, repeat fees, pension contributions, or any other monies whatsoever.

13. ARBITRATION: Any controversy or claim arising out of or relating to this agreement or any breach thereof shall be settled by arbitration in accordance with the Rules of the American Arbitration Association; and judgment upon the award rendered by the arbitrator may be entered in any court having jurisdiction thereof. The prevailing party shall be entitled to reimbursement for costs and reasonable attorneys' fees. The determination of the arbitrator in such proceeding shall be final, binding and non-appealable.

14. EMPLOYMENT ELIGIBILITY: All of Producer's obligation herein are expressly conditioned upon Performer's completion, to Producer's satisfaction, of the I-9 form (Employee Eligibility Verification Form), and upon Performer's submission to Producer of original documents satisfactory to demonstrate to Producer Performer's employment eligibility.

IN WITNESS WHEREOF, the parties have executed this agreement on the day and year first above written.

AGREED TO AND ACCEPTED:

_____

(signature)

_____

"Player" (print name),

Player address: _____

Player Phone number: _____

Player Social Security #_____

AGREED TO AND ACCEPTED:

Big Deal Entertainment, Inc.,

By:_____

   Pat Producer, its President

RIDER TO DAY-PLAYER AGREEMENT
BIG DEAL ENTERTAINMENT

1. SERVICES/TERM: Producer engages Player as an actor in the Role set forth in the Principal Agreement and shall cause Player to render all services customarily rendered by actors in feature-length motion pictures at such times and places designated by Producer and in full compliance with Producer's instructions in all matters. Without limiting the foregoing, Player's services shall be in accordance with the following:

   (a) Start Date: Principal Photography of the Picture shall commence on or about _____, 19__ but no later than _____, 19__. The Start Date shall be automatically extended without notice for a period equal to the duration of any default, disability and/or force majeure (as such terms are defined below and regardless of whether Player's services are suspended therefore), or due to any location requirements, director and/or cast availability, weather conditions, and/or other similar contingencies.

DEALMAKING
IN THE
FILM AND
TELEVISION
INDUSTRY

148

(b) Exclusivity: Player's services hereunder shall be non-exclusive first priority during the Pre-Production, exclusive during Production Periods, non-exclusive, but on a first-priority basis, during the Post-Production Period.

(c) Retakes and Other Additional Services: During and after the Term, Player shall render such services as Producer may desire in making retakes, added scenes, transparencies, closeups, soundtrack (including dubbing and looping), process shots, trick shots and trailers for changes in and foreign versions of the Picture. Compensation for such additional services shall be payable pursuant to Paragraph 1 of the principal agreement; provided, however, that no compensation shall be payable for such additional services to the extent they are rendered during any period for which Producer is otherwise obligated to pay or has paid Player compensation, or its entitled to Player's services without compensation.

(d) Nights, Weekends, Holidays, Work Time: No increased or additional compensation shall accrue or be payable to Player for services rendered by Player at night or on weekends or holidays, or after the expiration of any number of hours of service in any period.

2. CREDIT: There shall be no obligation to accord Player credit in paid advertising and/or publicity, although Producer may from time to time elect, in its sole discretion, to accord Player such credit. Producer shall accord Player customary shared screen credit.

3. RIGHTS: Player grants, and Producer shall have, the perpetual and universal right to photograph and re-photograph Player (still and moving) and to record and re-record, double and dub Player's voice and performances, by any present or future methods or means and to use and authorize others to use Player's name, voice and likeness for and in connection with the Picture, the soundtrack (including a soundtrack album), trailers, and documentary and/or "making of" pictures, and all advertising (including Player's name and likeness on sleeves, jackets and other packaging for soundtrack albums, video cassettes, video-discs, written publications and the like), merchandising, commercial tie-ups, publicity, and other means of exploitation of any and all rights pertaining to the Picture and any element thereof. Producer shall own all results and proceeds of Player's services hereunder, including the copyrights thereof, and as such owner shall have the right (among all other rights of ownership): (i) to include such results and proceeds in the Picture and in advertising and publicity relating to the Picture, (ii) to reproduce such results and proceeds by any present or future means, (iii) to

combine such results and proceeds with photographs and recordings made by others for use in the Picture, (iv) to exhibit and
perform such results and proceeds in theaters, on the radio and
television, and in or by any other present or future media, for
profit and otherwise, and for commercial or non-commercial
purposes and purposes of trade, and (v) to license and assign its
rights to any other person or producer. Without in any way
limiting the foregoing, the results and proceeds of Player's
services hereunder include any and all material, words, writings,
ideas, "gags," dialogue, melody and lyrics composed, submitted
or interpolated by Player in connection with the preparation or
production of the Picture (hereinafter referred to as "material").
All said material, the copyright therein, and all renewals, extensions or reversions of copyright now or hereafter provided, shall
automatically become the property of Producer, which shall be
deemed the author thereof, it being agreed and acknowledged
that all of the results and proceeds of Player's services hereunder
are a specially ordered and commissioned "work made for hire"
within the meaning of the 1976 Copyright Act for the compensation provided in the Principal Agreement. Player hereby expressly waives and relinquishes any moral rights or "droit mo-
rale" in and to any material created by or contributed to the
Picture by Player including all of Player's performance.

4. FORCE MAJEURE: As used herein, the term "force majeure"
means epidemic, act of God, strike, lockout, labor condition,
unavailability of materials, transportation, power or other commodity, delay of common carrier, civil disturbance, riot, war or
armed conflict (whether or not there has been an official declaration of war), the enactment of any law, the issuance of any
executive or judicial order or decree, breach of contract by, or
disability of, the Producer, Director, other principal cast member,
breach of contract by a financier or completion guarantor, or
other similar occurrence beyond the control of Producer, which
causes an interruption of or materially hampers or materially
interferes with the production of the Picture.

5. INSURANCE: Player warrants that, to the best of Player's
knowledge, Player is in good health and has no condition which
would prevent Producer from obtaining life, health, accident,
cast or other insurance covering Player at premium rates normal
to Player's age and sex, without any unusual exclusion or
limitation of liability on the part of the insurer.

6. WITHHOLDING: Producer may deduct and withhold from any
monies otherwise payable under this Agreement such amounts
as Producer may reasonably believe it is legally required to
deduct and withhold.

DEALMAKING
IN THE
FILM AND
TELEVISION
INDUSTRY

150

7. ASSIGNMENT: Producer shall have the right to assign this Agreement and any of the rights granted herein, in whole or in part, to any person, firm, corporation or entity, and nothing contained herein shall imply anything to the contrary. Upon the assignee's assumption of the obligations of Producer with respect to the rights so assigned, Producer shall be relieved of all such obligations. Producer shall also have the right to lend the services of Player to any person, firm or corporation which is a subsidiary, parent or affiliate of Producer or the successor to Producer by a merger or by a transfer of substantially all of Producer's assets hereunder. In the event of any such lending, Player agrees to render his services to the best of his ability to the person, firm, or corporation to whom his services are loaned hereunder.

AGREED TO AND ACCEPTED:

_____
Player

EXTRA AGREEMENT

Producer:

MOTION PICTURE:

EMPLOYEE EMPLOYMENT DATE(S): _____

ROLE: _____

EMPLOYEE NAME: _____

ADDRESS: _____

PHONE: Home: _____
            Work: _____

SOCIAL SECURITY # _____

RATE: $_____

OTHER TERMS: _____

TERMS AND CONDITIONS OF EMPLOYMENT

1. Payment of Wages: Wages shall be paid to all employees no later than Friday following the week in which services were performed. Pay date may be delayed by reason of an intervening federal or state holiday. Employee is responsible for submitting her/his time card at the end of the work week to insure timely payment. No employee will be paid without fully completing these forms.

2. Employee shall not be beneficiary of additional overtime, turnaround or other hourly payments except as expressly provided in this deal memo.

3. Nights, Weekends, Holidays, Work Time: Unless expressly provided elsewhere in this deal memo, no increased or additional compensation shall accrue or be payable to employee for the rendering of services at night or on weekends or holidays, or after the expiration of any particular number of hours of service in any period.

4. The Producer will provide meal breaks and/or food service at approximately six (6) hour intervals.

5. Immigration Reform and Control Act of 1986 (IRCA): Employment (or the engagement of services) hereunder is subject to

DEALMAKING
IN THE
FILM AND
TELEVISION
INDUSTRY

152

employee providing the requisite documents required by IRCA and completing and signing the required Form I-9 pursuant to IRCA Section 274a.2. Employee shall comply with the immigration verification employment eligibility provisions required by law.

6. Use of alcohol or drugs during hours of employment will result in employee's immediate termination.

7. Employee's services are on an exclusive basis to the production of the motion picture (the "Picture") referred to in this deal memo for such period of time as required unless otherwise specified in this deal memo.

8. Screen credit is at Producer's discretion subject to employee's performing all services required through completion of term.

9. Unless expressly provided elsewhere in this agreement, employee's employment hereunder shall not be for a "run of the show" or for any guaranteed period of employment. Production reserves the right to discharge employee at any time, subject only to the obligation to pay the balance of any guaranteed compensation due. Producer will attempt to notify employees a minimum of twenty-four (24) hours in advance of layoff. This agreement is subject to immediate suspension and/or termination (at Production's election) without further obligation on the part of Production in the event of any incapacity or default of employee or in the case of any suspension, postponement or interference with the production by reason of labor controversy, strike, earthquake, act of God, governmental action, regulation, or decree or for any other customary force majeure reason.

10. The terms and conditions of this deal memo are binding on Producer and employee and shall not be waived or altered by any method.

11. Producer shall be the owner of all of the results and proceeds of employee's services and shall have the right to use employee's name, voice, picture and likeness in connection with the Picture, the advertising and publicizing thereof, and any promotional films or clips respecting the Picture without additional compensation therefore.

12. Any controversy or claim arising out of or relating to this agreement or any breach thereof shall be settled by arbitration in accordance with the Rules of the American Arbitration Association; and judgment upon the award rendered by the arbitrator may be entered in any court having jurisdiction thereof. The prevailing party shall be entitled to reimbursement for costs and reasonable attorneys' fees.

EMPLOYEE ACCEPTS ALL CONDITIONS OF EMPLOYMENT AS DESCRIBED ABOVE

AGREED TO AND ACCEPTED:

EMPLOYEE SIGNATURE: _____

DATE: _____

PRODUCER SIGNATURE: _____

DATE: _____

EXTRA RELEASE

FOR GOOD AND VALUABLE CONSIDERATION, I hereby grant to Big Deal Entertainment, Inc. ("Producer"), and to its licensees, assignees, and other successors-in-interest all rights of every kind and character whatsoever in perpetuity in and to my performance, appearance, name and/or voice and the results and proceeds thereof (the "Performance") in connection with the motion picture currently entitled _____ ("The Picture"), and I hereby authorize Producer to photograph and record (on film, tape, or otherwise) the Performance; to edit same at its discretion and to include it with the performance of others and with sound effects, special effects and music; to incorporate same into Picture or other program or not; to use and to license others to use such recordings and photographs in any manner or media whatsoever, including without limitation unrestricted use for purposes of publicity, advertising and sales promotion; and to use my name, likeness, voice, biographic or other information concerning me in connection with the Picture, commercial tie-ups, merchandising, and for any other purpose. I agree that Producer owns all rights and proceeds of my services rendered in connection herewith.

AGREED TO AND ACCEPTED:

_____DATE: _____
Extra Player

DEALMAKING
IN THE
FILM AND
TELEVISION
INDUSTRY

154

PRODUCERS

Producers are not as powerful as they used to be. In the studio era producers working for a studio could exercise a great deal of authority over stars and directors employed under long-term contracts. Today, however, producers, directors and stars operate as independent contractors. Studios often value their relationships with stars and directors more than their affiliation with producers. If there is a clash between a producer and director, a studio may find it less costly and disruptive to remove a producer than a director. Moreover, some stars and directors have established their own production companies and hire producers to work for them. Obviously, these producers can exercise little authority over their employers.

Producers are often referred to as "independent producers." While they may not be tied exclusively to one studio, most are hardly independent. They may rely heavily upon studios for financing and distribution of their pictures.

A producer's role varies a great deal depending on his skills and background, the strengths and weaknesses of his collaborators and whether a film being made for a studio or is financed independently. A producer like Steven Spielberg with substantial experience as a filmmaker is often much more involved in the creative aspects of producing than a producer with a background in finance or distribution. A veteran producer working with a novice director will play a larger role than a novice producer working with a veteran director. A producer who raises his own financing has more power and control over a production than a producer working on a studio film.

Films today often contain numerous producing credits. I have seen movies with a couple of "Executive Producers," several "Producers," "Co-Producers," and "Associate Producers," and an "Executive in Charge of Production" or two. Why have producer credits proliferated?

The Producer's Guild is not recognized as a union or a guild by the studios. They consider producers part of management and have refused to enter into a collective-bargaining agreement that would restrict the studio's ability to grant credits.

Unlike the agreements reached with the DGA and WGA, which severely restrict the studio's ability to allocate credit for directors and writers, studios can assign producer credits as they please. Thus, studios can give producing credits away as perks to persons who have not earned them. A personal manager, for instance, might receive an "Executive Producer" for bringing his client into a project, even though the manager doesn't perform any producing function. The proliferation of producer credits has devalued their worth.

The producer function is often divided into "Executive Producer" and "Line Producer." The "Executive Producer" is the dealmaker, the financier. He may be producing several projects at once. He will often hire a "Line Producer" to work for him. The line producer is the person in charge of logistics for the shoot. He will hire crew, order supplies and equipment and make sure that everything the director needs to make the film is available when needed. During production a line producer will only be able to handle one project at a time.

Producer deals vary a great deal in their compensation and terms. Here is a sample line producer contract for a low-budget feature film.

DEALMAKING
IN THE
FILM AND
TELEVISION
INDUSTRY

156

LINE PRODUCER EMPLOYMENT AGREEMENT

THIS AGREEMENT is made and entered into as of the _____ day of _____, 19__, by and between _____ Entertainment, Inc., a California corporation (hereinafter "Production Company"), and _____ (hereinafter "Employee").

This Agreement is entered into with reference to the following facts:

A. Production company intends to produce a theatrical motion picture (hereinafter the "Picture") based upon that certain screenplay tentatively entitled "_____" (hereinafter the "Screenplay"), which Picture is intended for initial theatrical exhibition.

B. Production company wishes to utilize the services of Employee as line producer in connection with the production and delivery of the Picture upon the terms and conditions herein contained.

ACCORDINGLY, IT IS AGREED AS FOLLOWS:

1. ENGAGEMENT: Subject to events of force majeure, default, or the disability or death of Employee, Production company hereby engages the services of Employee on a "pay or play" basis, and Employee agrees to render exclusive services as line producer, in connection with the production of the Picture upon the terms and conditions herein contained. Subject to Production Company's final approval, Employee shall supervise and be responsible for the preparation of the budget and the production schedule of the Picture, the testing of persons proposed for the cast, scouting for shooting locations, assembling the crew, the supervision of the photography of the Picture, the supervision of the editing, and sound mixing, assisting in the selection of music, the supervision of the final dubbing and scoring, the supervision of all other post-production requirements of the Picture, the delivery of the final answer print and all other customary delivery items to Production company and its principal distributors, foreign and domestic, and perform such other services as are reasonably required by Production company and are usually and customarily performed by producers in the motion picture industry. Employee will report to such place(s) as are reasonably designated by Production company and will be available at all times and for such periods of time as are reasonably designated by Production company. Employee will advise Production company of Employee's whereabouts so that Employee may be reached at any reasonable hour of the night or day. During the term of

employment, Employee will render his services at all places and at all times reasonably required by Production company, including nights, Saturdays, Sundays, and holidays.

In addition, Employee shall assist in the preparation and delivery to Production company of a fully detailed and comprehensive preliminary and final below-the-line budget ("Budget") for the Picture, which Budget shall not exceed the sum of _____ , exclusive of contingency, completion-bond fee, insurance, and any "above the line costs." Employee shall also consult with and assist Production company, as and when requested by Production company, in connection with Production company's negotiations for the services of the production personnel and cast for the Picture.

2. TERM: Employee shall render the services required of him as set forth in Paragraph 1 hereof during the period commencing on _____ 19__, and continuing thereafter for such time as pre-production, principal photography, and customary post-production and delivery of the Picture as required by Production company. It is contemplated that principal photography of the Picture will commence approximately on _____, 19__, and subject to extension for events beyond Production company's control and other events of force majeure, Employee's exclusive services shall not be required beyond _____ 19__, but he shall nevertheless supervise the delivery of the Picture hereunder.

3. COMPENSATION: In consideration for all of the services to be rendered by Employee hereunder and for all of the rights granted by Employee to Production company, and on condition that Employee is not in default hereunder, and subject to the terms and conditions specified herein, Production company agrees to pay Employee, and Employee agrees to accept: _____, contingent compensation as described in subparagraph (a) below and other valuable consideration. Payment of the _____ shall be within ten days of execution of this agreement.

(a) Contingent Compensation: If employee is entitled to a line producer credit in accordance with Paragraph 9 of this agreement, Production company shall pay employee five percent of one-hundred percent (5% of 100%) of the "net profit" in accordance with Production Company's agreement with the Domestic Distributor of the Picture. Notwithstanding the foregoing, "Net Profit" shall be the monies remaining, if any, after all customary deductions, including but not limited to, all production expenses, interest, overhead, debts, deferred expenses and the cost of prints, advertising and marketing are deducted in accordance with Production Company's distribution agreement. Production Company shall only be obliged to pay Producer his share of "net profits" upon receipt of same from the distributor.

DEALMAKING
IN THE
FILM AND
TELEVISION
INDUSTRY

158

Disbursements of contingent compensation shall be on a semi-annual basis, on a pro-rata basis, beginning no later than six months after completion of the picture.

4. SERVICES: At all times during the term of Employee's services hereunder, Employee will promptly and faithfully comply with all of Production company's reasonable instructions, directions, requests, rules and regulations. Employee will perform his services conscientiously and to the full limit of his talents and capabilities when wherever reasonably required or desired by Production company and in accordance with Production company's reasonable instructions and directions in all matters, including those involving artistic taste and judgment. Employee will perform such service as Production company may reasonably require of him, and as customarily and usually rendered by and required of producers employed to produce low-budget theatrical motion pictures in the motion-picture industry.

5. INSURANCE: Employee agrees that Production company may at any time or times, either in Production company's name or otherwise, but at Production company's expense and for Production company's own benefit, apply for, and take out life, health, accident, and other insurance covering Employee whether independently or together with others in any reasonable amount which Production company may deem necessary to protect Production company's interests hereunder. Production company shall own all rights in and to such insurance and in the cash values and proceeds thereof and Employee shall not have any right, title, or interest therein. Employee agrees to the customary examinations and correctly preparing, signing and delivering such applications and other documents as may be reasonable required.

6. CONTROL: Production company shall have complete control of the production of the Picture including, but not limited to, all artistic controls and the right to cut, edit, add to, subtract from ,arrange, rearrange, and revise the Picture in any manner. Production company shall not be obligated to make any actual use of Employee's services or to produce or to release or to continue the distribution or release of the Picture once released.

7. RIGHTS: In addition to Employee's services as a line producer, Production company shall be entitled to and shall own all of the results and proceeds thereof throughout the world in perpetuity (including, but not limited to, all rights throughout the world of production, public performance, manufacture, television, recordation, and reproduction by any art or method, whether now known or hereafter devised, copyright, trademark and patent), whether such results and proceeds consist of literary, dramatic, musical, motion picture, mechanical or any other form of works, ideas, themes, compositions, creations, or prod-

ucts and without obligation to pay any fees, royalties or other amounts except those expressly provided for in this Agreement. Specifically, but without in any way limiting the generality of the foregoing, Production company shall own all rights of every kind and character in and to any and all acts, poses, plays and appearances of any and all kinds which Employee may write, suggest, direct or produce during the term hereof. In the event that Production company shall desire to secure separate assignments of any of the foregoing, Employee agrees to execute them upon Production company's request therefore. All rights granted or agreed to be granted to Production company hereunder shall vest in Production company immediately and shall remain vested in Production company and Production company's successors and assigns whether this Agreement expires in normal course or whether Employee's engagement hereunder is sooner terminated for any cause or reason. Production company shall have the right to use and authorize others to use the name, voice and likeness of Employee, and any results and proceeds of his services hereunder, to advertise and publicize the Picture including, but not limited to, the right to use the same in the credits of the Picture, in trailers, in commercial tie-ups, and in all other forms and media of advertising and publicity including merchandising, publications, records and commercial advertising and publicity tie-ups derived from or relating to the Picture.

8. REPRESENTATIONS, WARRANTIES AND INDEMNITY:

(a) Employee represents and warrants that all material of every kind authored, written, prepared, composed, and/or submitted by Employee hereunder for or to Production company shall be wholly original with him, and shall not infringe or violate the right of privacy of, or constitute libel against, or violate any copyright, common-law right or any other right of any person, firm or corporation. The foregoing warranties shall not apply to any material not authored, written, prepared, composed or submitted by Employee, but shall apply to all material, incidents and characterizations which Employee may add to or incorporate in or cause to be added to or incorporated in such material. Employee further represents and warrants that Employee is free to enter into this Agreement and to render the required services hereunder and that Employee is not subject to any obligations or disability which will or might interfere with Employee's fully complying with this Agreement; that Employee has not made, and will not make, any grant or assignment which might interfere with the complete enjoyment of the rights granted to Production company hereunder; and that Employee will not at any time render any services or do any acts which shall derogate from the value of Employee's services rendered pursuant to this Agreement or which shall interfere with the performance of any of

DEALMAKING
IN THE
FILM AND
TELEVISION
INDUSTRY

160

Employee's covenants or obligations pursuant to this Agreement. Employee hereby indemnifies Production company, its successors, assigns, licensees, officers and employees, and hold it harmless from and against any and all liability losses, damages and expenses (including attorneys' fees) arising out of (i) the use of any materials furnished by Employee for the Picture, or (ii) any breach by Employee of any warranty or agreement made by Employee hereunder.

(b) Production company represents and warrants that Production company has the right to enter into this Agreement, and to render the required obligations hereunder, and that Production company is not subject to any other obligations or disabilities which will or might interfere with Production company's fully complying with this Agreement; that Production company has not made, and will not make any grant or assignment which might interfere with the complete enjoyment of the compensation granted to Employee hereunder; that Production company has secured all necessary financing to make all payments hereunder, and complete the Picture as budgeted; and that Production company will not at any time render any services or do any acts which shall derogate from the value of Production company's obligations pursuant to this Agreement, or which shall interfere with the performance of any of Production company's covenants or obligations pursuant to this Agreement. Production company hereby indemnifies Employee and his successors and assigns, and holds them harmless from and against any and all liability, losses, damages, and expenses (including reasonable attorneys' fees) arising out of any breach by Production company of any warranty or agreement made by Production company hereunder.

9. CREDIT: Provided that Employee shall fully and completely keep and perform all of his obligations and agreements hereunder, and if the Picture has been produced substantially with the use of Employee's services hereunder, Employee shall receive a line producing credit on the positive prints and/or tape for the Picture in the main titles thereof and in all paid advertisements (subject to customary distributor exclusions). Production company shall determine in its sole discretion the manner of presenting and the size of such credits. No casual or inadvertent failure to comply with the provisions of this paragraph or failure of any third party to comply with same shall be deemed to be a breach of this Agreement by Production company. In the event of a failure or omission by Production company constituting a breach of its credit obligations under this Agreement, Employee's rights shall be limited to the right, if any, to seek damages at law, and Employee shall not have any right in such event to rescind this Agreement or any of the rights granted to Production company hereunder, or to enjoin the distribution, exhibition, or other

exploitation of the Picture or the advertising or publicizing thereof. Production company shall, however, upon receipt of written notice of any such breach of its credit obligations, cure such breach on a prospective basis on materials to be created in the future.

10. CONTINGENCIES: If Employee shall become incapacitated or prevented from fully performing his services hereunder by reason of illness, accident, or mental and physical disability and/ or if the production of the Picture is hampered or interrupted or interfered with for any event or reason beyond the control of Production company or any other event of force majeure (here-inafter collectively referred to as "incapacity"), Production company shall have the right to suspend Employee's services and the compensation payable to Employee during the continuance of any such incapacity. In the event any such incapacity continues for a period of seven (7) consecutive days or for an aggregate period of twenty-one (21) days, Production company shall have the right to terminate Employee's engagement hereunder. In the event that Employee should fail, refuse or neglect, other than because of incapacity, to perform any of his required services hereunder, Production company shall have the right at any time to suspend Employee's services and the compensation payable to Employee during the continuance of such default, and Production company shall have the right at any time to terminate Employee's engagement hereunder by reason of such default.

11. NO RIGHT TO CONTRACT: Employee acknowledges and agrees that he has no right or authority to and will not employ any person to serve in any capacity, nor contract for the purchase or rental of any article or material, nor make any commitment or agreement whereby Production company shall be required to pay any monies or other consideration or which shall otherwise obligate Production company, without Production company's express prior written consent.

12. TRAVEL AND EXPENSES: If Production company shall require Employee to render his services on location at any place(s) more than fifty (50) miles from his residence, Production company shall furnish Employee with transportation from his residence to such place(s) and return, or reimburse employee 25 cents per mile if employee uses his own means of transportation. Production company shall also furnish Employee with or reimburse Employee for actual reasonable expenses for each day Production company requires Employee to render services away from Employee's residence on a no-less-favorable basis than the expense allowance accorded the director. All transportation expenditures shall require the prior approval in writing by Production company or its designee. Any miscellaneous expenses that

DEALMAKING
IN THE
FILM AND
TELEVISION
INDUSTRY

162

Employee incurs relating to his employment shall be reimbursed by Production Company within seven days after receipts are submitted to Production Company.

13. ASSIGNMENT: Production company may transfer and assign this Agreement or all or any of its rights hereunder to any person, firm or corporation, but no such assignment or transfer shall relieve Production company of its executory obligations hereunder. This Agreement shall inure to the benefit of Production company's successors, licensees and assigns. Employee shall not assign or transfer this Agreement, or any of his rights or obligations hereunder, it being understood that the obligations and duties of Employee are personal to Employee, and any purported assignment shall be void. Employee may, however, assign his right to receive any monies hereunder.

14. LIMITATION OF REMEDY: All rights assigned by this Agreement shall be irrevocable under all or any circumstances and shall not be subject to reversion, rescission, termination or injunction. Employee agrees that he shall not have the right to enjoin the exhibition, distribution or exploitation of any motion picture produced hereunder or to enjoin, rescind or terminate any rights granted to Production company hereunder. Employee further agrees that Employee's sole remedy in the event of any default by Production company hereunder, including the failure by Production company to pay Employee any consideration payable to Employee pursuant hereto, or to accord Employee credit (to the extent that Production company is obligated to accord Employee such credit) pursuant hereto, shall be an action at law for damages and/or for an accounting (if applicable). At all times, the Production company shall have all rights and remedies which it has at law or in equity, pursuant hereto or otherwise.

15. PRODUCTION BUDGET AND SCHEDULE: Employee represents and warrants that Employee has read the Screenplay for the Picture, and based upon Employee's substantial experience in the production of motion pictures, Employee has advised Production company that based upon the current Screenplay, and an anticipated _____ week schedule for principal photography, the Picture can be produced for a below-the-line cost of $_____, excluding any contingencies, completion-bond fees, insurance, events of force majeure and all "above-the-line" costs. It is the essence of this Agreement that Employee produce the Picture in accordance with the approved production schedule and for a below-the-line cost not exceeding _____ thousand dollars ($_____). Employee agrees to timely notify Production company of any potential over-budget situations and further agrees not to proceed with any production cost overages without the prior written consent of Production company. If,

after such notification, the below-the-line cost of the Picture exceeds _____ dollars ($_____), or the approved production schedule through no fault of Employee, then Production company shall be solely responsible for said cost overruns. If, however, Employee fails to give such timely notification, and/or proceeds with production cost overages without the written consent of Production company, and as a result it reasonably appears, based upon Production company's good-faith judgment, that the below-the-line cost of the Picture will exceed $ _____, or the approved production schedule by Five Percent (5%), then Production company may, in addition to any other rights or remedies which Production company may have at law or in equity, terminate this Agreement, and any further payments or other obligations due Employee hereunder. Under no circumstances will the employee be personally liable for any cost overruns.

16. FURTHER DOCUMENTS: Employee agrees to execute any and all additional and further documents and instruments required by Production company to further the intents and purposes of this Agreement and to vest in Production company all right, title, and interest in and to the Picture. In the event Employee fails or refuses to execute such document or instrument, Employee hereby irrevocably appoints Production company his attorney-in-fact (such appointment being coupled with an interest) to execute such documents or instruments on behalf of Employee.

17. NOTICES: All notices or payments which Production company may be required to give or make to Employee hereunder may be delivered personally or sent by certified or registered mail or telegraph, or by fax to Employee at _____ .

All notices that Employee may wish to give to Production company hereunder may be delivered personally or sent by certified or registered mail or telegraph, or fax, to Production company at: _____.
The date of delivery, or attempted delivery, as the case may be, of any notice or payment hereunder shall be deemed to be the date of service of such notice or payment.

18. SECTION HEADINGS: The headings of paragraphs, sections or other subdivisions of this Agreement are for convenience in reference only. They will not be used in any way to govern, limit, modify, construe or otherwise be given any legal effect.

19. ARBITRATION: Any controversy or claim arising out of or relating to this agreement or any breach thereof shall be settled by arbitration in accordance with the Rules of the American Arbitration Association; and judgment upon the award rendered

DEALMAKING
IN THE
FILM AND
TELEVISION
INDUSTRY

164

by the arbitrators may be entered in any court having jurisdiction thereof. The prevailing party shall be entitled to reimbursement for costs and reasonable attorneys' fees. The determination of the arbitrator in such proceeding shall be final, binding and non-appealable.

20. ENTIRE AGREEMENT: This Agreement represents the entire understanding between the parties hereto with respect to the subject matter hereof, and this Agreement supersedes all previous representations, understandings or agreements, oral or written, between the parties with respect to the subject matter hereof, and cannot be modified except by written instrument signed by the parties hereto. This Agreement shall be governed by and construed in accordance with the laws of the State of California, and the exclusive venue for resolution of any dispute arising out of, or in connection with, this Agreement shall be in Los Angeles, California.

AGREED TO AND ACCEPTED:

_____
"Employee"

AGREED TO AND ACCEPTED:

_____ Entertainment, Inc.,

By:_____

  President

CHAPTER 7

ADVICE FOR WRITERS, DIRECTORS & ACTORS

Writers, directors and actors are often vulnerable to exploitation by producers and studios. Here are some specific suggestions and strategies for protection:

WRITERS

Most industry insiders believe that the script is the single most important element in the success of a movie. That is because the screenplay is the foundation on which everyone else's efforts rest. Mediocre direction and mundane acting won't ruin a great script. But a terrible script can't be saved with brilliant direction and exceptional performances.

Since the script is the most important element of any package, one would think that writers would be the most highly sought-after talent in Hollywood. That is not the case. Top writers are not paid anywhere near as much as leading directors or stars. Nor are writers accorded the respect and credit given directors. Writers exercise little influence and power and are often treated like second-class citizens.

DEALMAKING
IN THE
FILM AND
TELEVISION
INDUSTRY

166

Writers lack clout because their contributions are made during development, not production. Studios own the copyright to writers' work and can change it without their permission. Few of the many scripts written are ever produced, and when a studio executive wants to produce a script, pleasing the writer is not a high priority. The executive is usually more concerned with attracting a director or star to the project. Without these elements, the movie can't get made.

When a director or star comes aboard, they often want to change the script. A power struggle may ensue with the writer intent on protecting her work. Although non-writers may have little writing ability, they often think they can improve a screenplay. Scripts are not accorded the respect given other art forms.

Consider, for example, a producer who spends $100,000 to buy a Picasso painting. Can you imagine him looking at this masterpiece and saying to his wife, "You know honey, I think the picture could use some more blue. Where are the paints? It will just take me a moment to fix this." Or would a producer spend $100,000 on a piece of sculpture, bring it home and say to his spouse: "You know the nose looks a little big. Where's the chisel?" Of course, no producer in his right mind would buy a $100,000 piece of fine art and change it. But it is not uncommon for a producer to spend $100,000 or more on a script and promptly rewrite it.

Since the writer has already provided her services, she can't withhold them as a bargaining chip. Nobody cares if the writer threatens to lock herself in her Winnebago. Indeed, she usually doesn't get a Winnebago, and she may not even be welcome on the set.

Thus, scripts are often changed, and sometimes ruined, by those with more clout. Imagine, if you will, a top star who tells the studio executive that he will only participate in a project if his pet dog stars opposite him. When the writer hears this suggestion, he goes ballistic: "You can't turn the romantic interest into a dog. That changes the entire story!" But the star insists: "I promised Fluffy that he would be in my next movie. Either Fluffy gets the part, or I'm history."

The studio executive is faced with a dilemma. Without a star, the project doesn't get made and a lot of development expenses may have to be written off. On the other hand, the worse that happens if the writer is alienated is that he refuses to work for the executive again.

Aware of their lack of power, seasoned writers use diplomacy to protect their work. One veteran screenwriter advises novice writers not to be disagreeable with studio executives, no matter how silly their suggestions. If *Jaws* was last week's hit, the executive may suggest that you add a shark to your story. It doesn't matter that you've written a Western with no water in sight.

If you argue, you get a reputation for being obstreperous, and they may replace you with a more malleable writer. Better to take copious notes, and if the suggestions are moronic, ignore them. Often the executive will forget what he suggested at the last meeting. If he asks, simply say, "I tried the shark. It was a good idea, but it just didn't work."

ADVICE
FOR
WRITERS,
DIRECTORS &
ACTORS

167

HOW WRITERS ARE EXPLOITED

There are many ways that writers are exploited. The methods are only limited by the imaginations of unscrupulous producers— and in this regard writers concede that producers are a creative force to be reckoned with.

Some of the more common abuses are:

1. **BAIT:** Producers may hire a prestigious writer to help attract an important director or star to a project. The writer's script is later rewritten and ruined.

2. **IDEA THEFT:** Producers may steal a writer's story idea. As explained in Chapter 12, one cannot copyright an idea. The writer pitches his idea to the producer. He responds: "Oh, my gosh. Just this morning in the shower I had the same thought. What a coincidence. I guess brilliant minds think alike. See you around." If the writer is not represented by an attorney or agent, and he doesn't know how to protect himself by contract law, he is especially vulnerable.

    There are several strategies writers can employ to foil

DEALMAKING
IN THE
FILM AND
TELEVISION
INDUSTRY

168

idea thieves. First, don't talk about your story until you put it in writing. Remember that old Navy saying: "Loose lips sink ships." Don't tell *anyone* about your brilliant idea. The listener may forget he was told it in confidence, or he may inadvertently let it slip out. Since ideas are as free as the air, anyone who hears it can legally use it as the basis for his own screenplay.

While ideas cannot be copyrighted, a treatment or screenplay can be. The embellishment upon the idea is what copyright law protects. Thus, the more you write out and express your story, the more protection you will obtain.

As soon as you write your story, register it with the Writers Guild. You don't need to be a member to register a script with either their East or West coast office. Registration with the WGA does not grant the writer any additional legal rights. It does, however, create some great evidence that can be used in the event of a plagiarism dispute. The outcome of such a lawsuit may turn on which party can convince the jury that they created the story first. The first writer will be presumed to be the creator of the original, while the second will be presumed to be a copier.[1]

How do you prove that you came up with the story first? You could bring your spouse

REGISTERING A SCRIPT WITH THE WGA

WHAT CAN BE REGISTERED:
LITERARY PROPERTIES WRITTEN FOR MOTION PICTURES AND TELEVISION AS CONCEPTS, TREATMENTS AND SCRIPTS.

WHAT CANNOT BE REGISTERED: BOOK MANUSCRIPTS OR STAGE PLAYS.

PROCEDURE: SUBMIT ONE $8^1/_2$ X 11 UNBOUND COPY WITH A CHECK FOR $20.00 (NON-MEMBERS), $15.00 (STUDENTS), OR $10.00 (MEMBERS).

DURATION OF REGISTRATION:
FIVE YEARS BUT IT IS RENEWABLE.

MAILING ADDRESS:
8955 BEVERLY BLVD.,
WEST HOLLYWOOD, CA 90048-2456.
PHONE: (310) 205-2540.
IN NEW YORK CALL (212) 767-7800.
NEW YORK ADDRESS: 555 W. 57TH ST.,
STE. 1230, NEW YORK, 10019.

Pre-Recorded Information Tape: L.A.: (310) 205-2500;
NEW YORK: (212) 757-4360.

---

[1] If the second writer can prove that he independently created the same story, without copying the first writer, he will be entitled to the copyright to the second story just as the first writer will have the copyright to the first story. Thus, both writers will own the copyright to their own work, notwithstanding their similarities. Of course, if two stories are very similar, it is highly unlikely that one writer didn't copy from the other.

ADVICE
FOR
WRITERS,
DIRECTORS &
ACTORS

169

into court to testify as a witness that he/she read an early version of the manuscript. Or you could mail a copy of the manuscript to yourself, registered mail, in a postmarked and sealed envelope. But spouses are not impartial witnesses, and envelopes can be steamed open and their contents changed. The best evidence is a signed declaration by a neutral third-party custodian who swears that he received your manuscript on a certain date and has kept it in seclusion ever since. This is what registration with the Writers Guild accomplishes.

Another way to protect oneself from story theft is to establish an implied or oral contract between the producer and the writer. While ideas cannot be copyrighted, they have value and can be the subject of a contract. As described in Chapter 2, a writer can make a binding oral contract before disclosing his idea.

It is also advisable to put a copyright notice on your work before you publish it. Typically scripts are not published, and under the new copyright law, notice is optional anyway. Nevertheless,

ADMISSION REQUIREMENTS TO THE WRITERS GUILD

YOU NEED **12** CREDITS FOR ADMISSION, ACCUMULATED WITHIN THE PRECEDING TWO YEARS.

CREDITS ARE ALLOCATED AS FOLLOWS:

2 UNITS: FOR EACH WEEK OF EMPLOYMENT ON A WEEK-TO-WEEK OR TERM BASIS.

4 UNITS: FOR A THEATRICAL SHORT

6 UNITS: FOR A "CREATED BY" CREDIT

8 UNITS: FOR A STORY FOR A RADIO PLAY OR TELEVISION PROGRAM OF MORE THAN ONE HOUR (BUT LESS THAN TWO HOURS).

12 UNITS: FOR A STORY FOR A FEATURE OR TWO HOUR TELEVISION PROGRAM, OR SCREENPLAY FOR A FEATURE, TELEVISION OR RADIO PROGRAM OF ONE HOUR OR MORE; OR

A SCREENPLAY FOR A FEATURE-LENGTH FILM OR TELEVISION PROGRAM OR RADIO PLAY FOR A RADIO PROGRAM OF MORE THAN ONE HOUR; OR

A BIBLE (LONG-TERM STORY PROJECTION).

INITIATION FEE: $2,500.

CALL THE WRITERS GUILD AT (310) 550-1000 FOR ADDITIONAL INFORMATION.

DEALMAKING
IN THE
FILM AND
TELEVISION
INDUSTRY

170

copyright notice prevents anyone from claiming that they innocently infringed on your copyright.[1] Innocent infringers may be liable for less damages than willful infringers.

Idea theft will be deterred if you are represented by an agent or entertainment attorney. A studio executive will think twice before ripping off a client of a powerful agency. Foul play may jeopardize his access to other agency clients.

I believe most idea theft occurs between fringe producers and novice writers. Sometimes the theft is inadvertent and done by lower-level staffers who don't understand the fine points of copyright law. I don't believe most successful producers regularly steal ideas—it doesn't make any sense. There is little reason for Steven Spielberg to rip off a writer. The best writers are anxious to work with him and their fees comprise a small part of a production budget. Besides, Spielberg can make so much money legitimately that it would be foolish for him to steal a story. No one wants to become enmeshed in expensive and lengthy litigation, not to mention the bad publicity and harm to reputation that such a lawsuit can generate.

Writers are well advised to try to deal only with reputable producers. Find out who the sleazy operators are and avoid them. In my experience, most producers who have bad reputations have earned them.

Although writers should be careful, they shouldn't become so paralyzed with fear that they refrain from submitting their work to potential buyers. I have found that those writers who most fear story theft are novices who have the least to worry about. Many of their scripts are so bad they couldn't be given away.

3. **FREE CONSULTING SERVICE:** Another industry abuse involves veteran writers who are brought in to consult on a project on the pretext that they are being considered for a rewrite. Let's say you have a producer who has commissioned and received a first draft of a screenplay. He likes the script but there are certain problems. Despite the producer's and writer's efforts, they cannot fix the

---

[1] See page 270, Chapter 12, for the requirements of a copyright notice.

script. So the producer calls the agents of several veteran writers and says, "I'm thinking of hiring your client to rewrite my script. I'd like to send him a copy of the first draft and have him come in to discuss with me how he would rewrite it, if I hired him."

The writers dutifully come in and offer their suggestions, but the producer doesn't hire any of them. He uses their suggestions, however, to rewrite the script. The producer has essentially used these writers as a free consulting service. Novice writers need not worry about this abuse, as producers don't value your suggestions enough to steal them.

ADVICE
FOR
WRITERS,
DIRECTORS &
ACTORS

171

4. SHOPPING: Shopping refers to the practice of producers pitching a story that they do not own or have an option on. Let's say you are a writer. You go in to see a producer and pitch your project. The producer says "Interesting. Let me think about it for a few days and get back to you." After you depart, the producer calls his buddy, an executive at ABC, and pitches your story without your knowledge. If there is interest, the producer takes an option on your project. If there is no interest, he passes. He never tells you that he pitched your story behind your back to ABC and it was rejected.

You go on your merry way and pitch your story to a more ethical buyer. Let's call him producer Bob. He takes an option on your story before pitching it. When he goes in to ABC they inform him that they already heard your story and passed on it. Producer Bob is unhappy that you did not mention this fact to him.

Shopping is a widespread practice. Producers who do not risk any money on an option tend to hastily package and pitch a project. The tendency is to throw the project up against the wall to see if it will stick. A more careful approach could produce better results. Shopping can tarnish a project. Once ABC has heard and passed on your story, it is unlikely that they will reconsider, even if the second pitch is better.[1]

---

[1] See page 18 as to how to deter unauthorized presentation of your project by establishing an agreement that your story be kept in confidence.

DEALMAKING
IN THE
FILM AND
TELEVISION
INDUSTRY

172

A writer may choose to let a producer pitch a property without taking an option. Essentially, the writer is giving the producer a free option. The writer may feel that the project will get its best shot if an experienced producer pitches it rather than a novice writer. Perhaps the writer doesn't have the stature or contacts needed to arrange a pitch meeting himself. As long as the writer gives the producer permission to pitch the project, there is no abuse.

The Writers Guild Minimum Basic Agreement (MBA) provides some protection for its members. For theatrical motion pictures, a writer may restrict, in writing, the extent to which a company may shop material to third parties. In television, shopping is not permitted *unless* the writer gives written permission. Violations are punishable by a fine of $750 for an unauthorized submission. The Guild also prohibits companies from distributing their critiques or script coverage to persons outside the company unless the writer consents.[1]

5. **WRITING ON SPEC:** Writing on speculation, which is writing on the promise that you will be paid subject to some contingency (e.g. the producer likes the script or can obtain financing), is strictly prohibited by the Writers Guild. Writers must receive the minimum fixed compensation as set forth in the Guild's schedule. Additional payments above and beyond the minimum may be predicated on a contingency (i.e., bonus, deferred, contingent and additional compensation).

Although writers naturally resist working on only a promise of payment, clever producers may persuade them otherwise. Let's say you are called in to see a producer who has read your script. The producer gushes with praise of your work, saying he loves your characters, the first act is brilliant, and the second is even better. After raving about your creation, he tells you that he has just one reservation: "That third act just doesn't work for

---

[1] The MBA makes an exception for those individuals with whom the company has a business relationship, such as a development deal or production deal. See 1988 MNA, article 60.

me." He claims that if you had written it differently, he would have bought it. Well, you can read between the lines. You run home and spend two months revising the script. You submit it to him and he turns it down again. The producer has essentially gotten you to work for free.

6. **STIFFING THE WRITER:** Sometimes writers are not paid for their work despite their contract with a producer. Agreements typically provide that the writer receives half her fixed compensation when she begins writing and half when she turns in the completed work. Suppose she turns in the finished manuscript and the producer refuses to pay the balance due. The producer professes dissatisfaction with the script. His disappoinment, however, is not a valid excuse because the producer bears the risk of the script not turning out well.

What remedy does the writer have? If the amount owed is $5,000 or less, the writer could sue in California's small claims court. However, if the amount owed is more than $5,000, but not enough to justify hiring a lawyer to litigate, the writer is caught in a bind.[1]

If the writer is a member of the Writers Guild, and the producer a signatory, the Guild will attempt to secure payment for the writer. Ultimately, the Guild can threaten to put the production company on the Unfair or Strike list.[2] This means that all WGA members are prohibited from working for the production company. This would appear to be a crushing blow to any production entity.

But what if the producer dissolves his company, incorporates a new legal entity, and signs another agreement with the WGA? Then he goes his merry way, exploiting a new crop of writers. The WGA is now trying to crack down on unethical producers who attempt this ruse. The Guild keeps a cross-reference of producer names and companies. Producers who dissolve and re-incorporate

---

[1] This is when it is great to have an arbitration clause in your agreement. See page 29 in Chapter 2 for more information on binding arbitration.

[2] The Unfair List is for producers whom the Guild has determined are unreliable as to payment or are financially insolvent. The Strike List is comprised of producers who refuse to bargain or sign the basic agreement after hiring a WGA member.

DEALMAKING
IN THE
FILM AND
TELEVISION
INDUSTRY

174

must satisfy all prior obligations to WGA members before a new agreement is signed.

7. **UNNECESSARY REWRITES:** Writers' scripts may be rewritten for extraneous reasons. Not all rewrites are bad; some may improve the work. But often the maxim "Too many cooks spoil the broth" reflects what can happen when a script is rewritten too many times. Such scripts may lose their distinctive point of view and become homogenized, limp stories.

Rewrites can not only ruin the writer's work but can have significant impact on compensation. As discussed in Chapter 6, the amount of a writer's bonus and contingent compensation may be tied to whether he receives sole or shared screenplay credit.

CASES

ROSSNER V. CBS, INC.

FACTS: Rossner (P) wrote a novel entitled *Looking for Mr. Goodbar* about a young woman who was picked up in a singles bar and murdered. The novel was loosely based on a true story that was widely reported in the press.

Rossner's novel became a best seller. She sold the movie rights to Paramount, which produced a movie titled *Looking for Mr. Goodbar*. Rossner first conceived of the term "Goodbar" to identify a fictional character in her book.

After Rossner's novel was published, but before Paramount's movie was released, a newspaper reporter who covered the murder wrote several magazine articles titled "Finding Mr. Goodbar" and "Finding the Real Mr. Goodbar." The journalist subsequently wrote a book, *Closing Time: The True Story of the "Goodbar" Murder*. The publications were widely disseminated. While Rossner was aware of these publications and the use of the word "Goodbar" in their titles, she didn't bring any legal action.

As a result of the publicity surrounding the murder, and the various publications and movie, the public began to

ADVICE
FOR
WRITERS,
DIRECTORS &
ACTORS

175

associate the word "Goodbar" with the murder and with the singles scene or a dangerous pick-up.

CBS subsequently made a television movie entitled *Trackdown: Finding the Goodbar Killer* based on the true story of the murder investigation. Rossner objected to the use of the term "Goodbar" in the title, claiming that viewers were likely to believe CBS's movie was based upon Rossner's work. CBS claimed the term "Goodbar Killer" was in the public domain.

ISSUE: Can CBS use the term "Goodbar" in the title of their movie without Rossner's permission?

HOLDING: Yes, although the court directed that CBS must broadcast a disclaimer in the credits informing viewers that the CBS movie is not based on Rossner's novel.

RATIONALE: Rossner claimed the term "Goodbar" had become associated in the public mind with her work. Having thus acquired a "secondary meaning," it became her trademark, and CBS's use of the term was unfair competition. The court said that while the term was associated with Rossner when her novel was first published, the strength of her trademark was diminished by the later use of the mark by others.

In other words, Rossner's failure to police the mark, and prevent others of using it, caused the mark to loose its association with her. It lost its secondary meaning. The court did require, however, that a disclaimer be included in the broadcast to prevent any viewer confusion about the origin of the television movie.

ROGERS V. GRIMALDI [1]

FACTS: Federico Fellini conceived, co-wrote and directed a film entitled *Federico Fellini's "Ginger and Fred."* The movie was a fictional work about two retired dancers. The dancers used to make a living in Italian cabarets imitating Fred Astaire and Ginger Rogers, thus earning the nickname "Ginger and Fred." The story was a satire about the world of television. According to Fellini, the characters did not resemble or portray Fred Astaire and Ginger Rogers. Ginger Rogers (P) brought suit, claiming that Fellini violated her rights of privacy and publicity.

---

[1] *Rogers v. Grimaldi*, 695 F. Supp. 112 (1988).

DEALMAKING
IN THE
FILM AND
TELEVISION
INDUSTRY

176

ISSUE: Has Rogers' rights been violated?

HOLDING: No.

RATIONALE: Fellini's movie is a work protected by the First Amendment. The work is protected expression rather than a use for a purely commercial purpose.

Sometimes a person's right to protect their privacy and personality come into conflict with another's rights under the First Amendment. The courts draw a distinction between "commercial speech," which entails the use of someone's name or likeness on a product or in an advertisement, from artistic expression, which is protected by the First Amendment. In this case, the court determined that Fellini's rights under the First Amendment outweighed any infringement of Rogers' rights.

RIGHTS OF WRITERS GUILD MEMBERS

The Writers Guild agreement, also known as the Minimum Basic Agreement (MBA),[1] sets the minimum terms for options and purchases of material from professional writers and the minimum terms for the employment of writers for feature films and television programs. The agreement is more than 400 pages long, and its terms are incorporated by reference in every WGA writer's contract.

The MBA only binds signatory companies. Smaller production companies and fringe producers may not be signatories to the agreement. Guild members are prohibited from writing for non-signatory companies. Furthermore, members cannot work for less than minimum-scale compensation and can never write on spec. All agreements between writers and producers must be in writing, and a writer may not work without a contract.

Although the MBA sets forth the minimum terms that producers must grant Guild writers, the Guild encourages writers to negotiate more favorable terms. Such agreements are known as "overscale" deals.

---

[1] The Writers Guild also has a PBS agreement that covers certain public television stations and producers. See the 1988 Public TV Freelance Agreement.

SUMMARY OF WGA BASIC AGREEMENT

ADVICE
FOR
WRITERS,
DIRECTORS &
ACTORS

177

Coverage

The WGA Basic Agreement applies to both writer-employment agreements and acquisition of literary material from "professional" writers that is unpublished and unexploited. A professional writer is one who has a theatrical motion picture or television credit or has had at least thirteen weeks of prior employment, or has a credit for a produced play or published novel.

A signatory company must pay guild minimums to non-professional writers and non-guild members if *employing* them. The minimums do not apply, however, if the company merely *buys* a literary property unless a writer is a "professional" writer and the material has not been previously exploited. In other words, the MBA does not cover contracts for purchase of literary properties that have been published or exploited in any medium, or contracts to buy literary material from non-professional writers.

Compensation

Unless the writer defaults or fails to deliver the work, minimum compensation is guaranteed. Producers cannot withhold payment because they do not like the material, can't secure financing or any other condition. Overscale payments may be tied to conditions.

For literary purchases, the minimum payments are the same as for a flat deal. The MBA provides that in no event may the week-to-week or term writer receive less for the material than he would have received had he worked on a free-lance basis at minimum compensation.

Going rate and bonus payments apply in certain situations. When a producer hires a "qualified" writer to write a story and teleplay for a network prime-time series or a MOW, minimum compensation is at the "going rate," which is higher than the minimum rate. A "bonus" is generally payable upon delivery of the teleplay. A qualified writer is one who has written within the genre and received compensation equal to the going rate, or a writer who has written twice within the genre.

DEALMAKING
IN THE
FILM AND
TELEVISION
INDUSTRY

178

Writers are entitled to other payments. The producer must furnish first-class transportation, board and accommodations if the writer works on location. A signatory must contribute 5% of gross compensation to the Pension plan, and 4% to the Health Fund. Producers do not have to make payments on amounts paid to purchase literary material, on residuals, certain additional compensation, supplemental payments and compensation in excess of $100,000 for a single feature film.

For writers who work through a loan-out company, the loan-out company is initially responsible for these contributions, but the production company must reimburse it.

Credits

Upon completion of principal photography, the producer must file with the Guild a "Notice of Tentative Writing Credits" and send a copy to each writer. If any writer protests, the guild arbitrates.

Credit must be given in a form authorized by the MBA. The agreement requires credit be given in most publicity and advertising when credit is given a producer or director.

Sometimes a writer may choose to use a pseudonym. For a feature, a writer who receives compensation of $200,000 or less has the right to use a pseudonym. In television, a writer may use pseudonyms if paid less than three times the minimum.[1]

---

[1] The writer must promptly request a pseudonym, however. For features, the request must be made within five business days after the credits are final.

TERMS & DEFINITIONS

TREATMENT: THE ADAPTATION OF A STORY OR LITERARY MATERIAL AS A BASIS FOR A SCREENPLAY.

SCREENPLAY: FINAL SCRIPT WITH SCENES, DIALOGUE AND CAMERA SETUPS. SCRIPTS WRITTEN FOR TELEVISION ARE CALLED "TELEPLAYS."

FIRST-DRAFT SCREENPLAY: FIRST COMPLETE DRAFT OF ANY SCRIPT IN CONTINUITY FORM, INCLUDING FULL DIALOGUE.

REWRITE: SIGNIFICANT CHANGES IN PLOT, STORY LINE OR INTERRELATIONSHIP OF CHARACTERS IN A SCREENPLAY.

POLISH: CHANGES IN DIALOGUE, NARRATION OR ACTION, BUT NOT INCLUDING A REWRITE.

FORMAT: THE FRAMEWORK WITHIN WHICH THE CENTRAL RUNNING CHARACTERS WILL OPERATE AND BE REPEATED IN EACH EPISODE, INCLUDING DETAILED CHARACTERS, AND THE SETTING, THEME, PREMISE OR GENERAL STORY LINE OF THE PROPOSED SERIES.

BIBLE: FORMAT FOR A MINI-SERIES BUT MORE DETAILED.

CONTINUED

Revisions

Generally, when a producer hires a writer to write a story, the company has the right to request one revision. The request must be made within fourteen days of the first submission. When a producer pays for a teleplay, the producer gets two sets of revisions if requested in the allocated time.

The writer of an original screenplay or teleplay who grants an option to a producer has the right to do the first rewrite during the option period. After acquisition, the producer usually must offer the writer the first rewrite.[1]

Residuals

Residuals are payments for re-runs, foreign telecasts and certain other uses. For example, when there is a foreign theatrical exhibition of a television movie, additional compensation is due the writer. The amount owed is equal to 100% of the minimum of the initial compensation or minimum scale for a feature, whichever is greater. If there is a domestic theatrical exhibition, additional compensation of 150% or minimum scale for a feature, whichever is greater, is payable.

The company and writer may agree by contract that any portion of the compensation paid to the writer beyond twice the applicable initial minimum, may be applied against amounts due for theatrical exhibition.

[1] See MBA, Article 16.A.3.c and 16.B.3.h.

ADVICE
FOR
WRITERS,
DIRECTORS &
ACTORS

179

TERMS & DEFINITIONS
(CONTINUED)

MERCHANDISING RIGHTS: UNDER THE MBA, THE RIGHT TO SELL OBJECTS DESCRIBED IN LITERARY MATERIAL PROVIDED SUCH OBJECTS ARE FULLY DESCRIBED AND ARE UNIQUE AND ORIGINAL. FOR FEATURES, A WRITER HAS NO MERCHANDISING RIGHTS BUT IS ENTITLED TO 5% OF ABSOLUTE GROSS OF MONIES REMITTED BY THE MANUFACTURER. THIS APPLIES EVEN TO WRITERS NOT ENTITLED TO SEPARATION OF RIGHTS.

DRAMATIC RIGHTS: ESSENTIALLY "PLAY" RIGHTS.

SEQUEL: NEW FILM WITH THE SAME CHARACTERS AS FIRST FILM BUT IN A NEW PLOT.

WGA LOW-BUDGET FEATURE: COSTS LESS THAN $2.5 MILLION

WGA HIGH-BUDGET FEATURE: COSTS $2.5 MILLION OR MORE.

PILOT SCRIPT: STORY AND/OR TELEPLAY FOR A PROPOSED EPISODIC SERIES.

BACK-UP SCRIPT: STORY AND/OR TELEPLAY FOR A PROPOSED EPISODIC SERIES OTHER THAN A PILOT SCRIPT.

CONTINUED

DEALMAKING
IN THE
FILM AND
TELEVISION
INDUSTRY

180

Separation of Rights

An unusual aspect of the MBA is that signatory companies are required to grant WGA members certain rights although the writer, as an employee for hire, doesn't own the copyright to the material. These rights are granted to a credited writer who originates material as follows:

TERMS & DEFINITIONS
(CONTINUED)

SINGLE UNIT: A PROGRAM INTENDED FOR BROADCAST AS A SINGLE SHOW AND NOT A PART OF A SERIES.

UNIT SERIES: A SERIES OF FILMS WITH A COMPLETE STORY WITHOUT CHARACTERS IN COMMON BUT HELD TOGETHER BY THE SAME TITLE (I.E., ANTHOLOGY).

EPISODIC SERIES: A SERIES OF FILMS, EACH WITH A SEPARATE COMPLETE STORY BUT CHARACTERS IN COMMON.

ASSIGNED MATERIAL: STORY MATERIAL GIVEN THE WRITER. IN OTHER WORDS, THE WRITER DIDN'T CREATE THE WORK FROM SCRATCH—THE PRODUCER GAVE HIM ASSIGNED MATERIAL (E.G., CHARACTERS, STORY OUTLINE) FROM WHICH TO WORK.

FLAT DEALS: OPPOSITE OF WEEK-TO-WEEK OR TERM EMPLOYMENT. THE WRITER IS HIRED TO WRITE A CERTAIN TYPE OF WORK (E.G., TREATMENT OR SCREENPLAY) AND COMPENSATION IS TIED TO THE TYPE OF WORK, LENGTH OF PROGRAM AND WHETHER IT IS HIGH-BUDGET OR LOW-BUDGET. PRODUCERS MUST PAY THE WRITER IN INSTALLMENTS ACCORDING TO GUILD STANDARDS.

FEATURES

Publication rights: the writer has a license that he cannot exercise until six months after the general release of the picture or three years from the date of the employment (or purchase) agreement, whichever is earlier. The producer retains a limited right of publication for publicity purposes. The writer has the first opportunity to write the novelization.

Dramatic rights: If a producer fails to exploit these rights within two years after general release, these rights revert to the writer. In any event, the writer is entitled to royalty payments if a stage show is produced.

Sequel payments: The writer doesn't have sequel rights but a right to payment upon production of a sequel. For a feature sequel: 25% of initial fixed compensation for writing services, 15% for sale of literary material. If the sequel is a television series or program, the writer receives (subject to offsets) the sequel payments provided in the MBA.

ADVICE
FOR
WRITERS,
DIRECTORS &
ACTORS

181

Writers entitled to separation of rights retain all rights other than television film and television sequel rights. The production company owns exclusive film television rights for four years from delivery of the material. After that, the company and the writer own these rights non-exclusively.

Sequel rights: Company has the exclusive right for a limited time. Then rights revert to the writer.

The rights reserved to the writer include legitimate stage rights, theatrical motion picture rights, publication rights, merchandising rights, radio rights and live television rights. Some of these rights are subject to hold-back periods, during which the writer cannot exploit them.

Two-Meeting Rule

In no event may there be a third meeting between the writer and a company regarding an assignment unless a firm commitment has been made or is made in the third interview.

If in the first interview the writer proposes a story, then a second meeting at the request of the company entitles the writer to a story commitment at minimum compensation.

Warranties and Indemnification

The company must indemnify the writer against claims or actions respecting material assigned to the writer, and the writer must be named an additional insured on the Errors and Omissions policy.

Collaborating with Others

Writing can be a lonely profession. The writer has to sequester himself for long periods and possess the self-discpline to work unsupervised. Some writers find it helpful to collaborate with others.

DEALMAKING
IN THE
FILM AND
TELEVISION
INDUSTRY

182

I think it is very difficult to find a good writing partner. Personalities must mesh, and both parties need to be willing to put their egos aside and do what is best for the project. Moreover, for a collaboration to last, each party must bring something valuable to the partnership that the other lacks.

Many writers embark upon a collaborative endeavor with high hopes, only to discover later that the partnership is not working. Not only has time been wasted, but difficult questions may arise as to ownership of the work that has been created. Antagonism between the parties may make it difficult to resolve outstanding issues. If ownership of the embryonic story is unclear, neither party may safely use it. Thus, writers are well advised to enter a collaboration agreement beforehand.

The collaboration agreement is useful because it forces the parties to deal with important issues before a lot of time and effort have been invested in the venture. If the relationship is not going to work, it is best to know early.

The WGA-West has a model collaboration agreement for screenwriters and teleplay writers. Copies are available for free. Call (310) 550-1000.

Here is a sample agreement for writers collaborating on a book project.

COLLABORATION AGREEMENT

This Agreement between _____ [Writer A], residing at _____, City of _____, State of _____ (herein called Writer A), and _____ [Writer B], residing at _____, City of _____, State of _____ (herein called Writer B).

WITNESSETH

The parties desire to collaborate in the writing of a book on the terms hereinafter set forth.

NOW THEREFORE, in consideration of the promises, and of the mutual undertakings herein contained, and for other good and valuable considerations, the parties agree as follows:

1. The parties hereby undertake to collaborate in the writing of a certain non-fiction book (herein called the "Book"), dealing

ADVICE
FOR
WRITERS,
DIRECTORS &
ACTORS

183

with _____, and provisionally entitled
_____.

2. They have agreed on a tentative outline, a copy of which is annexed. In the outline, the name of Writer A has been placed opposite the titles of certain proposed chapters; and the name of Writer B has been placed opposite the titles of certain other chapters. It is the intention of the parties that the first draft of each chapter shall be prepared by the party whose name it bears, and shall be submitted to the other party for comments and suggestions. The final drafts shall be worked out by the parties together.

3. The parties contemplate that they will complete the manuscript of the Book by _____19__. If they fail to do so, they may by mutual agreement extend the time for completion. In the absence of any such extension, they shall endeavor to fix by negotiation their respective rights in the material theretofore gathered and written, and in the project itself (i.e., whether one or the other of them shall have the right to complete the Book alone or in collaboration with someone else, and on what terms). Their understanding as to these matters shall thereupon be embodied in a settlement agreement. If they are unable to agree, their respective rights and the terms pertaining thereto shall be fixed by arbitration. In either event, this agreement shall cease when the rights of the parties have been fixed as aforesaid; and thereafter they shall have only such rights and obligations as will be set forth in the settlement agreement or the arbitration award, as the case may be.

4. If the manuscript of the Book is completed, the parties shall endeavor to secure a publisher. Each shall have the right to negotiate for this purpose, but they shall keep each other fully informed with reference thereto. No agreement for the publication of the Book or for the disposition of any of the subsidiary rights therein shall be valid without the signature of both parties. However, either party may grant a written power of attorney to the other, setting forth the specific conditions under which the power may be exercised. For services rendered under such power of attorney, no agency fee or extra compensation shall be paid to the attorney-in-fact.

5. The copyright in the Book shall be obtained in the names of both parties, and shall be held jointly by them.

6. The parties shall receive equal authorship credit on the same line and in type of equal size, except that the name of Writer A shall precede that of Writer B.

7. All receipts and returns from the publication of the Book and from the disposition of any subsidiary rights therein shall be divided equally between the parties. All agreements for publication and for the sale of subsidiary rights shall provide that each

DEALMAKING
IN THE
FILM AND
TELEVISION
INDUSTRY

184

party's one-half share shall be paid directly to him.

8. If the parties by mutual agreement select an agent to handle the publication rights in the Book or the disposition of the subsidiary rights therein, and if the agent is authorized to make collection for the parties' account, such agent shall remit each party's one-half share directly to him.

9. After the completion of the manuscript of the Book, no change or alteration shall be made therein by either party without the other's consent. However, such consent shall not be unreasonably withheld. No written consent to make a particular revision shall be deemed authority for a general revision.

10. If either party (herein called the First Party) desires to transfer his one-half share in the Book or in the subsidiary rights thereof to a third person, he shall give written notice by registered mail to the other party (herein called the Second Party) of his intention to do so.

(a) In such case the Second Party shall have an option for a period of _____ days to purchase the First Party's share at a price and upon such terms indicated in the written notice.

(b) If the Second Party fails to exercise his option in writing within the aforesaid period of ____ days, or if, having exercised it, he fails to complete the purchase upon the terms stated in the notice, the First Party may transfer his rights to the third person at the price and upon the identical terms stated in the notice; and he shall forthwith send to the Second Party a copy of the contract of sale of such rights, with a statement that the transfer has been made.

(c) If the First Party fails for any reason to make such transfer to the third person, and if he desires to make a subsequent transfer to someone else, the Second Party's option shall apply to such proposed subsequent transfer.

11. All expenses which may reasonably be incurred in connection with the Book shall be subject to mutual agreement in advance, and shall be shared equally by the parties.

12. Nothing herein contained shall be construed to create a partnership between the parties. Their relation shall be one of collaboration on a single work.

13. If the Book is published, this agreement shall continue for the life of the copyright therein. Otherwise, the duration hereof shall be governed by the provisions of Clause 3.

14. If either party dies before the completion of the manuscript, the survivor shall have the right to complete the same, to make changes in the text previously prepared, to negotiate and con-

ADVICE
FOR
WRITERS,
DIRECTORS &
ACTORS

185

tract for publication and for the disposition of any of the subsidiary rights, and generally to act with regard thereto as though he were the sole author, except that (a) the name of the decedent shall always appear as co-author; and (b) the survivor shall cause the decedent's one-half share of the proceeds to be paid to his estate, and shall furnish to the estate true copies of all contracts made by the survivor pertaining to the Book.

15. If either party dies after the completion of the manuscript, the survivor shall have the right to negotiate and contract for publication (if not theretofore published) and for the disposition of any of the subsidiary rights, to make revisions in any subsequent editions, and generally to act with regard thereto as if he were the sole author, subject only to the conditions set forth in subdivisions (a) and (b) of Clause 14.

16. Any controversy or claim arising out of or relating to this agreement or any breach thereof shall be settled by arbitration in accordance with the Rules of the American Arbitration Association; and judgment upon the award rendered by the arbitrators may be entered in any court having jurisdiction thereof. The prevailing party shall be entitled to reimbursement of costs and reasonable attorneys' fees.

17. This agreement shall inure to the benefit of, and shall be binding upon, the executors, administrators and assigns of the parties.

18. This agreement constitutes the entire understanding of the parties.

IN WITNESS WHEREOF, the parties hereunto set their respective hand and seal this _____ day of _____, 19__.

_____
Writer A

_____
Writer B

DEALMAKING
IN THE
FILM AND
TELEVISION
INDUSTRY

186

DIRECTORS

Before a director can cut a deal, he must persuade investors and/or studio executives to let him direct. For the first-timer, this is a difficult task, for there is scant reason to hire an inexperienced director when so many veterans are available. First-time directorial candidates can exert leverage by threatening to withhold some other valuable commodity. For example, a star may refuse to accept a role unless he is also permitted to direct the film. A writer may refuse to sell a script unless she can direct it.

Once in the director's chair, the novice must have expertise in four areas to succeed. First, she must understand the basic principles of good storytelling. The director need not be a writer but she better be able to distinguish good writing from bad. A director who chooses material poorly will never shine. An uninteresting story will not involve an audience no matter how impressive the camera work or performances.

Second, the director must have a good visual sense. She must understand the basics of cutting, editing and cinematography. Pictures with crowd scenes, stunts and special effects require special expertise.

Third, the director must be able to manage a large endeavor. She must be well-organized, decisive and able to communicate well with her collaborators. The cast and the crew look to her for guidance, and if she is indecisive or unable to express her vision, the movie-making machinery will grind to a halt.

Fourth, the director must understand the art of acting. The director need not be an actor, but she must know how to talk to actors in their language. Actors need to understand the story and their character's motivation. Speaking to them about the size of the camera lense does not impart useful information.

Many directors believe that achieving a good performance is largely a function of casting the right person for the role. The best directors create a supportive atmosphere on the set that encourages the actors to take chances in an effort to give their best possible performance.

Directors share writers' concerns about liability for story theft and obscenity. Directors are also concerned that they not be unfairly penalized if the production goes over budget through no fault of their own. Directors' contracts may contain an EAT-IN CLAUSE, which provides that if a production goes over budget, the director's fees and profit participation may be eaten into (reduced). On the other hand, directors can ask that their contract provide that they share in any savings obtained if the production comes in underbudget.

To gain admission to the Directors Guild, directors need to direct a feature for a signatory company.

ADVICE
FOR
WRITERS,
DIRECTORS &
ACTORS

187

RIGHTS OF DIRECTORS GUILD MEMBERS[1]

Article seven of the Directors Guild Basic Agreement of 1990 guarantees DGA directors certain creative rights. The agreement acknowledges that the director contributes to all creative elements in the making of a motion picture. With few exceptions, a producer may assign only one director to a film at a time.

CREATIVE DECISIONS

As soon as the director is hired, she is entitled to participate in all decisions concerning the selection of cast and other creative personnel. The director needs to be consulted on any creative decisions regarding preparation, production and post-production, and the director's advice and suggestions need to be considered in good faith. No director may be discriminated against or be subjected to retaliation because she asserts her creative rights.

DISCLOSURE

Before a director is assigned to a film, the producer must give her:

1) a list of creative personnel already employed,

2) a description of any existing film footage contemplated to be used,

---

[1] A more detailed summary of Director's Creative Rights is available from the DGA.

DEALMAKING
IN THE
FILM AND
TELEVISION
INDUSTRY

188

3) a report of any rights of script or cast approval held by someone other than the employer or individual producer,

4) a copy of the motion picture's top sheet,

5) the story and script, if any, and

6) an explanation of all other creative commitments.

DEAL MEMO

Deal memos must designate the person with final cutting authority over the motion picture. Also, the intended post-production locale must be mentioned.

HIRING CREW

The employer must consult with the director about the selection of the Unit Production Manager for any theatrical motion picture and selection of the Second Unit Director. A director has the right to select the First Assistant Director on any theatrical motion picture and any non-series television motion picture that is 90 minutes or longer.

CASTING SESSIONS

Casting sessions are open only to persons who have a reasonable purpose for being there and are invited by the director, individual producer or employer.

FACILITIES

The director must be provided a private office at the studio. The office must be large enough for two people, have a door that shuts and possess a telephone, desk, chair and good lighting. Employers must use their best efforts to provide reasonable parking at no cost to the director.

STUNTS

The employer may not increase the difficulty of stunts or add a stunt to the script, unless the director consents.

ADVICE
FOR
WRITERS,
DIRECTORS &
ACTORS

189

DAILIES

The director must be permitted to see the dailies at a reasonable time. Before departing for a distant location, the director has the right to request interlocking sound and picture projection facilities for viewing of dailies on location. The studio must ship these dailies to the location within twenty-four hours of synchronization.

POST-PRODUCTION

A studio cannot replace a director who directs 100% of the scheduled principal photography except for gross willful misconduct. A director must be given the opportunity to direct additional photography and retakes. If a director directs 90% to 99% of scheduled principal photography, the director is entitled to all post-production creative rights, provided that the director was not primarily responsible for the motion picture going over budget.

These creative rights include the right to be present at all times and to be consulted throughout the entire post-production period. The director must have a reasonable opportunity to discuss the last version of the film before negative cutting or dubbing, whichever is first.

DIRECTOR'S CUT

The director supervises the editing of the first cut following completion of the editor's assembly. The director has the right to instruct the editor and to make whatever changes the director deems necessary in preparing his cut. No one may interfere with the editing during the period of the director's cut. Directors have the following time to complete their cut:

DEALMAKING
IN THE
FILM AND
TELEVISION
INDUSTRY

190

a) Theatrical Motion Picture: Ten weeks, or one day of editing for every two days of scheduled photography, whichever is longer. For low-budget films, six weeks or one day of editing for every two days of scheduled photography, whichever is longer.

b) Television Motion Picture:

   i)   Thirty minutes or less: within one day plus time, which is not to exceed one more day, to make changes if necessary.
   ii) Thirty-to-sixty minutes: four days
   iii) Sixty-to-ninety minutes: fifteen days
   iv) Ninty-to-one-hundred-twenty minutes: twenty days
   v)   Each additional hour: five days

PROTECTION AGAINST FALSE STORY-THEFT CLAIMS

Writers, directors and actors need to protect themselves from idea thieves. They also need to protect themselves from people who may falsely accuse them of theft. Generally, one is free to borrow ideas, concepts, themes and historical facts from others without paying compensation because these items are not copyrightable. However, if you agree to compensate another for such material, you may be liable under contract law.

What if someone sends you unsolicited material? Are you obligated to compensate the sender? The following case illustrates the issue:

CASE

YADKOE V. FIELDS (1944)[1]

FACTS: In 1938, Yadkoe (P) wrote W.C. Fields (D) a letter in which he provided Fields with material for use as an entertainer. Fields replied by letter, accepting the material and inviting Yadkoe to submit additional material

---

[1] *Yadkoe v. Fields*, 66 Cal. App. 2d 150, 141 P.2d 906 (1944).

without compensation. Fields stated that if he was able to use the material, he "might" enter into a contract with Yadkoe. Yadkoe sent additional material to Fields including scenes and dialogue for the movie *You Can't Cheat an Honest Man*. Fields used these materials but didn't compensate Yadkoe. A jury awarded Yadkoe judgment for $8,000 for breach of contract. Fields appealed.

ISSUE: Is an obligation incurred by the unsolicited submissions of ideas?

HOLDING: No. But once such ideas are solicited, this may give rise to an implied contract. Judgment affirmed.

ADVICE
FOR
WRITERS,
DIRECTORS &
ACTORS

191

To avoid liability to persons who submit unsolicited ideas, studios use release forms. Writers, directors and actors can use the same form to protect themselves. While this form does not protect the writer/director/actor if he intentionally steals another's work, it will make it more difficult for someone to successfully pursue a frivolous claim.

DEALMAKING
IN THE
FILM AND
TELEVISION
INDUSTRY

192

SUBMISSION RELEASE

Dan Director
1219 LaVine Ave
Hollywood, CA 90088

Dear Mr. Director:

I am submitting the enclosed material ("said material") to you: _____, an original screenplay. WGA REGISTRATION NO. _____. Copyright Registration No. _____.

The material is submitted on the following conditions:

1. I acknowledge that because of your position in the entertainment industry you receive numerous unsolicited submissions of ideas, formats, stories, suggestions and the like and that many such submissions received by you are similar to or identical to those developed by you or your employees or otherwise available to you. I agree that I will not be entitled to any compensation because of the use by you of any such similar or identical material.

2. I further understand that you would refuse to accept and evaluate said material in the absence of my acceptance of each and all of the provisions of this agreement. I shall retain all rights to submit this or similar material to persons other than you. I acknowledge that no fiduciary or confidential relationship now exists between you and me, and I further acknowledge that no such relationships are established between you and me by reason of this agreement or by reason of my submission to you of said material.

3. I request that you read and evaluate said material with a view to deciding whether you will undertake to acquire it.

4. I represent and warrant that I am the author of said material, having acquired said material as the employer-for-hire of all writers thereof; that I am the present and sole owner of all right, title and interest in and to said material; that I have the exclusive, unconditional right and authority to submit and/or convey said material to you upon the terms and conditions set forth herein; that no third party is entitled to any payment or other consideration as a condition of the exploitation of said material.

5. I agree to indemnify you from and against any and all claims, expenses, losses, or liabilities (including, without limitation, reasonable attorneys' fees and punitive damages) that may be asserted against you or incurred by you at any time in connection

with said material, or any use thereof, including without limitation those arising from any breach of the warranties and promises given by me herein.

6. You may use without any obligation or payment to me any of said material which is not protectable as literary property under the laws of plagiarism, or which a third person would be free to use if the material had not been submitted to him or had not been the subject of any agreement with him, or which is in the public domain. Any of said material which, in accordance with the preceding sentence, you are entitled to use without obligation to me is hereinafter referred to as "unprotected material." If all or any part of said material does not fall in the category of unprotected material, it is hereinafter referred to as "protected material."

7. You agree that if you use or cause to be used any protected material provided it has not been obtained from, or independently created by, another source, you will pay or cause to be paid to me an amount that is comparable to the compensation customarily paid for similar material.

8. I agree to give you written notice by registered mail of any claim arising in connection with said material or arising in connection with this agreement, within 60 calendar days after I acquire knowledge of such claim, or of your breach or failure to perform the provisions of this agreement, or if it be sooner, within 60 calendar days after I acquire knowledge of facts sufficient to put me on notice of any such claim, or breach or failure to perform; my failure to so give you written notice will be deemed an irrevocable waiver of any rights I might otherwise have with respect to such claim, breach or failure to perform. You shall have 60 calendar days after receipt of said notice to attempt to cure any alleged breach or failure to perform prior to the time that I may file a Demand for Arbitration.

9. In the event of any dispute concerning said material or concerning any claim of any kind or nature arising in connection with said material or arising in connection with this agreement, such dispute will be submitted to binding arbitration. Each party hereby waives any and all rights and benefits which he or it may otherwise have or be entitled to under the laws of the State of California to litigate any such dispute in court, it being the intention of the parties to arbitrate all such disputes. Either party may commence arbitration proceedings by giving the other party written notice thereof by registered mail and proceeding thereafter in accordance with the rules and procedures of the American Arbitration Association. The arbitration shall be conducted in the

ADVICE
FOR
WRITERS,
DIRECTORS &
ACTORS

193

DEALMAKING
IN THE
FILM AND
TELEVISION
INDUSTRY

194

County of Los Angeles, State of California, and shall be governed by and subject to the laws of the State of California and the then prevailing rules of the American Arbitration Association. The arbitrators' award shall be final and binding and a judgment upon the award may be enforced by any court of competent jurisdiction.

10. I have retained at least one copy of said material, and I release you from any and all liability for loss or other damage to the copies of said material submitted to you hereunder.

11. Either party to this agreement may assign or license its or their rights hereunder, but such assignment or license shall not relieve such party of its or their obligations hereunder. This agreement shall inure to the benefit of the parties hereto and their heirs, successors, representatives, assigns and licensees, and any such heir, successor, representative, assign or licensee shall be deemed a third-party beneficiary under this agreement.

12. I hereby acknowledge and agree that there are no prior or contemporaneous oral agreements in effect between you and me pertaining to said material, or pertaining to any material (including, but not limited to, agreements pertaining to the submission by me of any ideas, formats, plots, characters, or the like). I further agree that no other obligations exist or shall exist or be deemed to exist unless and until a formal written agreement has been prepared and entered into by both you and me, and then your and my rights and obligations shall be only such as are expressed in said formal written agreement.

13. I understand that whenever the word "you" or "your" is used above, it refers to (1) you, (2) any company affiliated with you by way of common-stock ownership or otherwise, (3) your subsidiaries, (4) subsidiaries of such affiliated companies, (5) any firm, person or corporation to whom you are leasing production facilities, (6) clients of any subsidiary or affiliated company of yours, and (7) the officers, agents, servants, employees, stockholders, clients, successors and assigns of you, and of all such person, corporations referred to in (1) through (6) hereof. If said material is submitted by more than one person, the word "I" shall be deemed changed to "we," and this agreement will be binding jointly and severally upon all the persons so submitting said material.

14. Should any provision or part of any provision be void or unenforceable, such provision or part thereof shall be deemed omitted, and this agreement with such provision or part thereof omitted shall remain in full force and effect.

15. This agreement shall be governed by the laws of the state of California applicable to agreements executed and to be fully performed therein.

16. I have read and I understand this agreement and no oral representations of any kind have been made to me and this agreement states our entire understanding with reference to the subject matter hereof. Any modification or waiver of any of the provisions of this agreement must be in writing and signed by both of us.

Sincerely,

ADVICE
FOR
WRITERS,
DIRECTORS &
ACTORS

195

_____

Signature

_____

Wally Writer

_____

Address

_____

Telephone Number

ACCEPTED AND AGREED TO:

_____

By Dan Director

STATE OF   )
) ss.:
COUNTY OF   )

On the ____ day of _____, 19__, before me personally came _____to me known and known to be the individual described in and who executed the foregoing instrument, and he did duly acknowledge to me that he executed the same.

_____

Notary Public

DEALMAKING
IN THE
FILM AND
TELEVISION
INDUSTRY

196

OBSCENITY

The First Amendment does not protect obscene works. The difficulty that creators, judges and everyone else confronts is understanding what is obscene. It is difficult, perhaps impossible, to articulate a useful definition. Here is the three-part test as set forth in *Miller v. California*:[1]

1) Whether the average person, applying contemporary community standards, would find that the work, taken as a whole, appeals to prurient interest;

2) Whether the work depicts or describes, in a patently offensive way, sexual conduct specifically defined by the applicable state law; and

3) Whether the work, taken as a whole, lacks serious literary, artistic, political or scientific value.

ACTORS

In the creative community actors have the worst lot. It is often said that they are always waiting to be invited to the party. They cannot perform their craft unless a director casts them in a role. They have little control over their careers.

Novices pursuing an acting career must be prepared for a long and difficult struggle with no assurance of success. Gaining admission to the Screen Actors Guild (SAG) is important because even "non-union" low-budget producers often hire SAG actors or become signatories to the SAG agreement.

ADMISSION TO SAG

A performer is eligible to join SAG under either of the following conditions:

1) Proof of SAG Employment. This can be either as:

---

[1] *Miller v. California*, 413 U.S. 15, 93 S.Ct. 2607, 37 L.Ed.2d 419 (1973).

a) a Principal Performer: upon proof of employment or prospective employment within two weeks or less by a SAG signatory company. Employment must be in a principal or speaking role in a film, videotape, television program or commercial.

b) Extra Player: upon proof of employment as a SAG covered extra at full SAG rates and conditions for a

ACTOR CAREER *CHECKLIST*

- Project energy and self-confidence at interviews and auditions. Be personable and friendly. Don't overstay your welcome. Learn to handle rejection.

- Prepare yourself for the long haul. Stories of overnight success are myths. Get a night job or employment that permits you to take off time for auditions. Be prepared to invest five to ten years before you expect to earn a living from acting. Even then, there are no guarantees.

- Obtain an answering machine or message service to take messages. You better know when your lucky break arrives.

- Get a good head shot and possibly a composite shot. The photo should be black and white, portray your appearance accurately and have your name and phone number on it.

- Prepare a neat and professional looking résumé listing your credits, the guilds you belong to, your training and any special abilities or skills you have (e.g., horseback riding, piano). Limit it to one page, don't lie, and don't clutter up the résumé with irrelevant work or educational background. List your agent's number if you have one. Staple resume, back to back, to your photos. Always have some of these handy when you go to an audition or an industry function. Keep some extras in your car.

- Build up your credentials: Perform in showcase plays [(Equity Waiver (L.A.), Off-Off Broadway (New York)] or non-Equity plays if you are not a member of Equity. In smaller cities, perform in community and little theater, or if you are a student, participate in university productions.

- When you obtain a part, invite agents to see you perform. Most theaters will allow them to attend free. Let agents know you are seeking representation. Have photos and résumés on hand in your dressing room. Invite producers and other industry folk you know to attend your performances.

- Consider working in non-union productions. Read all contracts carefully and recognize that you risk exploitation. But if you can obtain a good review of your performance, it may be worth the risk.

CONTINUED

DEALMAKING
IN THE
FILM AND
TELEVISION
INDUSTRY

198

minimum of three work days after March 25, 1990. Employment must be by a signatory company to the SAG Extra Players Agreement.

2) Employment by a sister union. You must have been a paid up member of an affiliated performer's union (AFTRA, AEA, AGVA, AGMA or ACTRA) for at least one year and

ACTOR CAREER *CHECKLIST* (CONTINUED)

- PREPARE A VIDEOTAPE COMPILATION OF YOUR WORK. IF YOU HAVE APPEARED ON TELEVISION OR IN FILMS, OBTAIN CLIPS OF YOUR PERFORMANCES AND PUT TOGETHER A PROFESSIONAL-LOOKING VIDEOTAPE THAT YOU CAN SUBMIT TO AGENTS AND CASTING DIRECTORS. HOMEMADE TAPES AND STAGED SCENES USUALLY DON'T IMPRESS AGENTS. NEVER SEND OUT YOUR ORIGINAL.

- JOIN THE APPROPRIATE GUILD(S):

    SCREEN ACTORS GUILD (SAG): FEATURE FILMS, FILMED TV SHOWS, FILMED COMMERCIALS AND INDUSTRIAL FILMS.

    AMERICAN FEDERATION OF TELEVISION AND RADIO ARTISTS (AFTRA): LIVE AND TAPED TV SHOWS, TAPED COMMERCIALS AND INDUSTRIALS, RADIO AND PHONOGRAPH RECORDS. ACTOR'S EQUITY ASSOCIATION (EQUITY OR AEA): PERFORMERS AND STAGE MANAGERS IN PLAY PRODUCTIONS.

    AMERICAN GUILD OF VARIETY ARTISTS (AGVA): LIVE PERFORMERS SUCH AS NIGHT-CLUB PERFORMERS.

    AMERICAN GUILD OF MUSICAL ARTISTS (AGMA): OPERA SINGERS, CLASSICAL DANCERS AND CHORAL SINGERS.

    IF YOU ARE A MEMBER OF ONE OF THE ABOVE AND YOU JOIN ANOTHER UNION, YOUR INITIATION FEES AND DUES MAY BE LESS.
    ANYONE CAN JOIN AFTRA. THE UNION ONLY REQUIRES AN APPLICANT TO PAY THE INITIATION FEE AND DUES.
    UNDER THE TAFT-HARTLEY LAW[1] YOU CAN WORK UP TO THIRTY (30) DAYS ON YOUR FIRST JOB ON A UNION SHOW BEFORE JOINING THE UNION. IN RIGHT-TO-WORK STATES, UNIONS CANNOT FORCE YOU TO JOIN.

- GET A REPUTABLE AGENT. SEEK OUT THOSE WHO ARE FRANCHISED BY THE GUILD THAT COVERS THE AREA YOU WANT TO WORK IN. FRANCHISED AGENTS HAVE TO ABIDE BY GUILD RULES. AGENTS GET PAID ON A CONTINGENT BASIS (10% IN CALIFORNIA). ANY AGENT ASKING FOR AN UP-FRONT FEE IS PROBABLY IN THE BUSINESS OF EXPLOITING ACTORS, NOT FINDING WORK FOR THEM. LISTS OF FRANCHISED AGENTS ARE AVAILABLE FROM NATIONAL AND LOCAL GUILDS.

CONTINUED

---

[1] 29 U.S.C. § 158 (a)(3).

worked at least once as a principal performer in that union's jurisdiction.

INITIATION FEE: Currently $932 plus the first semi-annual dues of $42.50.

ADVICE
FOR
WRITERS,
DIRECTORS &
ACTORS

199

ACTOR CAREER *CHECKLIST*
(CONTINUED)

AGENTS OFTEN DON'T ASK NEWCOMERS TO SIGN A WRITTEN CONTRACT UNTIL THEY SECURE WORK FOR THEM. ACTORS MAY PREFER NOT TO HAVE A WRITTEN AGREEMENT BECAUSE, IF THE AGENT CAN'T FIND WORK FOR THEM, THE ACTOR MAY NOT WANT TO BE ENCUMBERED WITH A CONTRACT.

- PERSONAL MANAGERS: IN CALIFORNIA AND OTHER STATES, PERSONAL MANAGERS ARE NOT FRANCHISED OR REGULATED. THEY OFTEN CHARGE 15% WHICH IS IN ADDITION TO THE FEE YOU PAY YOUR AGENT. TECHNICALLY, THEY ARE NOT ALLOWED TO SOLICIT WORK FOR CLIENTS ALTHOUGH THAT IS OFTEN WHAT THEY DO. BEGINNERS GENERALLY DON'T NEED SOMEONE TO TOUR WITH THEM OR MANAGE THEIR CAREERS, AND MANAGERS GENERALLY DON'T WANT TO WORK FOR BEGINNERS.

  DON'T CONFUSE BUSINESS MANAGERS WITH PERSONAL MANAGERS. A BUSINESS MANAGER TYPICALLY HAS AN ACCOUNTING BACKGROUND AND HELPS YOU MANAGE MONEY AND MAKE INVESTMENT DECISIONS.

- DON'T WAIT FOR YOUR AGENT TO OBTAIN WORK FOR YOU. PURSUE WHATEVER LEADS AND OPPORTUNITIES YOU CAN ON YOUR OWN. KEEP YOUR AGENT INFORMED OF ANY AUDITIONS OR INTERVIEWS YOU HAVE SET UP AND ANY PARTS YOU GET. LET THE AGENT NEGOTIATE THE DEAL EVEN IF YOU GET THE GIG.

- GET LISTED IN THE *ACADEMY PLAYERS DIRECTORY* (IF YOU LIVE IN L.A.) OR THE *PLAYERS GUIDE* (FOR THOSE IN NEW YORK) OR THE HEAD SHEET PUT OUT BY AGENTS IN LOCAL COMMUNITIES. FOR THE FIRST TWO PUBLICATIONS, A MODEST FEE WILL ENABLE YOU TO HAVE YOUR NAME, PHOTO AND AGENT'S NAME LISTED IN THOSE DIRECTORIES. MANY CASTING DIRECTORS REFER TO THESE PUBLICATIONS. FOR INFORMATION ON THE *PLAYERS DIRECTORY* CONTACT THE ACADEMY OF MOTION PICTURE ARTS AND SCIENCES, 8949 WILSHIRE BLVD, BEVERLY HILLS, CA 90211 (310) 247-3058. FOR INFORMATION ON THE *PLAYERS GUIDE* CALL (212) 869-3570.

- BE CAREFUL ABOUT MAKING COMMITMENTS. RECENTLY, ACTRESS KIM BASINGER WAS SUED BY PRODUCER CARL MAZZOCONE FOR BREACHING HER PROMISE TO APPEAR IN THE FILM *BOXING HELENA*. THE JURY AWARDED MAZZOCONE $8.92 MILLION IN DAMAGES PLUS REIMBURSEMENT OF ATTORNEYS' FEES.

DEALMAKING
IN THE
FILM AND
TELEVISION
INDUSTRY

200

NOTABLE SAG RULES

Once an actor joins SAG, she is subject to the Guild's rules and regulations. SAG members cannot work for non-signatory companies. They can be represented only by agents who are franchised by SAG. They cannot enroll in SAG under a name or professionally use a name that so closely resembles that of an existing member as to cause confusion. Members are required to carry their Guild card when working and not to turn possession of it over to any other person.

GUILDS

LOS ANGELES

SAG — 7065 Hollywood Blvd., Hollywood, CA 90028-6065, (213) 465-4600

AFTRA — 6922 Hollywood Blvd., 8th Floor, Hollywood, CA 90028, (213) 461-8111

AEA — 6430 Sunset Blvd., Ste. 700, Hollywood, CA 90028, (213) 462-2334

AGVA — 4741 Laurel Canyon Blvd., Ste. 208, N. Hollywood, CA 91607, (818) 508-9984

NEW YORK

SAG — 1515 Broadway, New York, NY 10036, (212) 944-1030

AFTRA — 260 Madison Ave., New York, NY 10016, (212) 532-0800

AEA — 165 W. 46th St., New York, NY 10036, (212) 869-8530

AGVA — 184 5th Ave., New York, NY 10016, (212) 675-1003

AGMA — 1727 Broadway, New York, NY 10019, (212) 265-3687

RIGHTS OF SAG MEMBERS [1]

ADVICE
FOR
WRITERS,
DIRECTORS &
ACTORS

201

Minimum Wages

SAG contracts cover film, television and commercial producers. The current film and TV scale is more than $400 a day. Additional payment is required for location work, holidays, travel time, overtime, stunts and wardrobe. Residual payments are required of producers who re-use film, television programs and commercials.

Working Conditions

The SAG contract requires first-class air travel, flight insurance, private dressing rooms, meal breaks, good meals and rest time between calls. The contract also sets minimum safety and first-aid standards, provides for the education of minors, requires arbitration of disputes and grievances, and mandates affirmative action in auditions and hiring.

Pension and Health Plans

A major SAG benefit is participation in the Pension and Health Plans. Performers who earn income of at least $5,000 a year are automatically enrolled for one year in the Health Plan, which includes coverage for spouses and dependent children. Dental benefits and life insurance are included.

Performers who earn more than $2,000 a year in SAG employment for ten years qualify for a pension plan upon retirement. Monthly payments range from $200 to $3,300 per month.

These benefits are paid by employers when they contribute 12½ of a performer's base salary to the Pension and Health fund.

---

[1] A more detailed description of SAG benefits is listed in the brochure *Basic Benefits, Acting In Your Interest*, available from SAG.

DEALMAKING
IN THE
FILM AND
TELEVISION
INDUSTRY

202

Questions and Answers

1. Does a director have the right to final cut on her picture?

Answer: The involvement and rights of director in post-production will depend on the terms of director's employment agreement, and the terms of the DGA Basic Agreement if it applies. The DGA Basic Agreement requires that a director be allowed to be present throughout the post-production period but does not give the director final cut. Most directors don't have final cut. If a producer or studio agrees to give you final cut, make sure the right is spelled out in your contract.

2. Who owns the copyright to a writer's script?

Answer: If the writer creates a work on his own, he will own all rights to it. If the writer is an employee of a producer, usually the producer will own all rights to the writer's work product.

CHAPTER 8

MUSIC

This chapter does not cover the many legal issues that concern composers and musicians as they pursue their careers.[1] The discussion is limited to the licensing of music for film and television soundtracks.[2]

SOUNDTRACKS

When it comes time to place music on a soundtrack, the producer has a choice: she can either obtain the right to use existing music (e.g., a popular song) or commission an original musical score (i.e., hire a composer to create something new for the movie). Of course, a producer could buy songs for part of the soundtrack and hire a composer for the remainder.

Buying Existing Music

Music is a work of authorship protected under copyright law. Determining ownership in music can be complex since several

---

[1] A good reference source for those who seek this information is *The Musician's Business & Legal Guide*, edited and compiled by Mark Halloran, which can be obtained from the Beverly Hills Bar Association.

[2] This area of music rights can be exceedingly complex. The author recommends that an experienced music attorney be retained by persons not familiar with the issues presented.

DEALMAKING
IN THE
FILM AND
TELEVISION
INDUSTRY

204

persons may share the copyright. For example, the composer may own the copyright to the composition, the lyricist may own the copyright to the lyrics, the musicians may own the copyright to their performances and the record label may own the copyright to the recording. So a film producer must determine which parties have ownership interests in each song and then license the appropriate rights.

Low-budget independent producers often run out of money by the time they reach post-production. One way to economize is by using songs by unknown songwriters that are available for little or no money. Fledgling songwriters often want to gain visibility and stature by having their music in a movie. The producer should keep in mind that a song performed in a movie that is broadcast can generate significant royalties for the songwriter (through ASCAP or BMI). Thus, songwriters have a financial incentive to have their music on a soundtrack, even if they receive no direct compensation from the producer. A Television Music Rights License is reprinted at the end of this chapter. This is a synchonization license for non-dramatic use only. It does not include any right to use the recording. For that right, the producer will need a Master Recording License.

Another way for a producer to reduce music acquisition costs is to use music that is in the public domain. One must make sure that *all* rights are in the public domain. Let's say a low-budget filmmaker decides to put Beethoven's Fifth Symphony on his soundtrack. He goes to the record store and buys the Boston Symphony Pops recording of Beethoven's Fifth. While the composition is in the public domain, this particular recording may not be. The filmmaker is free to use Beethoven's composition, but he will have to find a recording in the public domain or hire musicians and make his own recording.

To produce a new recording, a producer will have to strike a deal with a recording studio, musicians and/or vocalists. AFofM, AFTRA and SAG collective-bargaining agreements will apply to films made by Guild signatories. A star artist may receive $20,000 or more as a fee, as well as royalties based on the retail price of the soundtrack album. If the artist is exclusive to a record label, its permission will be needed.

If the producer wants to put recorded pre-existing music that is not in the public domain on the soundtrack, a MASTER USE LICENSE will be sought from the record company that owns the recording.[1] Fees range from several hundred dollars for use of a short excerpt to tens of thousands of dollars for the work of a superstar. The artist may have approval rights over licensing his music to another, in which case the artist's permission must also be obtained. Re-use payments to musicians and performers will be required if the recording was made by union members.

Commissioning an Original Score

The producer must take care in hiring a composer/lyricist or songwriter. The agreement between the parties will determine whether the artist is deemed an employee-for-hire or an independent contractor, which will in turn determine who is the author for copyright purposes. There can be joint ownership of a musical score (a participation agreement). Permission may also need to be obtained from a record company if you use an artist under contract.

The producer will usually want the work to be considered one that is "made-for-hire" so that he automatically owns the copyright. The composer will be entitled to a fee for his work and royalties from non-movie uses of his music.[2] A top songwriter may demand to share the copyright under a co-publishing agreement. The expenses of recording the soundtrack are borne by the producer.

For low-budget movies, a composer may wear several hats.[3] He may write, arrange, orchestrate, conduct and perform the

---

[1] A producer who has obtained synchronization and performance licenses from the artist's publisher could make its own sound-alike recording if the artist's record label refuses to grant a license to use its recording. That is, the producer could create his own recording that sounds exactly like the original as long as it was not copied from the orginal. See *Soundtrack Music* by Lionel S. Sobel, Chapter 184A, *Entertainment Industry Contracts*, Volume 4, Mathew Bender.

[2] Composer's royalties from soundtrack albums are typically 50% of the mechanical license fees paid the studio by the record company that releases the album. Also, the composer will receive 50% of the public performance fees collected by the agencies ASCAP or BMI, which is paid directly to the composer by his agency. Additionally, the composer will receive a royalty from the sale of sheet music and in some circumstances may receive a royalty for conducting and/or producing the soundtrack album.

[3] Composers are not unionized. However, the American Federation of Musicians represents orchestrators and conductors, a role often performed by composers in delivering soundtracks.

DEALMAKING
IN THE
FILM AND
TELEVISION
INDUSTRY

206

music. A composer may even agree to produce and deliver a finished master recording at his own expense. Some producers minimize costs by using non-union musicians or electronic synthesizers.

Sometimes artists anxious to break into movie composing will compose a soundtrack or song on speculation. Here the producer is not obligated to pay for the work unless he uses it.

A producer could also proceed under a step deal. The songwriter[1] is paid a modest upfront payment for composing the song, and then the producer decides if he wants to use it. If the producer uses the song, he will pay an additional fee. If he doesn't use the song, the writer will retain all rights to it. In that event, the producer may seek reimbursement of the upfront payment if the song ever generates income. A sample composer employment agreement is reprinted at the end of this chapter.

When a popular artist is commissioned to provide a song, the studio will pay him a creative fee for his services. The deal can be structured by providing the artist with a fund that includes payment for all writing and recording expenses. Thus the artist is paid a flat fee and is responsible for delivering the song and master and paying all recording expenses. Such a deal limits the studio's liability for recording costs and can provide greater compensation to the artist if expenses can be minimized.

Complications arise with popular songwriters because many have entered agreements granting a publisher the exclusive right to the songwriter's services. Both the publisher and the studio, which may have its own music publishing arm, may want copyright ownership and management of a song written for a movie. The parties will need to reach an agreement, unless the artist has already fulfilled his songwriting contract.

Similarly, a soundtrack artist may be exclusive to a record label for recordings over a term of years or for several albums. The recording company may demand a royalty from the film studio in return for granting permission to use the artist on the soundtrack. Often the label and the artist share royalties.

There are other areas where the studio's interests and those of

---

[1] The songwriter creates a song for the soundtrack while the composer creates an entire score. The employment agreements are similar.

the record label may conflict. Studios want to release singles to promote movies and soundtrack albums. Record labels, on the other hand, want to use the single to promote their artists' albums.

Ownership and control of a music video created to promote the movie is another issue. The studio will want to use the video as an integral part of the film's publicity campaign. The recording company will want to release the video in a manner that will best promote the artist.

Assuming all necessary permissions have been obtained from the artist's record label, a Soundtrack Recording Agreement will be used to employ an artist. The agreement will give the studio both the right to use the song on the soundtrack and the right to include it on a soundtrack album.

Since several artists may contribute material to a soundtrack, each will want to ensure that they receive a fair deal compared to the others. An artist will often ask for a MOST-FAVORED NATIONS clause, which guarantees the artist as favorable terms as those given any other artist.

An artist may also seek to limit a studio's recoupment of recording costs and advances to those costs directly incurred by that artist. Thus, the artist's royalty will not be reduced by expenses attributable to others. If the studio agrees to such a provision, it must maintain a separate accounting for each artist.

NATURE OF MUSIC RIGHTS NEEDED

As discussed in Chapter 12, a copyright is a bundle of different rights, including the right to control the performance, copying, display, distribution (by sale, rental or lease) and alteration of a work. The producer who wants to incorporate music on a soundtrack has to license several of these rights.

The PUBLIC PERFORMANCE RIGHT is the right to recite, play, sing, dance or broadcast a musical composition in public. Music rights' owners virtually always use agencies such as ASCAP, BMI or SESAC to license their performance rights. These agencies issue a blanket license to users.

First, the music rights' owner selects an agency, (e.g., BMI) to

DEALMAKING
IN THE
FILM AND
TELEVISION
INDUSTRY

208

represent her. Each agency represents thousands of songs. Television and radio broadcasters, nightclubs, theaters, amusement parks, discos and other businesses that publicly perform music (except movie theaters) pay a yearly fee to the agencies. The agencies issue blanket licenses entitling the user to use any of the songs they represent without securing permission on an individual basis.

The fees collected from users are pooled, and after the agency deducts its administrative costs, the money is divided among the songwriters and music publishers that the agency represents. The agency divides the money according to the popularity of the songs, which is determined through surveys and random samples. Thus a famous songwriter will receive a larger check than some unknown songwriter whose song was played once on a local radio station.

The blanket license makes sense for everyone concerned. As a practical matter, the owner of rights to a piece of music can't monitor every public performance of his music and take action to enforce payment. Similarly, it would be cumbersome for a radio station to have to negotiate permission for every song it broadcasts.

Imagine a disc jockey having to share the broadcast booth with a dozen lawyers. After the D.J. selects a record, he shouts "Get me permission from Bob Dylan for 'Blowin' in the Wind'" as lawyers in pin-striped suits furiously dial phones and negotiate deals to obtain performance rights. Such a scheme would employ many lawyers but vex disc jockeys.

There are two important points to remember about the blanket license. First, it only covers non-dramatic or small perform-

---

MUSIC RIGHTS NEEDED FOR A THEATRICAL FEATURE FILM

1) **PERFORMANCE RIGHTS:** NO BLANKET LICENSE FOR MOVIE THEATERS SO THE PRODUCER MUST NEGOTIATE A LICENSE.

2) **SYNCHRONIZATION RIGHTS:** OBTAINED WITH ABOVE FOR ONE FEE IN ONE LICENSE.

3) **OTHER MARKETS:** HOME VIDEO, NON-THEATRICAL DISTRIBUTION, FREE TELEVISION, CABLE, SUBSCRIPTION TV, CLOSED CIRCUIT TV, IN-FLIGHT EXHIBITION.

ing rights. Performances such as a musical play or opera, where songs tell a story, are considered dramatic performances and one cannot obtain a blanket license for this use.

It can be difficult to distinguish a dramatic from a non-dramatic performance. A disc jockey who broadcasts a song would be making a non-dramatic use, whereas a small theater performance with props, costumes and sets would be making a dramatic use. But there are many uses that fall in between.

Second, U.S. exhibitors cannot obtain a blanket license to perform music.[1] They are not covered by the license issued by ASCAP or BMI. Consequently, the rights to perform music in movie theaters (i.e., on the soundtrack) must be obtained from the music right's owner. Since it would be very cumbersome to require every theater owner to obtain these rights for each song in every movie they exhibit, the producer or distributor will obtain these rights for all exhibitors who might show the film. However, if the music rights' owner refuses to license the music, or the parties cannot agree on terms, the producer/distributor can't use the music.

The SYNCHRONIZATION RIGHT is the right to reproduce the music[2] on the soundtrack of the movie in synchronization with video or filmed images. There is no blanket license available. Producers must negotiate with the music rights' owner. The fees are modest (e.g., a few thousand dollars) for television use since the music owners will receive fees from the blanket performance license. As a matter of convenience, the synchronization license is usually obtained simultaneously with the performance license for one fee and one license. Organizations like The Harry Fox Agency[3] license synchronization rights for many music owners.

ADAPTATION RIGHTS allow the producer to alter the musical composition by way of arrangement, parody, comedic use and lyric change. If you want to use the title or story set forth in a song, you may need to obtain DRAMATIC RIGHTS. As mentioned above, dramatic use includes a film or television produc-

---

[1] Movie theaters in Europe, however, do pay public-performance fees.

[2] For non-dramatic use of music. A non-dramatic use does not tell a story.

[3] The Harry Fox Agency is located at 205 East 42nd Street, 18th Floor, New York, NY 10017. Phone: (212) 370-5330.

DEALMAKING
IN THE
FILM AND
TELEVISION
INDUSTRY

210

tion of an opera or musical play. The composer or publisher may reserve certain rights, such as the right to make changes to the work.

Producers may also want to obtain the right to use the work in other markets such as home video, non-theatrical distribution, free television, cable television, subscription television, closed-circuit television and airline exhibition.

Producers can either negotiate for the necessary rights themselves, use an attorney or retain an organization like the The Clearing House, Ltd.[1] to negotiate for them. Producers should always obtain all needed licenses before placing the music on the soundtrack. Otherwise, the producer risks having to remix the soundtrack if he cannot obtain the requisite rights.

DISTRIBUTION OF THE SOUNDTRACK ALBUM

The motion-picture studio will negotiate an agreement with a record label for the production and distribution of the sound-track album. Record companies can earn significant revenue from such releases and will pay the studio a royalty and often an advance as well. Record companies prefer soundtracks with major artists and pop songs rather than orchestral performances.

The royalty will range from 10% to 19% of the retail price, although the studio will pay a portion to musical artists. The record company may ask the studio to put up matching funds for promotion. A studio will want the album's release to coincide with the film's release.

---

[1] The Clearing House, Ltd., 6605 Hollywood Blvd., Ste. 200, Hollywood, CA 90028, (213) 469-3186

TV MUSIC RIGHTS LICENSE

1. In consideration of the payment of _____, and upon the payment of it to the undersigned, the undersigned does hereby grant to Licensee the non-exclusive, irrevocable right and license to record the following copyrighted musical composition(s) (the "Compositions") in synchronization or timed-relation with a picture produced by Licensee (the "Picture") for television broadcast and exhibition only, and known as:

    Title:
    Composer:
    Publisher:
    Length of Composition & Manner of Use:

2. This is a license to record only, and the exercise of the recording rights herein granted is conditioned upon performance of the Composition(s) over television stations having valid licenses from the copyright owner (the "Owner"), or from the person, firm, corporation or other entity having the legal right to issue performance-rights licenses for the Owner in the respective territories in which the Composition(s) shall be performed. The Composition(s) shall not be used in any manner and media or be recorded for any other purpose, except those specifically set forth herein, without the express written consent of the Owner. No sound recordings produced pursuant to this license are to be manufactured, sold and/or used separately from the Picture; and the Picture shall not be exhibited in or televised into theaters or other public places of amusement where motion pictures are customarily exhibited.

3. This license is granted for the following territory: The United States, its territories and possessions.

4. This license shall end on _____. Upon such date rights herein granted shall immediately cease and end, and the right derived from this license to make or authorize any further use or distribution of the Picture with the licensed music shall also cease and end upon such date.

5. This license cannot be assigned or transferred without the express consent of the undersigned in writing.

6. The undersigned warrants, on behalf of the principal for whom the undersigned is acting, that it is the owner of the recording rights herein licensed, and this license is given without other warranty or recourse, except to repay the consideration paid for this license if said warranty shall be breached. The

DEALMAKING
IN THE
FILM AND
TELEVISION
INDUSTRY

212

undersigned's warranty is limited to the amount of consideration paid for this license; and the undersigned further reserves all rights and uses in and to the Composition(s) not herein specifically granted.

_____

Publisher

AGREED AND ACCEPTED:

_____

Producer

COMPOSER AGREEMENT

FOR LOW-BUDGET FEATURE

_____ 19__

Mr. John Doe
Melody Lane
Los Angeles, CA

Dear Mr. Doe:

This letter, when signed by you (the "Composer"), will confirm our mutual agreement whereby Very Independent Productions, Inc. (the "Producer"), has engaged you as an employee for hire to render certain services and to furnish a complete and original musical score (the "Work") for the documentary feature _____ (the "Picture").

Producer agrees to pay composer as full compensation, for all services required of him in connection with the Picture and for all the rights granted by the Composer, upon condition that the Composer shall fully and faithfully perform all the services required of him hereunder, the sum of $ _____ and other valuable consideration including one VHS copy of the Picture with musical score and a credit in the picture.

Producer employs Composer to write, compose, orchestrate, perform, record and submit to Producer music suitable for use as the complete background score for the Picture. Composer shall bear the full cost of any musicians, studio or equipment rental, guild or union fees or any other costs incurred in preparing the work except for tape stock costs.

The Composer grants the Producer the perpetual nonexclusive right to use and license others to use his name and likeness in any advertising or exploitation of the Picture.

The Composer agrees that Producer may perpetually use or authorize others to use any of the rights herein granted for commercial advertising or publicity in connection with any product, commodity or service manufactured, distributed or offered by the Producer or others, provided such advertising refers to the Picture, or to the Composer's employment by the Producer.

Composer warrants that all material written, composed, prepared or submitted by him during the term hereof or any extension of it

DEALMAKING
IN THE
FILM AND
TELEVISION
INDUSTRY

214

shall be wholly original with him and shall not be copied in whole or in part from any other work, except that submitted to the Composer by the Producer as a basis for such material. The Composer further warrants that said material will not infringe upon the copyright, literary, dramatic or photoplay rights of any person. Composer warrants and agrees to indemnify and hold Producer and Producer's officers, shareholders, employees, successors and assigns harmless from and against any claim, demand, damage, debt, liability, account, reckoning, obligation, cost, expense, lien, action and cause of action (including the payment of attorneys' fees and costs incurred) arising out of any breach or failure of any of Composer's warranties, representations or covenants herein contained.

The Composer further agrees that all the material which he may write, compose, prepare or submit under this agreement shall be the sole property of the Producer. All of the material shall be written, composed, prepared and submitted by him as the employee of the Producer, and not otherwise. The Producer shall be the author and first proprietor of the copyright, and the Composer shall have no right, title or interest in the material. Producer shall have the right to obtain copyrights, patents and/or other protection therefore. The Composer further agrees to execute, verify, acknowledge, and deliver any documents which the Producer shall deem necessary or advisable to evidence, establish, maintain, protect, enforce or defend its rights and/or title in or to the said material or any part of it. Producer shall have the right, but not the duty, to use, adapt, edit, add to, subtract from, arrange, rearrange, revise and change said material or any part of it, and to vend, copy, publish, reproduce, record, transmit, broadcast by radio and/or television, perform, photograph with or without sound, including spoken works, dialogue and/or music synchronously recorded, and to communicate the same by any means now known or from now on devised, either publicly and for profit, or otherwise.

Producer, its successors and assigns, shall in addition to the Composer's services be entitled to and own in perpetuity, solely and exclusively, all of the results and proceeds of said services and material, including all rights throughout the world of production, manufacture, recordation and reproduction by any art or method, whether now known or from now on devised, and whether such results and proceeds consist of literary, dramatic, musical, motion picture, mechanical, or any other form of work, theme, idea, composition, creation or product.

The Composer will at the request of the Producer execute such assignments or other instruments as the Producer may deem necessary or desirable to evidence, establish or defend his right or title in the Work. The Composer hereby appoints the Producer the true and lawful attorney-in-fact of the Composer irrevocably to execute, verify, acknowledge and deliver any such instruments or documents which the Composer shall fail or refuse to execute.

Producer shall have and is hereby granted the complete control of the publication of all or any of the musical material written by the Composer hereunder. Producer agrees, however, that in the event it publishes the musical material or causes the musical material to be published by a third party, Producer shall pay to the composer the following fees:

(a) Five cents (.05) per copy for each piano copy of the Composition and for each dance orchestration of the Composition printed, published and sold in the United States and Canada by Publisher or its licensees, for which payments have been received by Publisher, after deduction of returns.

(b) Ten percent (10%) of the wholesale selling price upon each printed copy of each other arrangement and edition of the Composition printed, published and sold in the United States and Canada by Publisher or its licensees, for which payment has been received, after deduction of returns, except that in the event the Composition shall be used or caused to be used, in whole or in part, with one or more other compositions in a folio, album or other publication, Composer shall be entitled to receive that proportion of said royalty which the Composition shall bear to the total number of compositions contained in such folio, album or other publication for which royalties are payable.

(c) Fifty percent (50%) of any and all net sums actually received (less any costs for collection) by Publisher in the United States from the exploitation in the United States and Canada by licensees of Publisher of mechanical rights, electrical transcription and reproducing rights, motion picture and television synchronization rights and all other rights (except printing and public performance rights) in the Composition, whether such licensees are affiliated with, owned in whole or in part by, or controlled by Publisher.

(d) Composer shall receive his public-performance royalties throughout the world directly from his own affiliated performing-rights society and shall have no claims at all against Publisher for any royalties received by Publisher from any performing-rights society which makes payment directly (or indirectly other than through Publisher) to writers, authors and composers.

DEALMAKING
IN THE
FILM AND
TELEVISION
INDUSTRY

216

(e) Fifty percent (50%) of any and all net sums, after deduction of foreign taxes, actually received (less any costs of collection) by Publisher in the United States from sales, licenses and other uses of the Composition in countries outside of the United States and Canada (other than the public-performance royalties as hereinabove mentioned in paragraph (d)) from collection agents, licensees, subpublishers or others, whether same are affiliated with, owned in whole or in part by, or controlled by Publisher.

(f) Publisher shall not be required to pay any royalties on professional or complimentary printed copies of the Composition which are distributed gratuitously to performing arts, orchestra leaders and disc jockeys or for advertising, promotional or exploitation purposes. Furthermore, no royalties shall be payable to Composer on consigned copies of the Composition unless paid for, and not until an accounting therefore can properly be made.

Notwithstanding anything to the contrary contained in this Agreement, Producer, its lessees, licensees and all other persons permitted by Producer to distribute, exhibit or exploit any picture in connection with which any material written, prepared or composed by Composer hereunder is used, shall have the free and unrestricted right to use any such material and to make mechanical reproductions of it without the payment of any sums at all, and in no event shall Composer be permitted or entitled to participate in any rentals or other forms of royalty received by Producer, its licensees or any other persons permitted by Producer to use any such material or mechanical reproductions of it in connection with the exhibition, distribution, exploitation or advertising of any present or future kind of motion picture, nor shall Producer be obligated to account to Composer for any sums received by Producer from any other persons from the sale or licensing or other disposition of any material written, created, or composed by Composer hereunder in connection with the exhibition, distribution, exploitation or advertising of any motion picture. Without limiting the foregoing, Composer shall not be entitled to any portion of any synchronization fee due to the use of the material or any portion of it in motion pictures produced by Producer or by any of its subsidiaries, affiliates or related companies.

Provided Composer fully and satisfactorily renders his services pursuant to the terms and conditions of this Agreement, and that all of the original music contained in the Picture as released is the product of Composer's services, Producer shall accord Composer billing on a separate card by the phrase "MUSIC BY JOHN DOE" or a phrase substantially similar thereto on the positive prints of said Picture. Except as set forth in the preceding sentence, all other matters about billing shall be decided in Producer's sole discretion.

If Producer, its successors or assigns shall exercise their right hereunder to make, distribute and sell, or authorize others to make, distribute and sell, commercial phonograph records (including, without limitation, discs of any speed or size, tape and wire demos and any and all other demos, whether now known or unknown, for the recording of sound) embodying the material for the Picture and if said records contain Composer's performance as a conductor, they shall pay or cause to be paid to Composer in connection with it a reasonable royalty as is customarily paid in the industry.

Composer's sole remedy for any breach hereof shall be an action at law for damages, if any. In no event shall Composer have the right to rescind this Agreement or any of the rights granted hereunder nor to seek or obtain injunctions or other equitable relief restraining or enjoining the production, exhibition or exploitation of any motion pictures based upon or using any portion of the Work.

Nothing contained in this Agreement shall be deemed to require Producer or its assigns to publish, record, reproduce or otherwise use the Work or any part of it, whether in connection with the Picture or otherwise.

This instrument is the entire Agreement between the parties and cannot be modified except by a written instrument signed by the Composer and an authorized officer of the Producer.

This agreement shall be deemed to have been made in the State of California and its validity, construction and effect shall be governed by and construed under the laws and judicial decisions of the State of California applicable to agreements wholly performed therein.

Very truly yours,

By John Smith
President, Very Independent Prods.

ACCEPTED AND AGREED TO:

_____
John Doe
Composer

I hereby certify that I wrote the material hereto attached, as an employee of Very Independent Productions, Inc., pursuant to an agreement dated the _____ day of _____, 19___, in performance of my duties thereunder, and in the regular course of employment, and that said Very Independent Productions, Inc., is the author of it and entitled to the copyright therein and thereto, with the right to make such changes therein and such uses of it, as it may determine as such author.

IN WITNESS WHEREOF, I have hereto set my hands this _____ day of 19__.

_____

John Doe

CHAPTER 9

THE ACQUISITION/
DISTRIBUTION
AGREEMENT

There are several ways to develop or produce a film. Beginning with an idea, or the movie rights to an existing literary property, a studio can hire a writer to create a script. The studio's development staff will work with the writer to develop the story. Most scripts developed by studios, however, never get produced.[1]

Other movies begin with a script developed outside the studio. Here a writer, working on his own or hired by an independent producer, writes a screenplay. After it is finished, it may be packaged (joined) with other elements (e.g., a star or director) and presented to the studio for financing and distribution. The big three talent agencies (CAA, ICM and William Morris) are responsible for most packaging.

Other films are both developed and produced away from the

---

[1] Development, like research and development in scientific endeavors, doesn't always succeed. Many ideas sound promising at the concept stage, but the finished work may not be impressive enough to justify an investment of millions of dollars for production.

DEALMAKING
IN THE
FILM AND
TELEVISION
INDUSTRY

220

studio that ultimately distributes them. These independently produced projects are often dependent on investors or pre-sale distribution deals (selling off various foreign-distribution rights) to finance production. The producer then enters an acquisition agreement with a distributor for release of the picture. This is called a NEGATIVE PICK-UP DEAL.

While the terms of negative pick-up deals vary, the studio/distributor typically pays for all distribution, advertising and marketing costs. The studio and producer share profits. Because the producer has taken the risk of financing production, he probably can obtain a better definition of net profits than if he made the film with studio financing. Profits may be split 50/50 between the studio and producer without a deduction for a studio distribution fee. A 50/50 net deal is illustrated on page 226. Of course, the independent producer takes the risk that if the film turns out poorly, no distributor will want it. In that case, the producer can incur a substantial loss.

In a negative pick-up deal, the distributor will often agree to give the producer an advance of his share of profits. The producer can use this money to repay investors. Producers will want to obtain as large an advance as possible because they know they may never see anything on the back end of the deal (i.e., no profits).

The distributor wants to pay as small an advance as possible, and usually resists giving an amount that is more than the cost of production. Its executives will propose, "We'll be partners. We will put up all the money for advertising and promotion. If the picture is successful, we will share in its success." Sound good?

Unfortunately, distributors have been known to engage in creative accounting, and profit participants rarely see any return on their share of "net profits" because of the way that term is defined. Consequently, the shrewd producer tries to get as large an advance as possible. He also tries to retain foreign rights and keep them from being cross-collateralized.[1]

---

[1] Cross-collateralized means the monies earned from several markets are pooled. For example, let's say your picture made $1 million in England and lost $1 million dollars in France. If those territories were cross-collateralized, and you were entitled to a percentage of the net revenue, you would get nothing. On the other hand, if the territories were not cross-collateralized, you would get your percentage of the English revenues and the distributor would absorb the loss incurred in France.

Cash-Flow from Domestic Theatrical Distribution of a Feature Film

(50/50-Net Deal)

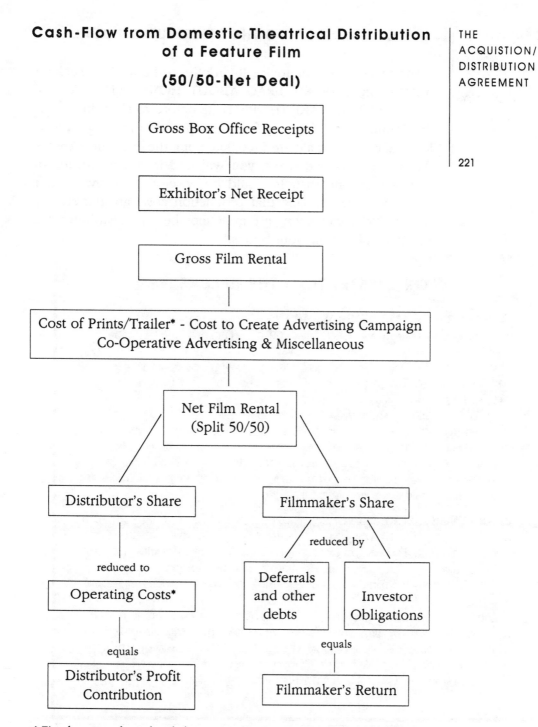

* Fixed costs and overhead charges applications vary with each distributor.
Source: Independent Feature Project, Orion Classics & Off-Hollywood.

DEALMAKING
IN THE
FILM AND
TELEVISION
INDUSTRY

222

ORCHESTRATING THE DISTRIBUTION DEAL

The most important advice I can offer to filmmakers seeking distribution is DON'T BRAG ABOUT HOW LITTLE MONEY YOU SPENT TO MAKE THE PICTURE before you conclude your distribution deal. You may feel justly proud of making a great-looking picture for a mere $400,000. But if the distributor knows that is all you have spent, you will find it difficult to get an advance beyond that. It would be wiser not to reveal your investment, recognizing that production costs are not readily discernible from viewing a film. Remember, the distributor has no right to examine your books.[1]

ORCHESTRATING THE RELEASE

1) KEEP THE FILM UNDER WRAPS: DON'T SHOW YOUR FILM UNTIL IT IS FINISHED. EXECUTIVES MAY ASK TO SEE A ROUGH CUT. THEY WILL SAY "DON'T WORRY. WE'RE PROFESSIONALS, WE CAN EXTRAPOLATE AND ENVISION WHAT THE FILM WILL LOOK LIKE WITH SOUND AND TITLES." DON'T BELIEVE THEM. MOST PEOPLE CAN'T EXTRAPOLATE. THEY WILL VIEW YOUR UNFINISHED FILM AND THINK IT AMATEURISH. FIRST IMPRESSIONS LAST.

THE ONLY REASON TO SHOW YOUR FILM BEFORE COMPLETION IS IF YOU ARE DESPERATE TO RAISE FUNDS TO FINISH IT. THE TERMS YOU CAN OBTAIN UNDER THESE CIRCUMSTANCES WILL USUALLY BE LESS THAN THOSE GIVEN ON COMPLETION. IF YOU MUST SHOW A WORK IN PROGRESS, EXHIBIT IT ON A MOVIOLA OR FLATBED EDITING TABLE. PEOPLE HAVE LOWER EXPECTATIONS VIEWING A FILM ON AN EDITING CONSOLE THAN WHEN IT IS PROJECTED IN A THEATER.

2) ARRANGE A SCREENING: INVITE EXECUTIVES TO A SCREENING; DON'T SEND THEM A VIDEOCASSETTE. IF YOU SEND A TAPE TO A BUSY EXECUTIVE, HE WILL POP IT IN HIS VCR. TEN MINUTES LATER THE PHONE RINGS AND HE PUSHES THE PAUSE BUTTON. THEN HE WATCHES ANOTHER TEN MINUTES UNTIL HE IS INTERRUPTED BY HIS SECRETARY. AFTER BEING DISTRACTED A DOZEN TIMES, HE PASSES ON YOUR FILM BECAUSE IT IS "TOO CHOPPY." WELL, OF COURSE IT'S CHOPPY WITH ALL THOSE INTERRUPTIONS.

YOU WANT TO GET THE EXECUTIVE IN A DARK ROOM, AWAY FROM DIVERSIONS, TO VIEW YOUR FILM WITH A LIVE AUDIENCE—HOPEFULLY ONE THAT WILL RESPOND POSITIVELY. SO RENT A SCREENING ROOM AT MGM, INVITE ALL THE ACQUISITION EXECUTIVES YOU CAN, AND PACK THE REST OF THE THEATER WITH YOUR FRIENDS AND RELATIVES, ESPECIALLY UNCLE HERB WITH HIS INFECTIOUS LAUGH.

CONTINUED

---

[1] Assuming the distributor has not provided any financing, what you have spent is between you, your investors and the I.R.S.

Negative pick-up deals can be negotiated before, during or after production. Often distributors become interested in a film after viewing it at a film festival and observing audience reaction. All the studios and independent distributors have one or more staffers in charge of acquisitions. It is the job of these acquisition executives to find good films to acquire.

It is not difficult to get acquisition executives to view your film. Once production has been announced, don't be surprised if they begin calling you. They will track the progress of your film so that they can see it as soon as it is finished—before their competitors get a shot at it.

From the filmmaker's point of view, you will get the best distribution deal if you have more than one distributor interested in acquiring your movie. That way you can play one off another to get the best terms. But what if one distributor makes a preemptive bid for the film, offering you a $500,000 advance, and you have only twenty-four hours to accept their offer? If you

ORCHESTRATING THE RELEASE
(CONTINUED)

3) MAKE THE BUYERS COMPETE AGAINST EACH OTHER: SCREEN THE FILM FOR ALL DISTRIBUTORS SIMULTANEOUSLY. SOME EXECUTIVES WILL ATTEMPT TO GET AN EARLY LOOK—THAT IS THEIR JOB. YOUR JOB IS TO KEEP THEM INTRIGUED UNTIL IT IS COMPLETE. YOU CAN PROMISE TO LET THEM SEE IT "AS SOON AS IT IS FINISHED." THEY MAY BE ANNOYED TO ARRIVE AT THE SCREENING AND SEE THEIR COMPETITORS. BUT THIS WILL GET THEIR COMPETITIVE JUICES FLOWING. THEY WILL KNOW THAT THEY BETTER MAKE A DECENT OFFER QUICKLY IF THEY HOPE TO GET THE FILM.

4) OBTAIN AN EXPERIENCED ADVISOR: RETAIN AN EXPERIENCED PRODUCER'S REP OR ENTERTAINMENT ATTORNEY TO NEGOTIATE YOUR DEAL. FILMMAKERS KNOW ABOUT FILM, DISTRIBUTORS KNOW ABOUT DISTRIBUTION. DON'T KID YOURSELF AND BELIEVE YOU CAN PLAY IN THEIR ARENA AND WIN. THERE ARE MANY PITFALLS TO AVOID. GET YOURSELF AN EXPERIENCED GUIDE TO PROTECT YOUR INTERESTS. ANY DECENT NEGOTIATOR CAN IMPROVE A DISTRIBUTOR'S OFFER ENOUGH TO OUTWEIGH THE COST OF HIS SERVICES.

CONTINUED

DEALMAKING
IN THE
FILM AND
TELEVISION
INDUSTRY

224

pass, you may not be able to get a better deal later. It is possible you may fail to obtain any distribution deal at all. On the other hand, if you accept the offer, you may be foreclosing the possibility of a more lucrative deal that could be offered you later. Consequently, it is important to orchestrate the release of your film to potential distributors to maximize your leverage.

SELF-DEFENSE TIPS FOR FILMMAKERS

I recently represented a filmmaker who had signed an agreement with a small distributor. The filmmaker was entitled to an

ORCHESTRATING THE RELEASE
(CONTINUED)

5) **INVESTIGATE THE DISTRIBUTOR**: ALWAYS CHECK THE TRACK RECORD AND EXPERIENCE OF POTENTIAL DISTRIBUTORS. AS AN ENTERTAINMENT ATTORNEY WHO REPRESENTS MANY INDEPENDENT FILMMAKERS, I OFTEN FIND MYSELF IN THE POSITION OF TRYING TO GET UNSCRUPULOUS DISTRIBUTORS TO LIVE UP TO THEIR CONTRACTS. I AM AMAZED AT HOW MANY DISTRIBUTORS REFUSE TO ABIDE BY THE CLEAR TERMS OF THEIR OWN DISTRIBUTION AGREEMENTS.

I AM NOT TALKING HERE ABOUT THE MAJOR STUDIOS. WHILE THEY ENGAGE IN CREATIVE ACCOUNTING BY INTERPRETING AMBIGUOUS CLAUSES IN THEIR FAVOR, THEY OFTEN FEEL OBLIGED TO COMPLY WITH THE CLEAR TERMS OF THEIR CONTRACTS. I AM TALKING ABOUT THE MANY SMALL INDEPENDENT DISTRIBUTORS WHO FLAGRANTLY BREACH CONTRACTS AND TAKE UNCONSCIONABLE ADVANTAGE OF INEXPERIENCED FILMMAKERS. THEIR ATTITUDE SEEMS TO BE: PROMISE ANYTHING TO GET THE FILM. THEN DEFRAUD, DECEIVE AND FLEECE WITH ABANDON. IF THE VICTIM HAS THE AUDACITY TO COMPLAIN, THE DISTRIBUTOR USUALLY:

1) LIES;
2) CLAIMS THE FILM WASN'T ANY GOOD AND THEREFORE ITS OBLIGATIONS ARE TERMINATED, OR;
3) OFFERS TO SETTLE FOR TEN CENTS ON THE DOLLAR.

THE SAVVY FILMMAKER WILL CAREFULLY INVESTIGATE POTENTIAL DISTRIBUTORS BY CALLING FILMMAKERS WHO HAVE CONTRACTED WITH THEM. I ONCE READ A STANDARD & POORS REPORT ON A DISTRIBUTOR AND WAS SHOCKED TO LEARN THAT THE COMPANY WAS $2.3 MILLION IN ARREARS ON ROYALTY PAYMENTS. ONE CAN ALSO CHECK THE SUPERIOR COURT DOCKETS IN LOS ANGELES TO SEE IF A COMPANY HAS BEEN SUED.

advance, payable in four installments. After the second installment was paid, the company changed hands and the new
owners simply refused to make payments. There was no question that the company owed my client the money and that my
client had lived up to all his obligations. The only excuse the
distributor offered was that they were experiencing "financial
problems." We offered to accept monthly payments to work off
the debt. Payments were promised but never made. Only after I
went to court and had the sheriff seize the distributor's film
library did they cough up the dough.

Distributors of low-budget films know that the amounts at
stake are often not enough for the filmmaker to hire an attorney. Consequently, filmmakers should include an arbitration
clause in their contracts. This provision provides that, in case of
a dispute, the matter will be settled through binding arbitration,
not litigation. Arbitration clauses and procedures are discussed
in Chapter 2.

My experience with distributors has taught me that filmmakers
need to be very careful when entering distribution agreements.
The experienced filmmaker will try to add incentives and/or
penalties to the contract that will encourage the distributor to
live up to its terms. In one contract, I inserted a special clause
which said that if the distributor breached any promise, my
client could recover all the money owed him AND regain all
rights to his film. Nevertheless, the distributor breached the
contract. My client got his money and film back and promptly
sold the distribution rights to another distributor, from whom he
received a second advance.

One of my current cases involves a dispute with a home-video
distributor. The filmmaker made an oral agreement with the
distributor and delivered his film. The distributor began advertising
and promoting the picture. Six weeks later, before the paper-
work was signed, the company reneged on the deal and
coerced the filmmaker into renegotiating the deal and granting
better terms.

To protect yourself from such tactics, make sure all promises
are in writing. Don't deliver any materials until the deal is
signed. Try to retain possession of your film negative; give the
distributor a lab-access letter. Have your lab directly report to

DEALMAKING
IN THE
FILM AND
TELEVISION
INDUSTRY

226

you how many copies are duplicated for the distributor. Make sure your agreement guarantees a minimum amount to be spent on advertising.

An experienced negotiator can obtain many important provisions just for the asking. Don't sign the "sucker" contract the distributor sends out to unwary filmmakers. Remember, the terms of the proposed contract are negotiable.

CHECKLIST FOR SELECTING A DISTRIBUTOR

1) AMOUNT OF ADVANCE.

2) EXTENT OF RIGHTS CONVEYED. DOMESTIC AND/OR FOREIGN. ANCILLARY RIGHTS? ARE ANY MARKETS CROSS-COLLATERALIZED?

3) IS THERE A GUARANTEED MARKETING COMMITMENT?

4) DOES THE PRODUCER HAVE ANY INPUT OR VETO POWER OVER ARTWORK AND THEATER SELECTION IN THE TOP MARKETS?

5) TRACK RECORD AND FINANCIAL HEALTH OF DISTRIBUTOR.

6) ARE MONTHLY OR QUARTERLY ACCOUNTING STATEMENTS REQUIRED?

7) TO WHAT EXTENT DOES THE DISTRIBUTOR PLAN TO INVOLVE THE FILMMAKERS IN PROMOTION?

8) MARKETING STRATEGY: DEMOGRAPHICS OF INTENDED MARKET, GRASSROOTS PROMOTION EFFORTS, FILM FESTIVALS, ETC.

9) SPLIT OF REVENUES AND ACCOUNTING OF PROFITS: IS THERE A DISTRIBUTION FEE? OVERHEAD FEES?

10) DISTRIBUTOR LEVERAGE WITH EXHIBITORS. CAN THE DISTRIBUTOR COLLECT MONIES OWED?

11) ANY COMPETING FILMS HANDLED BY DISTRIBUTOR? CONFLICTS OF INTEREST?

12) DOES THE PRODUCER HAVE THE RIGHT TO REGAIN DISTRIBUTION RIGHTS IF THE DISTRIBUTOR PULLS THE PLUG EARLY ON DISTRIBUTION?

13) PERSONAL CHEMISTRY BETWEEN PRODUCER AND DISTRIBUTION EXECUTIVES.

ACQUISITION/DISTRIBUTION AGREEMENT
Theatrical Release

Agreement dated _____ between _____ ("Production Company"), a California corporation at _____ and, _____ ("Distributor"), a California corporation at _____.

1. PICTURE: The term "Picture" refers to the Theatrical Motion Picture set forth in Schedule "A" hereof.

2. TERRITORY AND TERM:

(a) Territory: The territory covered hereby ("Territory") is set forth in Schedule "A."

(b) Distribution Term: The term of this Agreement and the rights granted Distributor hereunder for each country or place of the Territory shall be the period of time specified in Schedule "A" ("Distribution Term"). The term of this Agreement shall commence on the date hereof and expire upon the expiration of the Distribution Term as extended unless sooner terminated as provided herein.

3. RIGHTS GRANTED:

(a) Grant: Production Company hereby grants to Distributor throughout the Territory the exercise of all rights of theatrical, television (free, pay and syndication) and home-video (cassette and disc) exhibition and distribution with respect to the Picture and Trailers thereof, and excerpts and clips therefrom, in any and all languages and versions, including dubbed, subtitled and narrated versions. The rights granted herein shall include without limit the sole and exclusive right:

(i) Titles: To use the title or titles by which the Picture is or may be known or identified.

(ii) Music and Lyrics: To use and perform any and all music, lyrics and musical compositions contained in the Picture and/or recorded in the soundtrack thereof in connection with the distribution, exhibition, advertising, publicizing and exploiting of the Picture;

(iii) Versions: To make such dubbed and titled versions of the Picture, and the Trailers thereof, including without

DEALMAKING
IN THE
FILM AND
TELEVISION
INDUSTRY

228

limitation, cut-in, synchronized and superimposed versions in any and all languages for use in such parts of the Territory as Distributor may deem advisable.

(iv) Editing: To make such changes, alterations, cuts, additions, interpolations, deletions and eliminations into and from the Picture and trailer subject to prior written approval of Production Company and Director as Distributor may deem necessary or desirable, for the effective marketing, distribution, exploitation or other use of the Picture.

(v) Advertising and Publicity: To publicize, advertise and exploit the Picture throughout the Territory during the Distribution Term, including without limitation, the exclusive right in the Territory for the purpose of advertising, publicizing and exploiting the Picture to:

(A) Literary Material: Publish and to license and authorize others to publish in any language and in such forms as Distributor may deem advisable, synopses, summaries, adaptations, novelizations, and stories of and excerpts from the Picture and from any literary or dramatic material included in the Picture or upon which the Picture is based in book form and in newspapers, magazines, trade periodicals, booklets, press books and any other periodicals and in all other media of advertising and publicity whatsoever not exceeding 7,500 words in length taken from the original material;

(B) Radio and Television: Broadcast by radio and television for advertising purposes and to license and authorize others to so broadcast, in any language, or any parts or portions of the Picture not exceeding five minutes in length, and any literary or dramatic material included in the Picture or upon which the Picture was based alone or in conjunction with other literary, dramatic or musical material; and

(C) Names and Likenesses: Use, license and authorize others to use the name, physical likeness and voice (and any simulation or reproduction of any thereof) of any party rendering services in connection with the Picture for the purpose of advertising, publicizing or exploiting the Picture or Distributor, including commercial tie-ins.

(6) Use of Name and Trademarks: To use Distributor's name and trademark and/or the name and trademark of any

of Distributor's licensee's on the positive prints of the Picture
and in Trailers thereof, and in all advertising and publicity
relating thereto, in such a manner, position, form and sub-
stance as Distributor or its licensees may elect.

(7) Commercials: To permit commercial messages to be
exhibited during and after the exhibition of the Picture.

(8) Trailers: To cause trailers of the Picture and prints
thereof and of the Picture to be manufactured, exhibited and
distributed by every means, medium, process, method and
device now or hereafter known.

(b) Grant of Other Rights: Production Company hereby
grants to Distributor throughout the Territory the sole and
exclusive right, license and privilege to exercise all literary
publishing rights, live television rights, merchandising rights,
music publishing rights, soundtrack recording rights, radio
rights, additional motion picture rights, remake rights and
sequel motion rights subject to the terms and conditions of
the agreements pursuant to which Production Company acquired the foregoing rights with respect to the literary, dramatic and/or musical material used by Production Company
in connection with the Picture. Production Company agrees
that at the request of Distributor, Production Company will
execute and deliver to Distributor for recordation purposes a
separate document pursuant to which Production Company
confirms the transfer and assignment to Distributor of said
rights.

(c) Rights Free and Clear: The above-stated rights are
granted by Production Company to Distributor without quali-
fication and free and clear from any and all restrictions,
claims, encumbrances or defects of any nature and Production Company agrees that it will not commit or omit to
perform any act by which any of these rights, licenses,
privileges and interests could or will be encumbered, diminished or impaired, and that Production Company will pay or
discharge, and will hold Distributor harmless from, any and
all claims that additional payments are due anyone by reason
of the distribution, exhibition, telecasting, or re-running of
the Picture or the receipt of its proceeds. Production Company further agrees that during the Distribution Term (as
extended) with respect to each country or place, Production

DEALMAKING
IN THE
FILM AND
TELEVISION
INDUSTRY

230

Company shall neither exercise itself nor grant to any third party the rights granted to Distributor pursuant to the terms hereof.

(d) Production Company's Reservation of Rights: Production Company reserves for its use non-theatrical distribution.

(e) Credits: The statements of credits required to be given pursuant to Exhibit "2" shall conform to Distributor's standard credit provisions for comparable talent, including without limitation Distributor's standard art work title provisions as set forth in Exhibit "3," attached hereto.

4. PRODUCTION COMPANY'S WARRANTIES AND REPRESENTATIONS: Production Company represents and warrants to Distributor, its successors, licensees and assigns as follows:

(a) Quality: The Picture is completely finished, fully edited and titled and fully synchronized with language dialogue, sound and music and in all respects ready and of a quality, both artistic and technical, adequate for general theatrical release and commercial public exhibition.

(b) Content: The Picture consists of a continuous and connected series of scenes, telling or presenting a story, free from any obscene material and suitable for exhibition to the general public.

(c) Unrestricted Right to Grant: Production Company is the sole and absolute owner of the Picture, the copyright pertaining thereto and all rights associated with or relating to the distribution the absolute right to grant to and vest in Distributor, all the rights, licenses and privileges granted to Distributor under this Agreement, and Production Company has not heretofore sold, as signed, licensed, granted, encumbered or utilized the Picture or any of the literary or musical properties used therein in any way that may affect or impair the rights, licenses and privileges granted to Distributor hereunder and Production Company will not sell, assign, license, grant or encumber or utilize the rights, licenses and privileges granted to Distributor hereunder.

(d) Discharge of Obligations: All the following have been fully paid or discharged or will be fully paid and discharged by Production Company or by persons other than Distributor:

(i) All claims and rights of owners of copyright in literary, dramatic and musical rights and other property or rights in or to all stories, plays, scripts, scenarios, themes, incidents, plots, characters, dialogue, music, words, and other material of any nature whatsoever appearing, used or recorded in the Picture;

(ii) All claims and rights of owners of inventions and patent rights with respect to the recording of any and all dialogue, music and other sound effects recorded in the Picture and with respect to the use of all equipment, apparatus, appliances and other materials used in the photographing, recording or otherwise in the manufacture of the Picture;

(iii) All claims and rights with respect to the use, distribution, exhibition, performance and exploitation of the Picture and any music contained therein throughout the Territory, and

(e) No Infringement: To the best of Production Company's knowledge and belief, neither the Picture nor any part thereof, nor any materials contained therein or synchronized therewith, nor the title thereof, nor the exercise of any right, license or privilege herein granted, violates or will violate or infringe or will infringe any trademark, trade name, contract, agreement, copyright (whether common law or statutory), patent, literary, artistic, dramatic, personal, private, civil or property right or right of privacy or "moral rights of authors" or any other right whatsoever of or slanders or libels any person, firm, corporation or association whatsoever. In connection therewith, Production Company shall supply Distributor with a script clearance in a form acceptable to Distributor.

(f) No Advertising Matter: The Picture does not contain any advertising matter for which compensation, direct or indirect, has been or will be received by Production Company or to its knowledge by any other person, firm, corporation or association.

(g) No Impairment of Rights Granted: There are and will be no agreements, commitments or arrangements whatever with any person, firm, corporation or association that may in any manner or to any extent affect Distributor's rights hereunder or Distributor's share of the proceeds of the Picture. Production Company has not and will not exercise any right

DEALMAKING
IN THE
FILM AND
TELEVISION
INDUSTRY

232

or take any action which might tend to derogate from, impair or compete with the rights, licenses and privileges herein granted to Distributor.

(h) Contracts: All contracts with artists and personnel, for purchases, licenses and laboratory contracts and all other obligations and undertakings of whatsoever kind connected with the production of the Picture have been made and entered into by Production Company and by no other party and no obligation shall be imposed upon Distributor thereunder and Production Company shall indemnify and hold Distributor harmless from any expense and liability thereunder. All such contracts are in the form customarily in use in the Motion Picture industry and are consistent with the provisions of this Agreement, particularly with reference to the warranties made by Production Company and the rights acquired by Distributor hereunder. Said contracts shall not, without Distributor's prior written consent, be terminated, canceled, modified or rescinded in any manner which would adversely affect Distributor's rights hereunder.

(i) All Considerations Paid: All considerations provided to be paid under each and all the agreements, licenses or other documents relating to the production of the Picture have been paid in full, or otherwise discharged in full, and there is no existing, outstanding obligation whatsoever, either present or future, under any of said contracts, agreements, assignments or other documents, unless disclosed in Schedule "A."

(j) Full Performance: All terms, covenants and conditions required to be kept or performed by Production Company under each and all of the contracts, licenses or other documents relating to the production of the Picture have been kept and performed and will hereafter be kept and performed by Production Company, and there is no existing breach or other act of default by Production Company under any such agreement, license or other document, nor will there be any such breach or default during the term hereof.

(k) No Release/No Banning: Neither the Picture nor any part thereof has been released, distributed or exhibited in any media whatsoever in the Territory nor has it been banned by the censors of or refused import permits for any portion of the Territory.

(l) Valid Copyright: The copyright in the Picture and the literary, dramatic and musical material upon which it is based or which is contained in the Picture will be valid and subsisting during the Distribution Term (as extended) with respect to each country or place of the Territory, and no part of any thereof is in the public domain.

(m) Peaceful Enjoyment: Distributor will quietly and peacefully enjoy and possess each and all of the rights, licenses and privileges herein granted or purported to be granted to Distributor throughout the Distribution Term (as extended) for each country or place of the Territory without interference by any third party.

(n) Guild Union Performing-Rights Society Participation Payments: Any payments required to be made to any performing-rights society or to any body or group representing authors, composers, musicians, artists, any other participants in the production of the Picture, publishers or other persons having legal or contractual rights of any kind to participate in the receipts of the Picture or to payments of any kind as a result of the distribution or exhibition of the Picture, and any taxes thereon or on the payment thereof will be made by Production Company or by the exhibitors and need not be paid by Distributor.

(o) Music Performing Rights: The Performing rights to all musical compositions contained in the Picture are: (i) controlled by the American Society of Composers, Authors and Publishers (ASCAP), Broadcast Music, Inc. (BMI), or similar organizations in other countries such as the Japanese Society of Rights of Authors and Composers (JASEAC), the Performing Right Society Ltd. (PRS), the Society of European Stage Authors and Composers (SESAC), the Societe des Auteurs Compositeurs et Editeurs de Musique (SACEM), Gesellscraft fur Misikalische Auffuhrungs und Mechanische Vervielfaltigunsrechte (GEMA) or their affiliates, or (ii) in the public domain in the Territory, or (iii) controlled by Production Company to the extent required for the purposes of this Agreement and Production Company similarly controls or has licenses for any necessary synchronization and recording rights.

(p) Television Restriction: The Picture will not be exhibited in or telecast in or cablecast in or into the Territory during

DEALMAKING
IN THE
FILM AND
TELEVISION
INDUSTRY

234

the Distribution Term for each country or place of the Territory by any one other than Distributor or its licensees.

(q) Authority Relative to this Agreement: Production Company has taken all action necessary to duly and validly authorize its signature and performance of this Agreement and the grant of the rights, licenses and privileges herein granted and agreed to be granted.

(r) Financial Condition: Production Company is not presently involved in financial difficulties as evidenced by its not having admitted its inability to pay its debts generally as they become due or otherwise not having acknowledged its insolvency or by its not having filed or consented to a petition in bankruptcy or for reorganization or for the adoption of an arrangement under Federal Bankruptcy Act (or under any similar law of the United States or any other jurisdiction, which relates to liquidation or reorganization of companies or to the modification or alteration of the rights of creditors) or by its not being involved in any bankruptcy, liquidation, or other similar proceeding relating to Production Company or its assets, whether pursuant to statute or general rule of law, nor does Production Company presently contemplate any such proceeding or have any reason to believe that any such proceeding will be brought against it or its assets.

(s) Litigation: To Production Company's knowledge, there is no litigation, proceeding or claim pending or threatened against Production Company which may materially adversely affect Production Company's exclusive rights in and to the Picture, the copyright pertaining thereto or the rights, licenses and privileges granted to Distributor hereunder.

5. INDEMNITY: Production Company does hereby and shall at all times indemnify and hold harmless Distributor, its subdistributors and licensees, its and their officers, directors and employees, and its and their exhibitors, licensees and assignees, of and from any and all charges, claims, damages, costs, judgments, decrees, losses, expenses (including reasonable attorneys' fees), penalties, demands, liabilities and causes of action, whether or not groundless, of any kind or nature whatsoever by reason of, based upon, relating to, or arising out of a breach or claim of breach or failure of any of the covenants, agreements, representations or warranties of Production Company hereunder or by reason of any claims,

actions or proceedings asserted or instituted, relating to or arising out of any such breach or failure or conduct or activity resulting in a breach or claim of breach. All rights and remedies hereunder shall be cumulative and shall not interfere with or prevent the exercise of any other right or remedy which may be available to Distributor. Upon notice from Distributor of any such claim, demand or action being advanced or commenced, Production Company agrees to adjust, settle or defend the same at the sole cost of Production Company. If Production Company shall fail to do so, Distributor shall have the right and is hereby authorized and empowered by Production Company to appear by its attorneys in any such claim, demand or action, to adjust, settle, compromise, litigate, contest, satisfy judgments and take any other action necessary or desirable for the disposition of such claim, demand or action. In any such case, Production Company, within 20 days after demand by Distributor, shall fully reimburse Distributor for all such payments and expenses, including reasonable attorneys' fees. If Production Company shall fail so to reimburse Distributor, then, without waiving its right to otherwise enforce such reimbursement, Distributor shall have the right to deduct the said amount of such payments and expenses, or any part thereof, from any sums accruing under this Agreement or any other agreement, to or for the account of Production Company. Also, in the event of any matter to which the foregoing indemnity relates, Distributor shall have the right to withhold from disbursements to or for the account of Production Company a sum which in Distributor's opinion may be reasonably necessary to satisfy any liability or settlement in connection with such matter, plus a reasonable amount to cover the expenses of contesting or defending such claim and shall have the further right to apply the amount withheld to the satisfaction of such liability or settlement and to reimbursement of such expenses.

6. COPYRIGHT:

(a) Ownership: Production Company warrants that Production Company has not heretofore transferred its ownership in and to all copyrights pertaining to the Picture throughout the world, including without limitation the rights to secure copyright registration anywhere in the world with respect to all copyrights in the Picture and to secure any renewals and extensions thereof wherever and whenever

DEALMAKING
IN THE
FILM AND
TELEVISION
INDUSTRY

236

permitted. Production Company warrants that upon delivery of the Picture to Distributor, Production Company will own all copyrights in the Picture throughout the world for the full period of copyright and all extensions and renewals thereof. The negative of the Picture shall contain a copyright notice complying with all statutory requirements of the copyright laws of the United States or any country which is a party to the Berne Union or Universal Copyright Convention, such notice to appear in the main or end titles of the Picture. Production Company and Distributor shall not have the right to change the copyright notice contained in the Picture.

(b) Defense of Copyright: Distributor hereby agrees to take all reasonable steps to protect such copyrights from infringement by unauthorized parties and in particular, at the request of Production Company, to take such action and proceedings as may be reasonable to prevent any unauthorized use, reproduction, performance, exhibition or exploitation by third Parties of the Picture or any part thereof or the material on which it is based which may be in contravention of the exclusive rights granted to Distributor in respect to the Picture.

For the purpose of permitting Distributor to defend and enforce all rights and remedies granted to Distributor hereunder, and to prevent any unauthorized use, reproduction, performance, exhibition or exploitation of the Picture or any part thereof or the material on which it is based, Production Company hereby irrevocably appoints Distributor its sole and exclusive attorney-in-fact, to act in Production Company's name or otherwise. Distributor agrees (consistent with commercially acceptable practices in the Motion Picture industry), in its own name or in the name of Production Company, to take all reasonable steps to enforce and protect the rights, licenses and privileges herein granted, under any law and under any and all copyrights, renewals and extensions thereof, and to prevent the infringement thereof, and to bring, prosecute, defend and appear in suits, actions and proceedings of any nature under or concerning all copyrights in the Picture and to settle claims and collect and receive all damages arising from any infringement of or interference with any and all such rights, and in the sole judgment of Distributor exercised in good faith to join Production Company as a party plaintiff or defendant in such suit, action or proceeding.

Production Company hereby irrevocably appoints Distributor as its sole and exclusive attorney-in-fact, during the Term of this Agreement, with full and irrevocable power and authority to secure, register, renew and extend all copyrights in the Picture and all related properties upon each thereof becoming eligible for copyright, registration, renewal and extension.

(c) Limitation of Liability: Distributor shall not be liable, responsible or accountable in damages or otherwise to Production Company for any action or failure to act on behalf of Production Company within the scope of authority conferred on Distributor under this Clause 8, unless such action or omission was performed or omitted fraudulently or in bad faith or constituted wanton and willful misconduct or gross negligence.

7. ERRORS AND OMISSIONS INSURANCE: As provided in Exhibit 2, Distributor shall obtain and maintain, or cause to be obtained and maintained throughout the Distribution Term (as extended), Motion Picture Distributor Errors and Omissions insurance in a form acceptable to Production Company, from a qualified insurance company acceptable to Production Company, naming Distributor and Production Company and each and all the parties indemnified herein as additional named insureds. The amount and coverage shall be for a minimum of $1,000,000/$3,000,000 with respect to any one or more claims relating to the Picture, or if Distributor pays an advance, the amount of the advance, whichever shall be greater. The policy shall provide for a deductible no greater than $10,000 and thirty (30) days notice to Production Company before any modification, cancellation or termination.

8. INSTRUMENTS OF FURTHER ASSURANCE: Production Company shall execute and deliver to Distributor, promptly upon the request of Distributor therefore, any other instruments or documents considered by Distributor to be necessary or desirable to evidence, effectuate or confirm this Agreement, or any of its terms and conditions.

9. NO DISTRIBUTOR REPRESENTATIONS AND WARRANTIES: Production Company acknowledges and agrees that Distributor makes no express or implied representation, warranty, guaranty or agreement as to the gross receipts to be derived from the Picture or the distribution, exhibition or exploitation thereof, nor does Distributor guarantee the performance by any

DEALMAKING
IN THE
FILM AND
TELEVISION
INDUSTRY

238

subdistributor, licensee or exhibitor of any contract for the distribution, exhibition or exploitation of the Picture, nor does Distributor make any representation, warranty, guaranty or agreement as to any minimum amount of monies to be expended for the distribution, advertising, publicizing and exploitation of the Picture. Production Company recognizes and acknowledges that the amount of gross receipts that may be realized from the distribution, exhibition and exploitation of the Picture is speculative, and agrees that the reasonable business judgment exercised in good faith of Distributor and its subdistributors and licensees regarding any matter affecting the distribution, exhibition and exploitation of the Picture shall be binding and conclusive upon Production Company.

10. DISTRIBUTION AND EXPLOITATION OF THE PICTURE: Distributor shall have the complete, exclusive and unqualified control of the distribution, exhibition, exploitation and other disposition of the Picture (directly or by any subdistributor or licensee) in the media granted to Distributor hereunder throughout the Territory during the Distribution Term with respect to each country or place, in accordance with such sales methods, plans, patterns, programs, policies, terms and conditions as Distributor in its reasonable business judgment may determine proper or expedient. The enumeration of the following rights of distribution and exploitation shall in no way limit the generality or effect of the foregoing:

(a) Terms: Distributor may determine the manner and terms upon which the Picture shall be marketed, distributed, licensed, exhibited, exploited or otherwise disposed of, and all matters pertaining thereto and the decision of Distributor on all such matters shall be final and conclusive. Production Company shall have no control whatsoever in or over (i) the manner or extent to which Distributor or its subdistributors or licensees shall exploit the Picture, (ii) the terms and provisions of any licenses granted by Distributor to third Parties or (iii) to the sufficiency or insufficiency of proceeds from the Picture.

(b) Refrain from Distribution, Exhibition or Exploitation. Distributor may refrain from the release, distribution, re-issue or exhibition of the Picture at any time, in any country, place or location of the Territory, in any media, or in any form. Production Company acknowledges that there is no obligation to exploit the soundtrack recording rights or music publishing rights or merchandising rights or literary publishing rights, it being agreed that Distributor may elect to exercise any or all of said rights as Distributor in its sole business judgment exercised in good faith may determine.

(c) "Outright Sales": Distributor may make outright sales of the Picture as Distributor in good faith may determine. Only net monies actually received and earned by Distributor with respect to outright sales of the Picture shall be included within gross film rentals.

(d) Contracts and Settlements: Distributor may distribute the Picture under existing or future franchise or license contracts, which contracts may relate to the Picture separately or to the Picture and one or more other Motion Pictures distributed by or through Distributor. Distributor may, in the exercise of its reasonable business judgment, exercised in good faith, make, alter or cancel contracts with exhibitors, subdistributors and other licensees and adjust and settle disputes, make allowances and adjustments and give credits with respect thereto.

(e) Means of Release: Distributor may exhibit or cause the Picture to be exhibited in theatres or other places owned, controlled, leased or managed by Distributor. Distributor may enter into any agreement or arrangement with any other major distributor for the distribution by such other major distributor of all or a substantial portion of Distributor's theatrical motion pictures. Distributor may also enter into any agreement or arrangement with any other major distributor or any other party for the handling of the shipping and inspection activities of Distributor's exchanges or the handling of other facilities in connection with the distribution of motion pictures.

(f) Time of Release: The initial release of the Picture in any part of the Territory shall commence on such date or dates as Distributor or its subdistributors or licensees in their respective sole judgment and discretion may determine. Such releases shall be subject to the requirements of censorship boards or other governmental authorities, the availability of playing time in key cities, the securing of the requisite number of motion picture copies, and delays caused by

DEALMAKING
IN THE
FILM AND
TELEVISION
INDUSTRY

240

reason of events of force majeure or by reason of any cause beyond the control of Distributor or its subdistributors or licensees. If any claim or action is made or instituted against Distributor or any of its subdistributors or licensees as to the Picture, Distributor or such subdistributors or licensees shall have the right to postpone the release of the Picture (if it has not then been released) or to suspend further distribution thereof (if it has been released) until such time as such claim or action shall have been settled or disposed of to the satisfaction of Distributor or such subdistributors or licensees.

(g) Duration of Release: Distribution of the Picture shall be continued in the Territory or any part thereof in which it is released by Distributor or its licensees only for _____ years. Distributor shall not be obligated to reissue the Picture at any time in the Territory but shall have the right to do so from time to time as it may deem desirable.

(h) Withdrawal of the Picture: Should Distributor or its subdistributors or licensees deem it inadvisable or unprofitable to distribute, exhibit or exploit the Picture in the Territory or any part thereof, Distributor or its subdistributors or licensees shall have the right to withhold or withdraw the Picture from such Territory or any part thereof.

(i) Banning of Release: If by reason of any law, embargo, decree, regulation or other restriction of any agency or governmental body, the number or type of motion pictures that Distributor is permitted to distribute in the Territory or any part thereof is limited, then Distributor may in its absolute discretion determine which motion pictures then distributed by Distributor will be distributed in the Territory or any part thereof, and Distributor shall not be liable to Production Company in any manner or to any extent if the Picture is not distributed in the Territory or any part thereof by reason of any such determination.

(j) Collections: Distributor shall in good faith every six months audit, check or verify the computation of any payments and press for the collection of any monies which, if collected, would constitute gross receipts. There shall be no responsibility or liability to Production Company for failure to audit, check, or verify or to collect any monies payable.

(k) Advertising: Distributor agrees to commit a minimum of $_____ to the advertising and publicity of the Picture.

(l) Expenses: Distributor may incur any expenses which Distributor, in the good faith exercise of its reasonable business judgment, deems appropriate with respect to the Picture or the exercise of any of Distributor's rights hereunder.

(m) No Preferential Treatment: Anything herein contained to the contrary notwithstanding, Production Company agrees that nothing herein shall require Distributor to prefer the Picture over any other motion picture distributed by Distributor or shall restrict or limit in any way Distributor's full right to distribute other motion pictures of any nature or description whether similar or dissimilar to the Picture.

11. IMPORT PERMITS: Distributor shall be under no duty to obtain any necessary licenses and permits for the importation and distribution of the Picture in any country or locality nor to utilize for the Picture any licenses or permits available to Distributor in limited quantity. Production Company shall, on request, use its best efforts to secure for Distributor any such licenses or permits. Distributor shall be entitled to the benefit of all import and/or export licenses and/ or quotas and/or similar benefits of Production Company with respect to the Picture which would entitle the Picture to be imported into any country or territory.

12. MOTION PICTURE PRINTS: Distributor shall be entitled to obtain such prints, dupe negatives and master prints of the Picture which Distributor shall deem advisable for distribution of the Picture in the Territory. All such prints shall remain the property of Distributor.

13. CENSORSHIP OR FORCE MAJEURE:

(a) Adjustment of Advance: If Distributor is required to pay or advance to Production Company any fixed or other sum before it is collected from the distribution of the Picture, and Distributor is unable to distribute the Picture in any country or area of the Territory for any reason, including without limitation, censorship, import restriction, force majeure or failure to secure permits, the fixed payment or advance shall be reduced by the amount reasonably allocable to such country or area. The amount allocable to such country or area shall be the amount indicated in Schedule "A" or in the

DEALMAKING
IN THE
FILM AND
TELEVISION
INDUSTRY

242

absence of such indication in Schedule "A," or if the country or area where distribution is prevented is one to which no allocation is made or which is a part of a country or area for which an overall allocation is made, then a reasonable allocation shall be made by Distributor for such country or area in which distribution is prevented. If the Picture is classified as unsuitable for children under 18 years of age or suitable for adults only in any country or area, the fixed payment or advance payable for such country or area shall be reduced by _____ percent.

(b) Adjustment of Distribution Expenses: If Distributor is for any reason unable to distribute the Picture in any country or area of the Territory and Distributor has incurred any Distribution Expenses in connection with the distribution of the Picture in such country or area, Producer will, on demand reimburse Distributor therefore or, at Distributor's election, Distributor shall be repaid by Production Company from any sum thereafter due from Distributor to Production Company.

14. DISTRIBUTOR'S DEFAULT: Production Company shall not be entitled to bring any action, suit or proceeding of any nature against Distributor or its subdistributors or licensees, whether at law or in equity or otherwise, based upon or arising from in whole or in part any claim that Distributor or its subdistributors or licensees has in any way violated this Agreement, unless the action is brought within one (1) year from the date of Production Company's discovery of such alleged violation. It is agreed that if Distributor breaches this Agreement and fails to begin to remedy such breach within a period of thirty (30) days after receipt by Distributor of written notice from Production Company specifying the alleged breach and fails to cure such breach within sixty (60) days thereafter, or if after delivery of the Picture, Distributor shall fail to make any payments at the time and in the manner provided and Production Company has given Distributor ten (10) days written notice to that effect, then in either of such events, Production Company shall have the right to proceed against Distributor for monies due to Production Company in accordance with any and all remedies available to Production Company both at law and in equity. In no event, however, shall Production Company have any right to terminate or rescind this Agreement, nor shall the rights acquired by

Distributor under this Agreement be subject to revocation, termination or diminution because of any failure or breach of any kind on the part of Distributor or its subdistributors or licensees. In no event shall Production Company be entitled to an injunction to restrain any alleged breach by Distributor or its subdistributors or licensees of any provisions of this Agreement.

15. ARBITRATION: Any controversy or claim arising out of or relating to this agreement or any breach thereof shall be settled by arbitration in accordance with the Rules of the American Arbitration Association; and judgment upon the award rendered by the arbitrators may be entered in any court having jurisdiction thereof. The prevailing party shall be entitled to reimbursement for costs and reasonable attorneys' fees. The determination of the arbitrator in such proceeding shall be final, binding and non-appealable.

16. WAIVER: No waiver of any breach of any provision of this Agreement shall constitute a waiver of any other breach of the same or any other provision hereof, and no waiver shall be effective unless made in writing.

17. RELATIONSHIP OF PARTIES: Nothing herein contained shall be construed to create a joint venture or partnership between the parties hereto. Neither of the parties shall hold itself out contrary to the terms of this provision, by advertising or otherwise, nor shall Distributor or Production Company be bound or become liable because of any representations, actions or omissions of the other.

18. ASSIGNMENT: Distributor may assign this Agreement to and/or may distribute the Picture through any of its subsidiaries, parents, or affiliated corporations or any agent, instrumentality or other means determined by Distributor, provided that Distributor shall not thereby be relieved of the fulfillment of its obligations hereunder. Production Company may assign the right to receive payment hereunder to any third party; provided, however, that Production Company shall not be permitted to assign any of its obligations hereunder.

19. NOTICES: All notices from Production Company or Distributor to the other, with respect to this Agreement, shall be given in writing by mailing or telegraphing the notice pre-

DEALMAKING
IN THE
FILM AND
TELEVISION
INDUSTRY

244

paid, return receipt requested, and addressed to Distributor or Production Company, as appropriate, at the address set forth in the preamble hereof. A courtesy copy of any notice to Production Company shall be sent to _____ , and a courtesy copy of any notice to Distributor shall be sent to _____ .

20. GOVERNING LAW: This Agreement shall be governed by the laws of the State of California, without giving effect to principles of conflict of laws thereof.

21. CAPTIONS: The captions of the various paragraphs and sections of the Agreement are intended to be used solely for convenience of reference and are not intended and shall not be deemed for any purpose whatsoever to modify or explain or to be used as an aid in the construction of any provisions.

22. AMENDMENTS IN WRITING: This Agreement cannot be amended, modified or changed in any way whatsoever except by a written instrument duly signed by authorized officers of Production Company and Distributor.

23. ENTIRE AGREEMENT: This Agreement, which is comprised of the general terms above ("Main Agreement") and the attached Schedule and Exhibits, represents the entire agreement between the parties with respect to the subject matter hereof, and this Agreement supersedes all previous representations, understandings or agreements, oral or written, between the parties regarding the subject matter hereof.

By signing in the spaces provided below, the parties accept and agree to all the terms and conditions of this Agreement as of the date first above written.

_____
("Production Company")
By
Its

_____
("Distributor")
By
Its

CHAPTER 10

NEGOTIATING TACTICS & STRATEGIES[1]

The top Hollywood dealmakers are sometimes referred to as "players." These agents, attorneys, studio executives and producers regularly conduct business with one another and observe an unwritten code of behavior. While players are admired for being tough and shrewd, dishonesty is not respected.

For an industry with a reputation for chicanery, outsiders may be surprised to find that many players take great pride in keeping their word. They make oral agreements with one another that are relied upon by their clients. An agent may commit his client to a project, and the written contract may not be signed until the project has been completed.

The honor code among players does permit a certain amount of hype and exaggeration. Agents talking about a client will stress the positive and ignore the negative. Other shenanigans are allowed, although these tactics may only work against the uninitiated.

HIGH-BALLING is asking for an excessive amount of money or staking out an extreme position in order to position oneself favorably for compromise. If a fair fee for an actor would be

---

[1] Portions of this chapter are derived from the author's prior work *Reel Power*.

DEALMAKING
IN THE
FILM AND
TELEVISION
INDUSTRY

246

$80,000, a request for $180,000 leaves plenty of room to compromise and still walk away with a good deal. If the other side counters with an unreasonably low bid, the stage is set for a protracted struggle.

LOW-BALLING is suggesting an unduly low amount. In attempting to persuade a studio to produce a picture, producers may give a low estimate of its budget. The producer may reason that once the studio is committed to a picture, and has invested a significant amount of money, it will be loathe to shut down a production if it goes over budget. However, if the producer has agreed to an EAT-IN CLAUSE, the studio may have the last laugh. An eat-in clause provides that a producer's profits and/or fees are eaten into if the film goes over budget.

High-balling and low-balling tactics don't work against experienced negotiators since they understand how salaries are set. The unwritten rule is that everyone is entitled to a modest raise over what they earned on their last deal. Salary information is hard to keep secret, so the parameters within which to negotiate are fairly narrow. Unless the artist has recently won an Academy Award or starred in a blockbuster film, he ordinarily cannot obtain a substantial increase in his fee.

Creating confusion is a technique some dealmakers use. If one party does not understand what is being discussed—and is too embarrassed to ask for clarification—it is difficult for him to protect his interests. Some people create confusion by being long-winded or going off on tangents. Some deals are so complex that no additional confusion need be added. Parties should always carefully read each draft to make sure the agreed changes have been made. As a courtesy, the drafting attorney will often send a "red-lined copy" showing changes from the previous draft.

Intimidation can be another ploy. Strong-arm tactics work only when one's opponent needs a deal so badly that he will submit to such abuse. This tactic is usually avoided among players because they deal with each other regularly. "[If] I use leverage and kill somebody, tomorrow he is going to kill me," says attorney Eric Weissmann. "In the old days negotiating was filled with much more histrionics. There was much more ranting and raving and screaming, barring people from the lot, and fistfights. . . . [Today] people try to reason with each other."

Even insanity can be useful, it being difficult to negotiate with the insane. "If one person is nuts, then he cannot be reached logically and the other person . . . who is desperately trying to reach him is already at a disadvantage," says Weissmann, who adds that the approach works best when the party is truly insane, since it's a hard thing to fake.

Bursts of irrational behavior can be useful. "There's nothing more unsettling when you are negotiating with someone and they do something completely unexpected," says Weissmann. "When I was a young lawyer . . . I was negotiating with the head of the legal department at a studio, who buzzed the secretary and told her to call the studio police and have me escorted from the place and to bar me from the lot forever. Well I decided right then that I didn't feel that strongly about the point."

A variation of these last two approaches could be called "my boss is insane." A negotiator will concede his opponent's position is reasonable but profess that he cannot agree to it because his employer is crazy. It is tough to argue with some-one who agrees with you and denounces the person he repre-sents.

Even silence can be a negotiating ploy. If it makes the other party uncomfortable, he may talk himself into compromising his position. A similar passive technique is for a negotiator never to propose solutions but to maneuver the conversation so that the other party suggests them.

The best negotiators are versatile, employing tactics appropri-ate to the situation and the personality of their counterpart. Often first encounters are a time of testing. Parties who regu-larly deal with each other, however, don't engage in a lot of gamesmanship.

The best dealmakers are not necessarily those who make the toughest demands. An attorney may build a reputation for being tough, but it is often at the expense of clients who suffer the consequences of blown deals. An attorney who has the client's best interests at heart will try to obtain the optimum deal available under the circumstances and will not blow a deal unless that is what the client wants.

DEALMAKING
IN THE
FILM AND
TELEVISION
INDUSTRY

248

TECHNIQUES TO INDUCE A STUDIO TO MAKE A DEAL

Here are some gambits that can be used to lure a studio into a development or production deal. Considering that these techniques have been around a long time, it is surprising that they still work. One would think that at some point everyone would wise up to them.

When a studio executive knows that OTHER BUYERS ARE INTERESTED in a project, his interest often grows exponentially. I suppose a Columbia executive who learns that his counterpart at Fox is actively pursuing you figures that you must be worth pursuing. Pretty soon you have several suitors fighting over you, and that can produce a lucrative deal.

Of course, one cannot directly inform a Columbia executive of Fox's interest in your project. The Columbia executive might ask, "If Fox is so interested in the project, how come you are here talking with us instead of making the movie at Fox?"

So the masters of this technique use the trade papers and the grapevine to spread the word that they have a hot project. With smoke and mirrors, and gossip and innuendo, they try to generate the illusion that they have something desirable. Their goal is to get several buyers into a feeding frenzy, and auction the project off to the highest bidder.

Another gambit capitalizes on studio executives' desire to SEE A PROJECT FIRST. Everyone wants a first look or at least an early look at a project. So if your screenplay has been making the rounds for a couple of years and is looking kind of ragged, you would be well advised to make a fresh photocopy. If your script looks like it has been rejected everywhere, buyers may assume that it can't be any good.

Remember that evaluating a screenplay is subjective and some people don't trust their own instincts. A common phenomenon is for a new writer to labor many years submitting scripts in an attempt to break into the industry. Then the writer sells his sixth screenplay to Steven Spielberg or another reputable buyer. Suddenly his old screenplays sell like hotcakes. Did those old screenplays on the shelf get better with age, like fine wine? Of course not. The sale to Spielberg gave this writer the imprimatur of success. Buyers now view his work in a different light. The unspoken assumption is, "If Spielberg bought a script from this guy, he must be good." The same screenplay that was rejected six months ago is now enthusiastically received.

Everyone loves a BARGAIN, including studio executives. Stars will sometimes agree to do a favorite project for scale wages. Such movies are often prestige films that cost little and have the potential of winning an Oscar. Status-hungry executives also like these projects.

Executives are often attracted to a HOT TOPIC. A story off the front page of the newspaper or a subject that "everybody is talking about" can be easier to market because the public is already aware of it. Studios will avoid topical stories, however, if they think television will tackle the subject first. Television movies can be produced in less than a year, while features generally take several years to develop and produce. No studio will want to invest a lot of money developing a story that is likely to appear on television first.

How then does one distinguish those stories appropriate for television from those meant to be features? Sexy or violent subject matter may prevent the networks from tackling certain stories. The most important difference, however, is budget. The typical network movie costs $2 to $3 million while feature films often cost more than $20 million. Any story that involves numerous locations, expensive sets, special effects, herds of wild animals, costly costumes or crowds of extras is probably too expensive to be made for television.

BUILDING RELATIONSHIPS: Savvy dealmakers know that the motives of studios differ from their executives. Studios want to make hit movies for as little money as possible. To some extent, studio executives want the same. However, realizing that their tenure is limited, executives want to prepare for their next job. That job is often as an independent producer, sometimes affiliated with the same studio they used to work for. What is important to these executives? They want to build relationships with important stars, directors and writers. As one executive told me, "Working as a studio executive is like going to producer school."

Thus, a smart dealmaker knows that one way to make a

DEALMAKING
IN THE
FILM AND
TELEVISION
INDUSTRY

250

project appealing to a studio executive is to present it as an opportunity for the executive to develop a relationship with an up-and-coming star. The executive may want to develop the project, because it presents an opportunity to have several meetings with the talent and forge a strong relationship.

Similarly, studios may develop or produce a project just to placate a star with whom the studio has an important relationship. What is a few hundred thousand dollars in development expenses if it keeps a major star happy and earning the studio millions of dollars?

Finally, keep in mind that experienced dealmakers always want to appear passionate about their project, but they never want to appear desperate to make a deal. The best attitude is one of great determination. You would love to work with the studio, but if they pass on your project, you intend to pursue it elsewhere. Sometimes playing hard-to-get can be useful. When an executive asks to read a screenplay and the producer tries to keep it under wraps, the executive's appetite may be whetted.

CHAPTER 11

CREATIVE ACCOUNTING

ART BUCHWALD V. PARAMOUNT

Art Buchwald was angry. The Pulitzer Prize-winning columnist had just seen the movie *Coming to America* while vacationing in Martha's Vineyard. The Paramount picture was about an African prince, played by Eddie Murphy, who came to America to find a bride. It seemed similar to a story Buchwald had optioned to Paramount several years earlier, a project the studio had developed for Eddie Murphy.

Buchwald's story, *King for a Day*, as written in his three-page treatment, was about an extremely wealthy, handsome and spoiled young emperor from an oil-rich African country who comes to Washington and is stranded after losing his throne and wealth in a coup d'état staged in his absence. The King must cope with life in the ghetto, where he works a menial job and falls in love with a former CIA call girl. Eventually he is able to reclaim his throne, return home and make the former call girl his queen.

Under Buchwald's agreement with Paramount, he was entitled to receive a fixed fee of $65,000 plus 1½% of the net profits if a film based on his story was made. Alain Bernheim signed a similar deal with the studio to produce the project; he was set to receive a fee of $200,000 and 17½% of the net

DEALMAKING
IN THE
FILM AND
TELEVISION
INDUSTRY

252

profits. Buchwald and Bernheim received $42,500 during the two years the story was in development at Paramount.

The film grossed more than $128 million the year it was released, making it the third-highest-grossing film of 1988. But neither Buchwald nor Bernheim received any further compensation, and Buchwald didn't receive a screen credit because Eddie Murphy claimed he had conceived the story.

Murphy earned $8 million for his starring role in the movie as well as 15% of Paramount's gross revenues from the film—an astronomical sum in light of the combined salaries of the rest of the cast: $906,000. Since the film's release, Murphy's salary has risen to a cool $9 million per picture. Nevertheless, he was reportedly dissatisfied with his five-picture deal at Paramount.

In 1987, Bernheim lunched with Paramount production chief Ned Tanen in the studio commissary and accused Paramount of stealing Buchwald's story. The conversation quickly degenerated into a heated disagreement and the two have not spoken since. Buchwald and Bernheim discussed the matter and decided they might have to sue.

TERMS

EACH STUDIO CAN DEFINE THE TERMS USED IN ITS AGREEMENTS AS IT LIKES. THERE ARE NO INDUSTRY-WIDE DEFINITIONS FOR "GROSS," "ADJUSTED GROSS" OR "NET" DEALS. WHAT ONE STUDIO CALLS AN ADJUSTED GROSS DEAL, ANOTHER CALLS A NET DEAL. BEFORE YOU CELEBRATE THE "GROSS" DEAL YOU OBTAINED, CHECK THE FINE PRINT AND SEE HOW THE TERM IS DEFINED.

GENERALLY, INDUSTRY TERMS ARE DEFINED AS FOLLOWS:

BOX OFFICE RECEIPTS: WHAT THE THEATER OWNER TAKES IN FROM TICKET SALES TO CUSTOMERS AT THE BOX OFFICE.

FILM RENTAL: WHAT THE THEATER OWNER PAYS THE DISTRIBUTOR FOR THE RIGHT TO SHOW THE MOVIE.

GROSS RECEIPTS: ALL REVENUES DERIVED FROM ALL MEDIA, INCLUDING FILM RENTALS, TELEVISION SALES, MERCHANDISING AND ANCILLARY SALES. THE AMOUNT OF REVENUES CONTRIBUTED BY HOME VIDEO SALES, HOWEVER, IS TYPICALLY ONLY 20% OF WHOLESALE.

GROSS PARTICIPATION: A PIECE OF GROSS RECEIPTS WITHOUT ANY DEDUCTIONS FOR DISTRIBUTION FEES OR EXPENSES OR PRODUCTION COSTS. HOWEVER, DEDUCTIONS FOR CHECKING AND COLLECTION COSTS, RESIDUALS AND TAXES ARE USUALLY TAKEN.

ADJUSTED GROSS PARTICIPATION: GROSS PARTICIPATION MINUS CERTAIN COSTS, SUCH AS COST OF ADVERTISING AND DUPLICATION.

ADVANCES: UP-FRONT PAYMENT THAT COUNTS AGAINST MONIES THAT MAY BE PAYABLE AT SOME TIME IN THE FUTURE. NON-RECOUPABLE ADVANCES ARE PAYMENTS THAT ARE NOT REFUNDABLE, EVEN IF FUTURE MONIES ARE NEVER DUE.

CONTINUED

First, however, Buchwald told his friend, Paramount Communications, Inc., Chairman Martin Davis, what had happened and of his intention to sue the studio. Davis responded by sending the writer a bottle of champagne and a record of a song titled "Sue Me." Buchwald did, and then promptly went on the Larry King radio show to denounce the film.

The trial gave outsiders a rare glimpse into the highest echelons of studio decision making. Buchwald and Bernheim asked the court for $5 million in damages for breach of contract as well as unspecified punitive damages. Paramount responded that *Coming to America* was not based on Buchwald's story. Furthermore, the studio said that even if the movie was based on the story, Buchwald wasn't due any "net profits" from the film according to the studio's contract with him. The film had generated an estimated $350 million dollars in revenue and was one of the top twenty highest-grossing movies of the decade.

Hollywood writers and other net-profit participants have long complained that studios engaged in creative accounting, cheating them out of participating in "profits." But most writers just grumble because they don't have the financial means to finance a protracted legal struggle, and attorneys often don't want to take such cases on a

TERMS (CONTINUED)

NET PROFIT: WHAT IS LEFT, IF ANYTHING, AFTER ALL ALLOWABLE DEDUCTIONS ARE TAKEN. THIS USUALLY AMOUNTS TO ZERO. TYPICALLY EXPRESSED IN TERMS OF 100% OF NET PROFITS, ALTHOUGH PAYABLE OUT OF THE PRODUCER'S SHARE (E.G., OUT OF HIS 50%).

THEATRICAL DISTRIBUTION FEES: GENERALLY BETWEEN 30% AND 40% OF GROSS RECEIPTS.

DOUBLE DISTRIBUTION FEES: WHERE DISTRIBUTOR USES A SUB-DISTRIBUTOR TO SELL TO A TERRITORY. IF BOTH DISTRIBUTORS ARE ALLOWED TO DEDUCT THEIR FULL FEES, THE FILMMAKER IS UNLIKELY TO SEE ANY MONEY.

TELEVISION DISTRIBUTION FEE: TYPICALLY 10% FOR NETWORK BROADCAST, 35% TO 40% FOR DOMESTIC SYNDICATION AND 45% TO 50% FOR FOREIGN DISTRIBUTION. MANY FILMMAKERS CONSIDER THESE FEES EXCESSIVE SINCE THE STUDIO DOESN'T INCUR A LOT OF EXPENSE TO DISTRIBUTE TO TELEVISION. THERE ARE MINIMAL DUPLICATION EXPENSES (I.E., THE STUDIO SENDS ONE VIDEO COPY TO THE BUYER).

DISTRIBUTION EXPENSES: INCLUDES TAXES, GUILD PAYMENTS, TRADE ASSOCIATION DUES, CONVERSION/TRANSMISSION COSTS, COLLECTION COSTS, CHECKING COSTS, ADVERTISING AND PUBLICITY COSTS, RE-EDITING COSTS, PRINTS, FOREIGN-VERSION COSTS, TRANSPORTATION AND SHIPPING COSTS, COPYRIGHT COSTS, COPYRIGHT-INFRINGEMENT COSTS, INSURANCE, ROYALTIES, AND LAWSUITS.

DEALMAKING
IN THE
FILM AND
TELEVISION
INDUSTRY

254

contigent-fee basis. Besides, many writers fear that instigating such a suit might make them unemployable.

Buchwald, however, was a nationally syndicated columnist and a wealthy man who didn't need the movie industry for his livelihood. Over the years he had written ten movie treatments, none of which were produced, but it didn't much matter because movie writing was merely a diversion for him. He could afford to challenge the studios on behalf of all writers.

Executives at other studios quietly griped that Paramount's refusal to settle the lawsuit could result in a legal precedent that would have disastrous repercussions for the industry. Insiders speculated that Paramount, on its own, would have preferred to quietly settle the case. Fear of alienating Eddie Murphy apparently drove the studio to trial.

Although Murphy was not a named party in the suit, his testimony was relevant. The star swore that he and his talk-show-host friend Arsenio Hall had conceived the story for *Coming to America*. But correspondence written by Murphy's manager, Bob Wachs, revealed that he knew Buchwald's story was being developed by Paramount for Murphy.

Other documents obtained through discovery revealed that within a few months of taking an option on Buchwald's story, Paramount began developing the story for Murphy. In a letter stamped "confidential," then-Paramount production head Jeffrey Katzenberg sent John Landis a list of thirteen projects in development for him to consider directing. On that list was *King for a Day*, which was described as a political satire for Eddie Murphy inspired by Art Buchwald.

Paramount spent approximately $500,000 to have screenwriters Tab Murphy and Francis Veber develop Buchwald's story into a

COMING TO AMERICA[1]

PROFIT PARTICIPATION STATEMENT, JUNE 23, 1990

GROSS RECEIPTS:	$140,566,278
LESS UNCOLLECTED BILLINGS:	300,300
LESS STUDIO DISTRIBUTION FEES:	47,137,610
LESS DISTRIBUTION EXPENSES:	38,233,946
BALANCE:	54,894,422
LESS NEGATIVE COST:	62,717,606
INTEREST ON NEGATIVE COST:	7,165,859
BALANCE (NET LOSS):	(14,989,043)

[1] Financial information on *Coming to America* from "Net Profits" by David Robb, *The Hollywood Reporter*, reprint of series appearing from August 17 to September 4, 1992.

screenplay. But when Paramount's management changed in 1985, the new regime let the option on Buchwald's story lapse. Bernheim then sold the story to Warner Bros. under the title *Me and the King.* Warner's spent more than $200,000 developing the concept. When they learned that Paramount had a similarly themed movie in production, they dropped the project.

The trial was presided over by Judge Harvey Schneider, an admitted film buff, who decided all factual issues himself after both sides waived a jury trial. After reviewing the evidence, Schneider ruled that *Coming to America* was based upon Buchwald's story. In a partial victory for Paramount, however, the judge ruled that the plaintiffs were not entitled to punitive damages. The studio had not acted in bad faith or with fraudulent intent, according to Schneider, when it failed to honor its contract with Buchwald and Bernheim. The ruling didn't settle all outstanding issues because now the court had to decide what the plaintiffs' share of net profits was worth. If, as Paramount contended, there were no net profits, Buchwald and his attorney would have won a Pyrrhic victory, having incurred more in legal fees than any recovery from Paramount.[1]

For the second part of the trial, Buchwald's attorney, Pierce O'Donnell, asked the court to invalidate Paramount's definition of net profits on the ground that it was unconscionable. According to O'Donnell, Paramount and other major studios exploit ambiguities in their contracts to the detriment of profit participants. They abuse their "awesome power," he said, by imposing terms on talent which allow the studios to make "hidden profits" and charge "exorbitant interest."

Defenders of the major studios point out that the studios bear all the financial risks of making movies and therefore deserve the lion's share of revenues. Paramount charged that Buchwald was trying to rewrite his agreement after the fact. The studio protested that it had hardly taken advantage of a vulnerable and unsophisticated writer, noting that Buchwald was represented in his negotiations by one of the top executives at the William Morris Agency.

According to Paramount's calculations, the movie cost more than $58 million. Buchwald claimed the studio spent $22.9 million

[1] Since Buchwald's attorney took the case on a contingent fee, the law firm was the big loser.

DEALMAKING
IN THE
FILM AND
TELEVISION
INDUSTRY

256

on the film. He claims that certain payments such as $1 million for Murphy's entourage, $900,000 for excessive fringe benefits and a uniform 15% overhead charge shouldn't be allocated to the production budget. According to Buchwald, $1.65 million of the $8 million in overhead charges was "merely for writing gross-participation checks to Eddie Murphy and [director] John Landis."

Buchwald won his case at the trial level. Paramount has appealed. There is a reasonable chance that Paramount will succeed in overturning the verdict. If Buchwald's contract is unconscionable, then many other contracts could be contested on the same grounds. Generally, courts have refused to rewrite contracts simply because they may be unfair to one party. Otherwise, courts would constantly be asked to intervene in contractual disputes. Hollywood anxiously awaits the outcome of the Buchwald appeal.

CREATIVE ACCOUNTING—TRICKS OF THE TRADE

Creative accounting problems are widespread in the industry. Most films are not profitable by any standard, so the profit participants don't bother with an audit. For those films that do generate significant revenue, audits invariably pay for themselves. Audits usually cost a minimum of $20,000 to $30,000.

There are two types of errors revealed by an audit. The first are clerical errors. For example, a studio accountant added up a row of numbers incorrectly, or expenses were deducted twice. For some mysterious reason, these errors usually favor the studio. Studios often correct such errors without a fuss when the profit participant points them out.

The other type of error arises out of contract interpretation. The philosophy of most studios is "When in doubt, resolve it in our favor and we will fight it out later if it is contested." Despite the great care taken by lawyers to draft contracts, new areas of ambiguity always arise.

Creative-accounting disputes frequently arise when a net-profit participant feels cheated. Gross-profit participants—people who receive a piece of the gross—usually don't experience problems because determining gross revenues is fairly straightforward since few deductions are permitted.

To understand the difference between a "net" and a "gross" deal, let us review the cash flow from ticket sales to the profit participant. BOX OFFICE RECEIPTS is the sum that the theater owner (exhibitor) takes in from ticket sales at the box office. A theater owner is entitled to retain some of these revenues to cover costs and hopefully earn a profit.

The exhibitor/distributor agreement states the terms on which the film is licensed to the exhibitor. For example, the exhibitor may agree to play the film for a minimum of eight weeks and make a guaranteed payment in advance. The agreement also sets the exhibitor's share of box office revenue. If a distributor is releasing a highly desirable picture, the revenues may be split on a 90/10 ratio[1] for the first few weeks. The distributor receives 90% of the revenue, the exhibitor 10%. In subsequent weeks the split may shift to 70/30, 60/40 or 50/50.[2]

A sliding scale gives the exhibitor an incentive to show the picture as long as possible. From the distributor's point of view, as long as the picture is in a theater, there is the possibility that someone may buy a ticket to see it. Once the film is no longer in the theaters, no revenue can be earned from this market.

Before revenues are split, the exhibitor may be allowed to deduct certain expenses or his house NUT. The nut is an amount that is supposed to represent the exhibitor's overhead expenses. This figure is arrived at through negotiation with the distributor, and often it is greater than the actual overhead expenses. In such a case, the figure has some AIR in it. The exhibitor retains 100% of all revenue from the concession stand. This is a major profit center for exhibitors.

After the exhibitor deducts his house nut and splits revenue according to the distribution/exhibition contract, he remits the distributor's share. This payment is called the film RENTAL. Generally, exhibitors retain about half of the box office receipts and pay the other half as rental payments.

The DISTRIBUTOR'S GROSS receipts comprises rentals from all exhibitors and revenue derived from other markets such as television, foreign sales, cable, home video and merchandising.

---

[1] The exhibitor typically gets to deduct his "house nut," or overhead expenses, before the split.

[2] These splits may be without any deduction for the house nut.

DEALMAKING
IN THE
FILM AND
TELEVISION
INDUSTRY

258

Profit participants with a PIECE OF THE GROSS share in gross revenue, although a few deductions like taxes are allowed. Only the top stars and directors have the clout to obtain a piece of the gross. Studios dislike gross deals because gross-profit participants share in revenue from a picture even if the studio has not earned its investment back.

Suppose a studio has given Paul Newman 10% of the gross from a film. If the film's gross revenues from all sources are $50 million, and if the film's production, marketing and distribution costs total $50 million, the distributor has broken even. However, Newman is due $5 million beyond his up-front fee. So the studio is losing money while Newman is making a bundle. To avoid this situation, studios prefer to pay participants after the studio recoups at least some expenses such as advertising and duplication costs. This arrangement is an ADJUSTED GROSS or MODIFIED GROSS deal.

Filmmakers and studios have devised all kinds of variations on these deals. For instance, a participant's piece of the gross might not be payable until the movie grosses two or three times its negative cost. The parties could also agree to split some markets (e.g., home video) off into separate profit pools and pay part of the gross in these markets to participants.

The least desirable deal from the profit participant's point of view is a NET PROFIT[1] deal. Here, so many deductions are allowed that what is left is often zero or less. Although the net-profit participant may not see any money from his POINTS, or percentage of profits, the studio may make a "profit" because it receives 30% to 40% of the gross as a distribution fee. This fee is usually far more than the actual costs the studio incurs to distribute a film. Thus the release of a picture may be very profitable to the studio although technically there are no "profits" for the participants.

Net profits, if there are any, are often shared 50/50 between the studio and the producer. Net profit participants typically receive their pieces of the profit pie from the producer's half. Nevertheless, net profits are customarily defined in terms of the whole (100%). We say the writer is entitled to 5% of 100% of the net profits. This

---

[1] A "net profit" deal does not represent anyone's economic net profit but is simply a net amount determined by a contract formula.

THREE MEN AND A BABY[1]

PROFIT PARTICIPATION STATEMENT, SEPTEMBER 30, 1991

FILM REVENUES

DOMESTIC THEATRICAL	$80,990,413
FOREIGN THEATRICAL	32,559,620
FREE TELEVISION	8,779,571
PAY TELEVISION	14,615,518
HOME VIDEO	13,242,932
NON-THEATRICAL	2,451,131
OTHER SOURCES	12,445
TOTAL REVENUE:	152,651,630
LESS ACCTS. RECEIVABLE	41,421
GROSS RECEIPTS:	152,610,209
DISTRIBUTION FEES:	49,798,213
ADVERTISING & PUBLICITY	35,125,096
CHECKING & COLLECTION	428,316
OTHER VERSIONS	621,920
RESIDUALS	2,990,426
TRADE DUES	50,000
TAXES, LICENSES, INSURANCE	2,289,052
PRINTS	4,617,978
TRANSPORTATION	696,350
MISCELLANEOUS	172,405
NET RECEIPTS AFTER DIST. COSTS & FEES	55,820,453

NEGATIVE COSTS

DIRECT COST	13,241,723
OVERHEAD @ 15%	1,986,258
INTEREST	1,291,866
GROSS PARTICIPANTS	1,983,750
TOTAL NEGATIVE COST	18,503,597
BALANCE	37,316,856
LESS OTHER PARTICIPATIONS & DEFERMENTS	10,284,593
NET PROFITS	$27,032,263

[1] Financial information on *Three Men and a Baby* from "Net Profits" by David Robb, *The Hollywood Reporter*, reprint of series appearing from August 17 to September 4, 1992.

means the writer is entitled to 5% of all the net profits, although his percentage comes from the producer's half. We define net profits this way to avoid ambiguity. If the contract simply said the writer was entitled to 5% of the net profits, the question might arise, is he due 5% of the producer's half (which would amount to 5% of 50%) or is he entitled to 5% of the whole?

There is more room for dispute when a participant is entitled to a piece of the net because the studio can deduct various expenses as well as interest, distribution and overhead fees. Any payments made to gross-profit partici-

DEALMAKING
IN THE
FILM AND
TELEVISION
INDUSTRY

260

pants are also deductible before payment is due a net-profit participant. Thus, even if there is no creative accounting, a net-profit participant is unlikely see any profits if the studio is obligated to pay gross-profit participants.

Other problems arise when improper deductions are made. For example, a studio may try to deduct the cost of an ad used to promote a different movie. Other deductions may seem unfair but are technically proper according to the terms of the distribution agreement.

Here are some problem areas to watch out for when reviewing a studio's accounting:

1) EXCESSIVE BILLS: If the studio used a film lab that is a subsidiary, has the film processing been charged at the prevailing rate? If the studio has used its own vehicles in a shoot, is it fair for them to charge the production the highest daily rate that Hertz might charge?

2) REBATES: If a studio receives year-end rebates, have all the films been credited with their fair share?

3) OVERHEAD CHARGES: Studio overhead charges may apply even if a film is not shot on a studio lot. This fee is meant to compensate a studio for the fixed costs of running the production and for the corporate functions performed by the studio. Distributors also may charge a 10% advertising overhead charge, which is meant to reimburse the studio for the fixed costs of operating the marketing division. But what if all the advertising work is contracted out? Is it proper to take an overhead fee? What does the contract say?

4) INTEREST: Studios charge the production interest on money used to make each film. They often mark up the rate. For example, they may borrow the money at prime and charge you prime plus two. Does the contract allow this? Also, advances from exhibitors are often not credited against interest charged. Thus the studio collects interest on advances while refusing to credit this interest against the interest charged the producer.

5) MISALLOCATION OF EXPENSES: It is in the studio's interest to tack on expenses to successful pictures to avoid having to pay profit participants. Unsuccessful pictures will never earn enough revenue to pay participants under any circumstances. Thus the cost of limos, lunches, executive travel and other expenses that were incurred on flops may find their way onto the books of hits.

6) MISALLOCATION OF REVENUES: If the studio sells a package of its films to television, how have the revenues been allocated? If one film is a hit and the others are flops, is it fair to apportion the revenue equally among the pictures? The studios prefer to allocate revenue to flops that have no chance of earning a profit to avoid paying profit participants.

7) HOME VIDEO: Many studios have home-video subsidiaries. These subsidiaries will typically pay the studio 20% of the wholesale price as a royalty for the right to distribute the movie in the home-video market. The royalty payments are then added to the studio's gross receipts, and a distribution fee is deducted. Is it fair for the studio to license the product to its own subsidiary for only 20%? Is it fair for both the subsidiary and the parent company to each make a profit from home video distribution?

8) ADVERTISING & MERCHANDISING REVENUE: The studio may earn a fee from putting a Coca-Cola commercial on its videocassettes, or a manufacturer may pay to have a product shown in a picture. Has the studio accounted for this revenue? A studio may license a manufacturer to produce spin-off toys and merchandise. Has the studio accounted for this revenue?

9) FOREIGN DUBS: Has the film been dubbed into a foreign language? Are the charges appropriate? What is the local practice? Pictures released in Japan, for example, are subtitled, not dubbed.

10) TAXES: Some governments impose a remittance tax on money taken out of the country. The U.S. government

DEALMAKING
IN THE
FILM AND
TELEVISION
INDUSTRY

262

allows a credit on these taxes on the distributor's U.S. tax return. If the tax doesn't really cost the studio anything, should it be deductible?

11) CALCULATION OF INTEREST: Studios may charge interest on items that are not out-of-pocket expenses. Did the studio charge simple interest or compound interest? What is the period for which interest is charged? Is the studio assessing interest based on a 360-day year? If interest is tied to the prime rate, was it properly calculated? What does the contract say?

12) PAYMENTS TO GROSS PARTICIPANTS: Are these payments considered part of the negative cost? Will an overhead fee be assessed on it? Suppose the gross-profit participants earn $5 million. The studio could deduct an overhead fee of $750,000 for the task of writing and mailing a few checks.

13) OVER-BUDGET PENALTY: this penalty may be added to negative cost, even if the studio was responsible for the film going over budget. Perhaps the budget never was realistic in the first place.

Because of all the creative-accounting disputes that have arisen in the industry, top talent demands large up-front payments or a piece of the gross. They know that it is unlikely that they will ever see anything from net points. Thus budgets escalate to accommodate large up-front fees, and talent has little incentive to keep production expenses down since it doesn't affect their earnings.

Remember that not all complaints about creative accounting are legitimate. Sometimes studios account according to the terms of their contracts. The contract may be unfair and the talent never bothered to read it. Now the film is a big hit, and the talent can't understand why they are not sharing in the riches. This is not creative accounting. This is an example of a studio using its clout to bargain hard and extort favorable terms. Is this unconscionable? The Buchwald appeal may let us know.

CHAPTER 12

COPYRIGHT

You are writing the Great American Screenplay. After completing 119 pages of your 120 page script, you put your work aside for the evening and leave your writer's garret for dinner.

Late that night, through a window you carelessly left open, a burglar enters. He is a literary thief who doesn't take your money or stereo but steals your almost-finished manuscript. The script has not been registered with the copyright office and you didn't place a copyright notice on it.

The thief takes the script to the nearest film studio, which immediately recognizes its value. Before one can say "Oprah Winfrey," the movie is produced, it becomes a blockbuster hit and the thief is interviewed on talk shows about "his" new work.

Question: Can you sue the thief for copyright infringement? Answer: Yes. You obtained the copyright to your work when you created it. It doesn't matter that you didn't put a notice on the manuscript, nor does it matter that you didn't register it with the Copyright Office. Incidentally, the thief may be liable for burglary, trespass and conversion, too.

There is a common misunderstanding that copyright registration is required for copyright protection.

Now, you may wonder in this situation how you could prove you wrote the script. That is a question of evidence. Both parties to the dispute will present their evidence and the jury

DEALMAKING
IN THE
FILM AND
TELEVISION
INDUSTRY

264

will decide whom to believe. Your attorney will have an opportunity to cross-examine the thief to discredit his claim of authorship. You could have your spouse testify that he/she read an early draft of the work. Of course, spouses may not have as much credibility as an impartial third party. That is why it is a good idea to register your manuscript with the Writer's Guild.[1]

BASICS OF COPYRIGHT LAW

Copyright law is derived from the United States Constitution (Article 1, § 8) which empowers Congress to protect the work of authors. "Authors" is defined broadly to encompass creators of all works eligible for copyright including photographers, painters and sculptors.

Congress has enacted Copyright Laws to protect authors.[2] Because the Act is a federal law it applies in all states. State law may provide additional remedies.

The United States has joined several international copyright conventions that protect American works abroad. These accords essentially say: If you protect the works of our authors in your country, we will protect the works of your authors here.

CRITERIA FOR COPYRIGHT PROTECTION

Not every work is copyrightable. To be eligible for copyright protection a work must meet four criteria. These criteria are:

1) It must be original

2) It must be an "expression of an author."

3) It must be of a non-utilitarian nature.

4) It must be in a fixed, tangible medium of expression.

A work has to meet all four criteria; three out of four is not good enough.

If a work meets all four criteria, the creator automatically has

---

[1] See Chapter 7 for information on how to register.

[2] See Title 17, United States Code (U.S.C.) or United States Code Annotated (U.S.C.A.).

a copyright in her work. The copyright comes into existence when the work has been created. The creator does not need to send any forms into the Copyright Office, say any magic words or perform any rituals in order to be protected under Copyright law. No Copyright notice is required to gain a copyright.[1]

Perhaps the simplest way of understanding copyright law is to view it as a three-tiered scheme. First, the author gets a copyright in his work when he *creates* it (assuming it meets the four

criteria). Second, before 1989 authors were obliged to put a copyright notice (the word copyright, or the abbreviation or the symbol ©; the name of copyright holder and the year of publication) *if* they choose to publish the work. And third, if the author *registers* the work, he will be eligible for some extra, super-duper benefits, like reimbursement of attorneys' fees and recovery of statutory damages in a copyright-infringement suit. But if the author does not publish or register the work, he is nevertheless protected under copyright law.

Note that since the United States joined the Berne international copyright convention in 1989,[2] notice is no longer required to protect a copyright. Nowadays an American author

TYPES OF WORKS THAT CAN BE COPYRIGHTED

LITERARY WORKS
MUSICAL WORKS
DRAMATIC WORKS
PANTOMIMES
PHOTOGRAPHS
GRAPHIC DESIGN
SCULPTURE
MOTION PICTURES
SOUND RECORDINGS
CHOREOGRAPHY
COMPUTER PROGRAMS

WHAT CAN'T BE COPYRIGHTED

INVENTIONS
IDEAS
THEMES
INDUSTRIAL DESIGN
TYPEFACE DESIGN
TITLES
HISTORICAL EVENTS
ANYTHING IN THE PUBLIC DOMAIN

Note that the categories are broad and they overlap. Lyrics for a song can fit into either the literary-work category or the musical-work category. Pantomimes and choreography can sometimes double as dramatic works.

---

[1] Although before March 1, 1989, failure to put a copyright notice on your work, if you published it, could result in the loss of the copyright.

[2] The Berne Convention Implementation Act of 1988 enabled the United States to establish copyright relations with twenty-five more countries. Notice requirements were dropped for works published after March 1, 1989. Recordation of an interest in a copyrighted work is no longer required as a prerequisite to bringing an infringement suit.

DEALMAKING
IN THE
FILM AND
TELEVISION
INDUSTRY

266

who publishes his work and fails to attach a copyright notice is protected anyway. However, it remains a good practice to routinely put a copyright notice on your work so that nobody can claim they didn't know it was copyrighted material. You don't need the Copyright Office's permission to put a copyright notice on your work.

The Four Criteria

1) THE WORK MUST BE ORIGINAL

In order for a work to meet the originality requirement it must be created through the independent effort of the author. The creator cannot copy it from another's work.

The work need not have any merit. No one at the copyright office reviews applications for copyright registration to determine artistic or literary value. You can register a badly written novel or a child's fingerpainted picture. You can register a brilliant scientific article or *The National Enquirer.* In other words, there are no esthetic or scholarly standards for copyright protection. The work has to be original, not good. Besides, artistic worth is subjective. What one person considers great art another may think is junk.

How much originality is required? Could you, for instance, take a picture of an ordinary white wall with a Brownie Instamatic camera and receive copyright protection for your work? Yes, because not much originality is required. Here, the creator choose how to frame the picture and how to light it. You may not think this picture is interesting or worth much, but it is original enough for copyright protection.

2) THE WORK MUST BE AN EXPRESSION OF AN AUTHOR

Ideas, themes and titles are never copyrightable. On the other hand, books, plays and movies are copyrightable. The former are not considered expressions of an author, while the later are.

Copyright law protects the craftsmanship of the writer, the writer's approach, and his skill in fashioning the material. But the writer can never copyright an idea—whether it is incorporated in a sentence or a 400-page book—and prevent others from creating works based on the same idea.

In other words, ideas are as free as the air. Nobody can possess them. If you want to write a book about George Washington, you may do so and be protected under copyright law. But you cannot preclude subsequent authors from writing their own books on George Washington as long as they don't copy your work.[1]

It is sometimes difficult to distinguish an idea from the expression of an author. I'm sure everyone would agree that a 500-page book is an expression of an author. But what about a 250-page book? A 100-page book? A ten-page book? A one-page book? What about a one-page book with just one letter on each page? We'll call it the Alphabet Book Series. The first book contains just the letter "A."

WHICH FORM TO FILE

REGISTER OF COPYRIGHT CLASSIFICATION SYSTEM FOR REGISTRATION HAS FOUR BROAD CATEGORIES:

CLASS TX: NON-DRAMATIC LITERARY WORKS

CLASS PA: PERFORMING ARTS

CLASS VA: VISUAL ARTS

CLASS SR: SOUND RECORDINGS

HOW A WORK IS CLASSIFIED CAN HAVE IMPORTANT IMPLICATIONS. FOR EXAMPLE, THE OWNER OF A COPYRIGHT IN A SOUND RECORDING DOES NOT ENJOY A PERFORMANCE RIGHT. ONLY NON-DRAMATIC MUSICAL WORKS ARE SUBJECT TO COMPULSORY LICENSE FOR REPRODUCTION. A LIBRARY'S REPRODUCTION RIGHT IS MUCH WIDER FOR LITERARY AND DRAMATIC WORKS THAN FOR OTHER CATEGORIES.

If this book deserves copyright protection, could I then prevent anyone else from using the letter "A" in their writings? Of course not. You can't copyright a letter or a word. But when you string together words, at a certain point you will be protected if somebody copies your

---

[1] Except they may be able to borrow small portions of your book under the Fair Use Doctrine, discussed on page 273, and they could borrow historical facts because these are in the public domain.

DEALMAKING
IN THE
FILM AND
TELEVISION
INDUSTRY

268

expression. At what point does that occur? It's not clear because it is difficult to determine precisely when an idea becomes sufficiently embellished to become an expression of an author. And even when a work is an expression of an author, the underlying idea is not protected.

To understand why Congress protects only expressions of authors, you have to understand the competing policy considerations underlying the Copyright Act. On one hand, Congress wants to protect the work of authors to encourage them to create new works. If anyone who owned a printing press could freely copy, sell and compete against authors, authors would not reap the full fruits of their labor. Authors would have little incentive to invest time and energy to create new works. Because Congress wants to encourage authors to create new works for the good of society, Congress gives the author certain exclusive rights over the use of their work—the so-called copyright.

But Congress also believes that, in an open and democratic society people should be able to freely exchange ideas and create new works based on the ideas of others. So the copyright is not absolute. The right is limited in several ways.

First, it is restricted in time. The creator (or the employer of the creator if it is a work-for-hire) has a copyright to his work for a limited term. Under current law, a copyright lasts for the lifetime of the author plus fifty years. Before 1978, the author of a work had a copyright in his work for twenty-eight years and could renew it for an additional twenty-eight years, for a total of fifty-six years of copyright protection.[1] If the work is a "work-for-hire," then the employer usually owns the copyright, and a different term applies.[2] Once a copyright expires, the work goes into the public domain and anyone can use it. Second, Congress restricts the copy-

---

[1] Works in the second term when the law changed received an extra nineteen year extension for a total of seventy-five years

[2] Since the employer could be a corporation, which doesn't die or have to ever dissolve, a different term is required. Otherwise, corporations would have an unfair advantage in being able to keep their work copyrighted indefinitely.

right by limiting it to expressions of authors. Mere ideas, titles and themes are not protected.[1]

3) THE WORK MUST BE OF A NON-UTILITARIAN NATURE

Works of a utilitarian nature are not eligible for copyright protection. An ordinary lighting fixture, for example, cannot be copyrighted. A bookkeeping ledger or the contest rules on the side of a cereal box are utilitarian forms of writing. If there is no other way, or few other ways, to express something, the writing will be considered utilitarian.

Note that works of an ingenious design, although utilitarian, may be eligible for patent protection.[2] There is some overlap between patent and copyright law, and some works can be protected by both.

Since a lighting fixture cannot be copyrighted, and a statue is an aesthetic work that can be copyrighted, what happens if you mount a lighting fixture on top of a piece of sculpture? In other words, you make the sculpture the base of a lamp. Can you obtain copyright protection for the hybrid work? Well, you retain copyright to the base, but you don't gain a copyright in the fixture.

On the other hand, what if an avant-garde artist welds 200 old lighting fixtures into an intricate design? Although lighting fixtures are not ordinarily copyrightable, here they are being used in a non-utilitarian way, so the work should be copyrightable.

4) THE WORK MUST BE IN A FIXED, TANGIBLE MEDIUM OF EXPRESSION.

The work must be expressed in a tangible form that is relatively stable and permanent. Such mediums as paper, videotape, audiotape, paint, clay, film and metal meet the requirement. A work that is comprised solely of an impromptu speech or an unrecorded live perfor-

---

[1] Protection could be obtained in some situations, however, under contract, trademark or unfair competition laws.

[2] Patents protect technological information and they arise from government grant. Copyrights protect expressive information and they arise automatically upon creation assuming all the criteria for copyright eligibility have been meet. Trademarks protect symbolic information (e.g., product marks and logos) and they arise from use.

DEALMAKING
IN THE
FILM AND
TELEVISION
INDUSTRY

270

mance, or a work embodied in an ice sculpture or a sand castle, will not be protected under copyright law.

The author or someone under his authorization must reduce the work to a tangible form. Recordation by an audience member listening to an improvised jazz performance would not constitute fixation for purpose of copyright protection.

Fixation before a public performance is preferred. But what about simultaneous fixation as a work is performed? The Copyright Act protects live broadcasts that are simultaneously recorded.

There is a practical reason for the requirement that copyrighted material be put in tangible form. How else could a judge determine the extent of a copyright in an ethereal work?

Can one copyright choreography? Yes, if it is put in a fixed form. Either written stage directions or a videotaped performance will suffice. Of course, choreography must meet the other criteria for copyright protection. You could not copyright a single dance step because that would not be considered an expression of an author.

COPYRIGHT NOTICE

Proper copyright notice contains three elements:

1) either the word "copyright," the abbreviation for the word copyright or the symbol ©,

2) the name of the copyright owner, and

3) the date of first publication.

The order of the elements does not matter. Authors may also add the phrase "All Rights Reserved," which can provide additional protection in foreign jurisdictions.

The date may be omitted where a pictorial, graphic or sculptural work with accompanying text matter, if any, is reproduced in or on greeting cards, postcards, stationary, jewelry, dolls, toys or any useful articles. The full name of the copyright owner is not required.

The notice should be located in such a manner as to give

reasonable notice. A copyright is not affected if notice is taken off a work without authorization of the copyright owner.

The 1976 Copyright Act reduces the importance of publication because federal copyright now begins when a work is created. For works created between 1978 and March 1, 1989, the 1976 act retains the notice requirement, although omission of notice can be cured by taking certain steps. Until the 1988 Amendments the United States was alone in the world in requiring compliance with notice formalities.

After March 1, 1989, notice is permissive. Omission of notice does not inject the work into the public domain.

The provisions of the 1988 amendments are not retroactive, so works that went into the public domain for failure to comply with notice provisions remain in the public domain.

Copyright notice remains important because section 405(b) limits remedies against innocent infringers misled by lack

CONTINUING IMPORTANCE OF PUBLICATION:

1) **DEPOSIT REQUIREMENTS**: FOR WORKS PUBLISHED SINCE THE BERNE AMENDMENTS, DEPOSIT REQUIREMENTS REMAIN. YOU HAVE THREE MONTHS TO DEPOSIT A COPY WITH THE LIBRARY OF CONGRESS. CRIMINAL FINES CAN BE ASSESSED.

2) **NEED TO REGISTER AFTER PUBLICATION TO OBTAIN CERTAIN ADVANTAGES**: AFTER PUBLISHING A WORK, ONE MUST REGISTER OR LOSE CERTAIN ADVANTAGES IN A SUIT FOR INFRINGEMENT.

    A) REGISTRATION WITHIN FIVE YEARS OF PUBLICATION CONFERS PRIMA FACIE EVIDENCE OF THE VALIDITY OF A COPYRIGHT. IN OTHER WORDS, IT WILL CREATE EVIDENCE SUFFICIENT TO PROVE COPYRIGHT OWNERSHIP IF NOT REBUTTED OR CONTRADICTED BY THE OTHER PARTY.

    B) ONE CAN OBTAIN STATUTORY DAMAGES AND ATTORNEYS' FEES FOR PUBLISHED WORKS ONLY IF REGISTRATION PRECEDED THE INFRINGEMENT OR IF THE WORK WAS REGISTERED THREE MONTHS AFTER PUBLICATION.

3) **INTERNATIONAL COPYRIGHT IMPLICATIONS**: UNDER BOTH BERNE AND UNIVERSAL CONVENTIONS, THE ACT OF PUBLICATION IS IMPORTANT. WORKS FIRST PUBLISHED IN A MEMBER STATE OR BY A NATIONAL OF A MEMBER STATE MUST BE GIVEN THE SAME PROTECTION IN EVERY OTHER COUNTRY AS WORKS FIRST PUBLISHED IN ITS OWN TERRITORY.

4) **DURATIONAL CONSEQUENCES**: THE DATE OF PUBLICATION DETERMINES LENGTH OF COPYRIGHT FOR CERTAIN CATEGORIES OF WORKS. UNDER THE 1976 ACT, THE TERM FOR ANONYMOUS AND PSEUDONYMOUS WORKS AND WORKS-FOR-HIRE IS MEASURED FROM THE YEAR OF FIRST PUBLICATION.

UNDER THE CURRENT COPYRIGHT TERM OF LIFE OF AUTHOR PLUS FIFTY YEARS, THE AUTHOR MAY BE PRESUMED DEAD FOR FIFTY YEARS IF, SEVENTY-FIVE YEARS AFTER PUBLICATION, COPYRIGHT RECORDS DON'T REVEAL EVIDENCE OTHERWISE.

DEALMAKING
IN THE
FILM AND
TELEVISION
INDUSTRY

272

of notice. An innocent infringer is shielded from actual damages and statutory damages and probably attorneys' fees as well. This limitation lasts until the infringer is put on notice of the claim of copyright.

Summary of Notice Requirements

For works published before 1978, the harsh notice provisions of the 1909 Act apply.

For works published between 1978 and March 1, 1989, the less-strict notice provisions of the 1976 Act apply.

For works published after March 1, 1989, the permissive notice requirements apply.

THE RIGHTS OF THE COPYRIGHT HOLDER

When you own a copyright, you possess a bundle of rights: the right to control the reproduction of your work, the right to control preparation of derivative works, the right to distribute copies of the work to the public by sale, rental or lease, the right to perform the works publicly[1] and the right to display the works publicly.[2] Graphic, pictorial, sculptural works and sound recordings, however, don't enjoy the same full range of exclusive rights as do literary, musical and dramatic works. The copyright owner of a sound recording, for example, cannot control the right of performance and display of the work. Also, graphic, pictorial or sculptural works do not enjoy a performance right.[3]

Moreover, a copyright is limited by various compulsory licenses—licenses required to be given to all persons who comply with the statutory requirements (i.e., payment of royalties).[4]

There are other limitations as well. The Distribution right is

---

[1] A performance is public at any place where a substantial number of persons outside of the normal circle of family and friends is gathered. Thus singing in the bathtub is not a public performance. Renting a movie and showing it in one's house to friends is not a public performance.

[2] These rights are subject to limitations in sections 107-118 of the Copyright Act.

[3] Moreover, section 106 limits the exclusive rights of performance and display to public performance and display.

[4] The 1976 Copyright Act increased the number of compulsory licenses to five: 1) Cable television license, 2) Mechanical recording license, 3) Jukebox license, 4) public broadcasting license and 5) Satellite retransmission license. Licenses are administered by the Copyright Royalty Tribunal, an administrative agency.

limited by the First Sale Doctrine, which permits the owner of a copy to sell or rent it. This doctrine allows a video retailer to buy a tape from a movie studio and rent it out repeatedly to customers. An owner of a copy can dispose of it physically, can resell it, rent, give it away and rebind it. He cannot, however, reproduce it or perform it publicly. Record stores cannot do the same, however, because they fall within an exception to the First Sale Doctrine that prevents the renting of sound recordings.[1]

THE FAIR USE DOCTRINE

A copyright owner's rights are further limited by what is known as the Fair Use Doctrine. This doctrine permits others to borrow portions of a copyrighted work for purposes such as criticism, comment, news reporting, teaching (including multiple copies for classroom use) and scholarship.

Perhaps you heard the maxim that if you steal from one person, you are a plagiarizer but if you steal from a hundred, you are a scholar. The Fair Use Doctrine enables scholars to borrow small excerpts from other works without infringing on another's copyright.

Whether the Fair Use Doctrine will protect a particular taking is often difficult to determine. The Copyright Act lists the following factors to be considered:

1) The purpose and character of the use, including whether such use is of a commercial nature or is for nonprofit educational purposes;

2) the nature of the copyrighted work;

3) The amount and substantiality of the portion used in relation to the copyright work as a whole; and

4) the effect of the use upon the potential market for or value of the copyrighted work.

Other factors can be considered as well.

---

[1] See section 109(b) of the Copyright Act. The Record Rental Amendment of 1984 prohibits an owner of a phonorecord which embodies a sound recording of a musical work from renting it to the public for direct or indirect commercial advantage. It does not apply to resale or other transfers, and it is limited to commercial establishments (i.e., does not apply to libraries and educational institutions).

DEALMAKING
IN THE
FILM AND
TELEVISION
INDUSTRY

274

OWNERSHIP OF COPYRIGHT

Works created pursuant to one's employment are works made for hire. Works created by the collaborative effort of several authors are joint works. Like other property, copyrights can be sold and transferred.[1]

Work for Hire

The employer is considered the copyright owner of works made for hire. The employee has no ownership rights at all.

How does one determine if a work is made for hire? First, all works prepared by employees within the scope of their employment are presumed to be works for hire unless the parties have expressly agreed otherwise in a written instrument signed by them.

Second, certain works[2] that are specially made or commissioned from independent contractors are considered works for hire if the parties expressly agree so in writing. The agreement must be signed by both parties and must consist of explicit wording that the work is a work for hire.[3]

Joint Works

A joint work is one prepared by two or more authors with the intention that their contributions be merged into inseparable or interdependent parts of a unitary whole.

Critical to determining whether a joint work exists is whether the authors intended when they created their contributions that they be integrated into one work. A joint work can be created if

---

[1] Grants made after 1978 can be terminated under certain circumstances by serving written notice and filing a notice with the copyright office thirty-five years from date of grant or if grant covers right of publication, then thirty-five years from date of publication or forty years from date of grant, whichever is earlier. Works for hire and dispositions by will cannot be terminated. See section 203 of the Copyright Act.

[2] Works that are contributions to a collective work, part of a motion picture or other audiovisual work, a translation, supplementary work, a compilation, an instructional text, a test, answer material for a test or an atlas. See 17 USC 101.

[3] The presumption differed under the 1909 Act, which provided that the commissioning party was the author unless the parties intended the contrary. The 1976 Act reversed that presumption.

the contributions of the authors are unequal, so long as the author makes more than a de minimus (trifling) contribution and intends his work to be part of a joint work.

A joint work can also be created when a copyright owner transfers a copyright to more than one person, or when a copyright passes by will or intestacy to two or more persons, or when a work is subject to state community property laws. Thus a joint work can be broadly defined as one in which copyright is owned in undivided shares by two or more persons.

DURATION OF COPYRIGHT

All works are either copyrighted or in the public domain. There is no twilight zone in between. Until the 1909 Copyright Act was revised in 1976 (effective 1978), copyright lasted for twenty-eight years and could be renewed for one additional twenty-eight year term. For works published before 1978, the 1909 Act's two twenty-eight-year-term scheme continues to apply.[1] The first term is measured from the date of publication.

The copyright for works created since 1978 will last for the lifetime of the author plus fifty years.[2] For anonymous works and works made for hire, copyright generally lasts seventy-five years from first publication or 100 years from creation, whichever expires first.

DIFFERENCE BETWEEN 1909 AND 1976 COPYRIGHT ACTS

Under the 1909 Copyright Act, a work enjoyed perpetual

---

[1] The renewal term reverted to the author automatically, upon filing for renewal between the twenty-seventh and twenty-eighth year. Failure to comply resulted in forfeiture of copyright. The 1976 Act retains this system for works copyrighted before 1978, and the second term has been lengthened from twenty-eight to forty-seven years. Moreover, works in their renewal term between December 31, 1976 and December 31, 1977, receive an extra nineteen years added to the second term, for a total copyright of seventy-five years.

[2] For works created but not copyrighted or published before 1978, copyright will not expire before December 31, 2002. If published before this expiration date, copyright protection will last until December 31, 2027. These works are often letters, diaries and other manuscripts that were never sold or publicly distributed.

DEALMAKING
IN THE
FILM AND
TELEVISION
INDUSTRY

276

protection (under state common-law copyright law) until it was published. Then the work became subject to federal protection, which limited the copyright to two twenty-eight year terms. Notice was required to be affixed to each copy; failure to do so could place the work in the public domain. Thus, publication divested common-law rights. The '76 Act reduces the importance of publication because federal copyright now begins when the work is created.

COPYRIGHT REGISTRATION AND DEPOSIT

No other country has anything like the United State's elaborate system of copyright registration. The advantage of our system is that it protects owners by establishing priority of authorship and provides evidence of the validity of a copyright. It also facilitates transfers, assignments and licenses of copyrighted works because prospective transferees have more confidence in the validity of a registered copyright than an unregistered one.

The registration system has several shortcomings, however. A search of copyright records may be unrewarding or misleading because the absence of any mention of a work in the records does not mean it is unprotected. Registration is voluntary and many copyright owners choose not to register.[1]

Furthermore, information in records may be inaccurate or incomplete. The copyright office assumes all information submitted is accurate. No independent investigation is conducted. Consequently, searches of copyright records are rarely conclusive.

ADVANTAGES OF REGISTRATION

1) Establishes a public record of copyright claim.

2) Secures the right to file an infringement suit for works whose country of origin is the United States.

---

[1] The only exceptions to voluntarily registration were for works copyrighted before 1978 (published with notice) when the copyright owner had to file a renewal registration to claim a second term. For unpublished works, copyright protection was perpetual. Also under the 1976 Act registration is required to preserve copyright when proper notice has been omitted on a significant number of published copies.

The 1976 Act originally required registration as a pre-requisite for bringing a lawsuit. Effective March 1, 1989, registration is only required for works whose country of origin is the United States. Once registration has taken place, a lawsuit can be brought for all infringing acts occurring before or after registration.[1]

3) It establishes prima facie validity of the copyright (if registration takes place within five years of publication).

4) It makes available a broader range of remedies in an infringement suit, allowing statutory damages and attorneys' fees (if registration has taken place before infringement).[2] Statutory damages are important because they often offer the copyright holder the only remedy worth pursuing.

5) Only if registration is made will recordation of a document in the Copyright Office give constructive notice of facts in the document. In other words, registration gives the world notice of the copyright claim, even to those who may be unaware of the registration.

TO REGISTER A COPYRIGHT

Send in the same envelope:

1) a properly completed application form;

2) a non-refundable fee and

3) a deposit copy.

Registration is effective on the date of receipt in the copyright office. The Copyright Office does not institute interference proceedings to determine who has priority between conflicting applications.

---

[1] Registration is not required for a work whose country of origin belongs to the Berne Convention. The situs of publication determines whether a work is published in a Berne country, not the nationality of the author.

[2] Statutory damages are not recoverable for 1) any infringement of copyright in an unpublished work commenced before the effective date of its registration and 2) any infringement of copyright commenced after first publication of the work and before the effective date of its registration, unless such registration is made within three months after the first publication of the work.

DEALMAKING
IN THE
FILM AND
TELEVISION
INDUSTRY

278

REGISTRATION AFTER BERNE

For causes of action arising after March 1, 1989, the Berne Convention Implementation Act has ended the requirement of registering as a prerequisite to bringing a suit for infringement for non-U.S. works. Registration remains important because it gives constructive notice to the world of one's copyright. This notice may be critical if there arises a conflict between two transfers of an interest in one copyright.

REQUIREMENT OF REGISTRATION UPON PUBLICATION

You are not required to publish your work. If you do publish it, however, you are required to deposit two copies of the work within three months of publication.[1] If you do not deposit the copies you may be fined but you do not forfeit your copyright.[2]

The deposit requirement serves two purposes. It adds a copy of the work to the collection of the Library of Congress, and it identifies the work with the copyright registration.

CASES

ESTATE OF HEMINGWAY V. RANDOM HOUSE, INC. (1966)[3]

FACTS: Hotchner wrote a book, *Papa Hemingway*. It incorporated long conversations between the author and Hemingway. They had been close friends for thirteen years and went on drinking escapades and travels together. Hotchner took notes and published several articles incorporating their conversations. Hemingway liked the articles. Hemingway's Estate sues Hotchner seeking an injunction against the book and damages for infringement of common-law copyright.

---

[1] §407. This requirement does not apply to published works not having notice and works published in foreign countries.

[2] Under the 1909 Act, failure to comply with the deposit and registration requirements after a Demand by the Register of Copyrights would subject the claimant to a fine and void his copyright.

[3] *Estate of Hemingway v. Random House, Inc.* 49 Misc.2d 726, 268 N.Y.S.2d 531 (1966).

ISSUE: Were Hemingway's conversations protected under common-law copyright?

HOLDING: No.

RATIONALE: It is presumed that, in ordinary conversations the parties are not reserving any rights. Here Hemingway's conduct demonstrates no intention to reserve rights; indeed, it appears he approved of Hotchner quoting him.

One cannot copyright an extemporaneous conversation unless it is put in a tangible form. Absent an express or implied agreement, the plaintiff has no remedy.

Common-law copyright refers to the rights authors have in unpublished works protected by state court decisions. Since the Copyright Act of 1976, federal copyright law extends to unpublished as well as published works. Thus, the field has now largely been preempted by federal statutory law.

SHELDON V. METRO-GOLDWYN PICTURES CORP. (1936)[1]

FACTS: MGM attempted to secure the movie rights to Edward Sheldon's copyrighted play "Dishonored Lady." The play was based, in part, on a true story. When MGM couldn't secure the movie rights from Sheldon, the studio produced a movie of its own, "Letty Lynton," based on the same historical incident. Although much of the movie was original, certain details and sequences of events were identical to those expressed in Sheldon's play. The lower court held for MGM on the grounds that the use of Sheldon's play only involved general themes or ideas. Sheldon appealed.

ISSUE: Did MGM infringe upon Sheldon's copyright?

HOLDING: Yes.

RATIONALE: MGM'S work was identical in details and sequence of events to Sheldon's work in matters unrelated to the underlying true story. This is more than merely appropriating an idea or a theme. It doesn't matter that the plagiarized material only comprises a small portion of the entire film. It is not okay to steal a little bit.

---

[1] *Sheldon v. Metro-Goldwyn Pictures Corp.*, 81 F.2d 49 (1936).

DEALMAKING
IN THE
FILM AND
TELEVISION
INDUSTRY

280

Sheldon wrote a play based on a historical event. Historical events are in the public domain, and anyone, including MGM, is free to use them.

MGM wanted to make a movie of Sheldon's play. The parties were unable to agree on terms. So MGM decided to make its own movie based on the historical events underlying Sheldon's play. MGM hired a writer to write a screenplay and the movie was made. Some incidents and sequences of events in the movie were similar to Sheldon's play, and these similarities were not matters of historical record. In other words, Sheldon wrote a play based on a historical event and other events he created from his imagination. Some of the imaginary material appeared in MGM's movie.

While MGM had every right to make a movie about the historical event in Sheldon's play, it had no right to borrow material created by Sheldon if that material was copyrightable. In other words, if the material was more than an idea. Here the court felt the MGM writer borrowed more than an idea.

MGM should have been more careful in hiring a writer. The studio should have declined to hire writers who had read Sheldon's play. Once hired, the studio should have told the writer not to read Sheldon's play to ensure against any inadvertent copying.

MUSTO V. MEYER (1977)[1]

FACTS: Plaintiff wrote an article in a medical journal titled "A Study in Cocaine: Sherlock Holmes and Sigmund Freud." It concerned the history of cocaine use in Europe in the 1800s and speculated that Holmes was a heavy cocaine user which led him to believe that Professor Moriarty was after him. The author also speculated that Holmes' famous disappearance was due to his going to see Freud for treatment of his cocaine addiction.

Nicholas Myer subsequently wrote a book titled *The Seven Percent Solution*. It had Watson tricking Holmes into seeing Freud for treatment of cocaine addiction, Freud curing Holmes, and both of them embarking on a Holmesian adventure. Universal Pictures made a movie from the book. Plaintiff sued, claiming the book and movie infringed his copyrighted article.

---

[1] *Musto v. Meyer*, 434 F.Supp. 32 (1977).

ISSUE: Was Plaintiff's copyright infringed?

HOLDING: No.

RATIONALE: The book is not similar to the article except for the idea that Holmes was addicted to cocaine and this addiction was cured by Freud. They are not similar as far as reader appeal, fashioning of plot, delineation of characters or literary skill.

Nicholas Meyer didn't deny that he read the plaintiff's article. Indeed, he gave the plaintiff a credit in his book.

Meyer's book resembles the plaintiff's article because both are based on the premise of Sherlock Holmes seeing Freud for cocaine addiction. Sherlock Holmes is a fictional character, a creation of Sir Arthur Conan Doyle, whose copyright in the work has long since expired. Therefore, Sherlock Holmes is in the public domain and is available to everybody. Freud was a real person, so clearly this meeting between Holmes and Freud never took place but is a product of the plaintiff's imagination. Articles, whether fiction or non-fiction, are copyrightable.

Nicholas Meyer prevailed because the court found that he only borrowed an idea, and it's permissible to borrow ideas. The facts of this case are not much different from the Sheldon case. But in Sheldon the court found infringement because the borrower took "certain details and sequence of events," while what Meyer took was characterized merely as an idea. Because it's not always easy to know when one has borrowed more than an idea, attorneys are often conservative when counseling their clients.

WARNER BROS. V. ABC (1983)[1]

FACTS: Plaintiff, Warner Bros., owns the copyright in various works embodying the character Superman and have exploited its rights in various media including *Superman, The Movie* and two sequels. In these works, Superman is a brave, fearless hero, endowed with superhuman powers. The commercial success of the Superman movie led defendant ABC to seek a license for a production to be called *Superboy*, based on the early adventures of Super-

---

[1] *Warner Bros. v. ABC.*, 720 F.2d 231 (1983).

DEALMAKING
IN THE
FILM AND
TELEVISION
INDUSTRY

282

man. Warner Bros., which was planning to make their own sequels and derivative works, refused ABC permission to proceed with the proposed project.

ABC then asked Cannell to create a pilot program for a TV series involving a super hero. The program "The Greatest American Hero," was described as what happens when an average person becomes Superman. Its protagonist, Ralph Hinkley, was an ordinary guy. He was a young high-school teacher attempting to cope with a recent divorce, a dispute over custody of his son and his relationship with his girlfriend.

While attractive, Hinkley was not physically imposing. He derived his superhuman powers from a magical caped costume—a red leotard with a tunic top, no boots and a black cape—which was a gift from an intergalactic visitor. However, he lost the instruction book and uses his powers awkwardly and fearfully, often making crash landings.

The "Hero" series contained several visual effects and lines that inevitably called Superman to mind, sometimes by mention of Superman or another character from Superman works, and by humorous parodying or ironic twisting of well-known Superman phrases. For example, when Hinkley first viewed himself in a mirror, he says, "It's a bird . . . It's a plane . . . it's Ralph Hinkley."

ISSUE: Did ABC infringe the copyright of Warner Bros.' character Superman?

HOLDING: No.

RATIONALE: The total perception of the Hinkley character is not substantially similar to that of Superman. Superman is portrayed as a brave, proud hero. Hinkley is a timid, reluctant hero who accepts his mission grudgingly and exercises his powers in a bumbling, comical fashion. In the genre of super heroes, Hinkley follows Superman as Inspector Clouseau follows Sherlock Holmes.

As for Superman phrases and references in the series, this is not an infringement. The lines are used to highlight the differences with Superman, often to laughable effect. The defendant is poking fun at, rather than copying, a copyrighted work.

While Warner Bros. has a copyright to the Superman character, they don't have a copyright on the idea of a superhuman hero and cannot prevent others from inventing their own superhuman characters.

Characters may be copyrightable, especially those with pictorial or visual elements such as comic-book characters. With literary characters that are not represented visually, protection may depend on how finely drawn the character is. One could not, for example, gain any rights over a character defined simply as "a hard-boiled private eye." Other authors would be free to borrow these personality traits. Note that names of characters might be protectable under unfair-competition law and trademark laws.

KING V. MISTER MAESTRO, INC. (1963)[1]

FACTS: Dr. Martin Luther King (P) delivered his "I have a dream" speech, before thousands during a civil rights march in Washington, D.C. The speech was widely reported by the news media, and they received an advance copy of the text. Defendant Mister Maestro (D) produced records that included the speech without P's permission. P sought an injunction and damages. D argued that the delivery of the speech was a general publication which divested it of common-law copyright.

ISSUE: Does the general publication of a speech occur when it is orally delivered to a vast audience or its text is distributed to the press?

HOLDING: No.

RATIONALE: Oral delivery does not constitute a dedication of the speech to the public, and distribution to the press is only a limited publication.

At common law there was a property right in unpublished works (the "common-law copyright"). After publication, the common-law copyright did not exist and a work would only be protected if it met the the criteria for statutory copyright (federal copyright).

Ordinarily, the public performance of a work is not considered a publication. Note that the copyright law has been changed since this case was decided. First, copyright law was

---

[1] *King v. Mister Maestro, Inc.*, 224 F.Supp. 101 (1963).

DEALMAKING
IN THE
FILM AND
TELEVISION
INDUSTRY

284

amended to provide ways to cure the effects of a general publication without proper notice, so the act of publication has lost some of its importance. Later, notice became optional.

GROSS V. SELIGMAN (1914)[1]

FACTS: Rochlitz, an artist, posed a model in the nude and produced a photograph that he named *Race of Youth*. He sold his copyrighted photo to Gross (P). Two years later, Rochlitz placed the same model in an identical pose, but the woman wore a smile and held a cherry stem between her teeth. This photograph, called *Cherry Ripe*, was published by Seligman (D). P contends that the new photo infringes his copyright of the first photo.

ISSUE: When an artist sells all rights in a work to another and then produces a similar work that is only marginally different, is the subsequent work an infringement?

HOLDING: Yes.

RATIONALE: If an author grants all his rights to another and then attempts to reproduce the identical work with minor differences, the latter work is an infringment of the owner's copyright. This is not true if the subsequent work, although substantially similar, was independently created without reference to the prior work.

The test of infringement is twofold. Copying exists where the infringer has had access to the original work and where the subsequent work is substantially similar to the first. The access does not have to be deliberate or in bad faith and access may be inferred from circumstantial evidence.

COPYRIGHT REQUIREMENTS

1) AN ORIGINAL WORK

2) AN EXPRESSION OF AN AUTHOR

3) NON-UTILITARIAN NATURE

4) FIXED IN A TANGIBLE MEDIUM OF EXPRESSION

COPYRIGHT NOTICE

1) EITHER THE WORD COPYRIGHT, ABBREVIATION OR THE SYMBOL ©.

2) NAME OF THE COPYRIGHT OWNER

3) DATE OF FIRST PUBLICATION

OPTIONAL: THE PHRASE "ALL RIGHTS RESERVED" MAY PROVIDE ADDITIONAL PROTECTION IN FOREIGN JURISDICTIONS.

---

[1] *Gross v. Seligman*, 212 F. 930 (2nd Cir. 1914).

Certain foreign countries recognize what is known as moral rights (droit moral), which are personal to authors. They are separate and apart from the author's copyright.

These rights include:

1) The right to be known as the author of a work;

2) The right to prevent others from falsely attributing to the writer authorship of work he has not written;

3) The right to prevent others from making deforming changes to the work;

4) The right to withdraw a published work from distribution if it no longer represents the views of the author;

5) The right to prevent others from using the work or the author's name in such a way as to reflect adversely on one's professional standing.

WHAT RIGHTS DOES THE COPYRIGHT HOLDER HAVE?

1) RIGHT TO REPRODUCE (COPY)

2) RIGHT TO PREPARE DERIVATIVE WORK (E.G., SCREENPLAYS)

3) RIGHT TO DISTRIBUTE COPIES TO THE PUBLIC BY SALE, RENTAL OR LEASE.

4) RIGHT TO PERFORM WORKS PUBLICLY

5) RIGHT TO DISPLAY WORKS PUBLICLY

United States copyright law does not mention moral rights, and several federal and state decisions have noted that moral rights are not recognized in the United States. However, American law accords protection to many of these rights under other legal doctrines such as unfair competition, defamation, invasion of privacy and breach of contract.

The Berne Convention, to which the United States is now a signatory, expressly recognizes moral rights. However, the treaty is not self-executing, which means that the terms of the convention are not binding without implementing American legislation. The American implementation act, however, prohibits the use of Berne as the basis for recognizing more moral rights while reaffirming the protection given under existing American law.

DEALMAKING
IN THE
FILM AND
TELEVISION
INDUSTRY

286

CASE

GILLIAM V. ABC (1976)[1]

FACTS: "Monty Python" (the plaintiffs) retained the copyright in its scripts that the BBC produced as television programs. While the BBC retained final authority to make revisions, plaintiffs exercised primary control over the scripts and only minor changes were permitted without consultation. Nothing in the agreement allowed the BBC to alter the scripts once they were recorded. The BBC owned the copyright to the recorded programs.

The BBC sold the U.S. distribution rights to Time-Life Films and gave Time-Life the right to edit the programs and add commercials. ABC obtained from Time-Life the right to broadcast two 90-minute specials, each comprised of three 30-minute programs. After editing for commercials, the original 90 minutes was reduced by 24 minutes. ABC deleted some material on the ground that it was obscene or offensive.

Plaintiffs claimed that showing a truncated and distorted version of their work was an impairment of the integrity of their copyright and caused the program to lose its iconoclastic verve. Plaintiffs sought an injunction to prevent any further showing.

ISSUE: Should the court grant the injunction?

HOLDING: Yes.

RATIONALE: The authors retained the copyright to their work. The license given the BBC does not give

---

[1] *Gilliam v. ABC*, 538 F.2d 14 (2nd Cir., 1976).

ADVANTAGES OF COPYRIGHT REGISTRATION

1) ESTABLISH A PUBLIC RECORD OF THE COPYRIGHT CLAIM.

2) IF MADE WITHIN FIVE YEARS OF PUBLICATION, REGISTRATION IS PRIMA FACIE EVIDENCE OF VALIDITY OF THE COPYRIGHT.

3) IF MADE BEFORE INFRINGEMENT OR WITHIN THREE MONTHS OF PUBLICATION, REGISTRATION WILL ENABLE ONE TO GET STATUTORY DAMAGES AND ATTORNEYS' FEES.

HOW TO REGISTER A COPYRIGHT

WRITE TO THE COPYRIGHT OFFICE FOR FORMS:

LIBRARY OF CONGRESS
WASHINGTON, D.C. 20559

THE FORMS ARE FREE, BUT ALLOW TWO WEEKS FOR DELIVERY. FOR FASTER SERVICE, CALL THE FORMS AND PUBLICATIONS HOTLINE: (202) 707-9100. ORDERS ARE RECORDED AUTOMATICALLY AND FILLED LATER.

it the right to broadcast a truncated version. The BBC can give ABC no greater rights than the BBC possesses.

Moreover, broadcasting the deformed version as the work of the plaintiffs misrepresents the work's origins, an instance of unfair competition.

While the United States does not expressly recognize the doctrine of moral rights, except as to fine art, legal remedies can often be found under other legal doctrines such as unfair competition.

In this case ABC was representing to the public that their program was the work of the plaintiffs but in a form that substantially departs from the original work. The Lanham Act was invoked to prevent misrepresentation that may injure one's business or personal reputation by creation of a false impression of the product's origin. Thus there is a statutory basis for the type of protection other countries recognize under the principle of author's moral rights.

Questions and Answers

1. If I write a screenplay, do I need to register each draft with the copyright office?

Answer: There is only one copyright for each work. You can make a supplemental filing to your original filing to protect any additions to the draft already registered. If subsequent drafts do not differ materially from earlier drafts, you may not want to bother with a supplemental filing. You might choose not to register early drafts if you plan extensive revisions and you're not going to show the work to anyone. In such a case there is little danger of copyright infringement.

2. During a bus ride I overheard two people engaged in an interesting conversation. Can I incorporate snatches of their talk in my screenplay?

Answer: Yes. Typically speakers don't have any rights in ordinary conversation because the conversation has not been put in tangible form. Assuming you don't identify the person and

DEALMAKING
IN THE
FILM AND
TELEVISION
INDUSTRY

288

violate any right of privacy or defame them, and assuming you are not party to an agreement not to quote them, you should be free to incorporate their conversation in your screenplay.

However, if you subsequently discover that the speakers were not engaged in an ordinary conversation but were actors rehearsing a play, you would not be privileged to borrow any of the conversation (assuming the play was copyrighted material).

CHAPTER 13

THE FIRST AMENDMENT AND THE RIGHT TO PUBLICITY

The Right of Publicity is the right that individuals have to control the use of their name and likeness[1] in a commercial setting. You cannot put a picture of another person on your spaghetti sauce without their permission. The right of publicity is typically exploited by celebrities, who earn large fees from endorsing products.

The Right of Publicity is similar to the appropriation form of invasion of privacy. The principal difference is that the right of publicity seeks to ensure that a person is compensated for the commercial value of his name or likeness while the right of privacy seeks to remedy any hurt feelings or embarrassment that a person may suffer from such publicity.

Celebrities might have difficulty proving invasion of privacy because they do not seek solitude and privacy. How can James Garner claim that the unauthorized use of his likeness on a product embarrassed and humiliated him at the same time that

---

[1] Voice and signature are also protected.

DEALMAKING
IN THE
FILM AND
TELEVISION
INDUSTRY

290

he appears in commercials encouraging consumers to eat beef or drive Mazda cars or use Polaroid film? By thrusting themselves into the public eye, celebrities waive much of their right of privacy. On the other hand, celebrities have an especially valuable property right in their name and likeness, for which they are often paid handsomely.

Under either a publicity or privacy theory, subjects can recover for some unconsented uses of their names and likenesses. A problem arises, however, when one person's publicity/privacy rights come in conflict with another person's rights under the First Amendment. Suppose a newspaper publisher wants to place a picture of Cher on the front page of its paper. Is her permission required? What if "60 Minutes" wants to broadcast an expose of a corrupt politician? What if Kitty Kelly wants to write a critical biography of Frank Sinatra?

In each of these instances, a person's name and likeness is being used on a "product" that is sold to consumers. Products such as books, movies and plays, however, are also forms of expression protected by the First Amendment. The First Amendment allows journalists and writers to freely write about others without their consent. Otherwise, subjects could prevent any critical reporting of their activities. When one person's right of publicity conflicts with another person's rights under the First Amendment, the rights under the First Amendment are often paramount.

When a person's name or likeness is used on a coffee cup or T-shirt or poster, however, there is no expression deserving protection. The seller of these products is not making a statement or expressing an opinion. He is simply trying to make money by exploiting the name and likeness of another. Since there are no competing First Amendment concerns, the right of publicity will prevent the unauthorized use of a subject's name or likeness. Thus the law draws a distinction between products that contain protected expression and those that don't.

Courts have struggled with the issue of whether the right of publicity descends to a person's heirs. In other words, when a celebrity dies, does his estate inherit his right of publicity? Can the estate continue to control the use of the celebrity's name or likeness, or can anyone use it without permission?

THE FIRST
AMENDMENT
AND THE
RIGHT OF
PUBLICITY

291

Some courts have held that the right of publicity is a personal right that does not descend. These courts consider the right similar to the right of privacy and the right to protect one's reputation (defamation). When a person dies, heirs don't inherit these rights. Suppose you were a descendent of George Washington. An unscrupulous writer publishes a defamatory biography claiming that George was a kleptomaniac and revealing the contents of his diary. You couldn't sue for defamation or invasion of privacy. Perhaps this is why many scandalous biographies are not published until the subject dies.

In California, the courts have held that the right of publicity is personal and doesn't descend.[1] In 1984, however, the California legislature changed the law. The legislators enacted Civil Code section 990, which provides that the right of publicity descends for products, merchandise and goods, but does not descend for books, plays, television and movies. A similar statute, California Civil Code section 3344 prohibits the unauthorized use of the name and likeness of living persons on products. News and public affairs uses are excepted. Both statutes attempt to balance First Amendment rights against rights of publicity and privacy.

In other states, the right to publicity may descend. The rights of the heirs, however, may be outweighed by other people's First Amendment rights when protected expression is at stake.

CASES

HICKS V. CASABLANCA RECORDS (1978)[2]

FACTS: Casablanca Records begins to film a movie called *Agatha* about the well-known mystery writer Agatha Christie. The story is a fictionalized account of an eleven-day disappearance of Christie in 1926. The film portrays Christie as an emotionally unstable woman who is engaged in a sinister plot to murder her husband's mistress. An heir to Christie's estate brings suit to enjoin Casablanca from distributing the movie, alleging infringement of Agatha Christie's right of publicity.

---

[1] See *Lugosi v. Universal Pictures*, 25 Cal. 3d at 819 (1979).
[2] 464 F. Supp. 426 (S.D.N.Y. 1978).

DEALMAKING
IN THE
FILM AND
TELEVISION
INDUSTRY

292

ISSUE: Can Casablanca use Agatha Christie's name and likeness without the estate's permission?

HOLDING: Yes—although the right of publicity descends, Casablanca's rights under the First Amendment are paramount to the estate's rights.

RATIONALE: The First Amendment outweighs the right of publicity because the subject was a public figure, and the events portrayed were obviously fictitious.

Here is a movie based on a real-life individual set in a fictional plot. In other words, Agatha Christie was a famous mystery writer, but the story presented in this movie is fictional.

Note that Christie's estate couldn't win a defamation action although the movie portrayed Christie as a criminal. A defamation action isn't possible because the right to protect one's reputation is a personal right that doesn't descend to the estate.

While the right of publicity in this jurisdiction descended, the Christie estate lost. The court felt Casablanca's First Amendment rights outweighed the estate's right to control the name and likeness of Christie.

ZACCHINI V. SCRIPPS-HOWARD BROADCASTING CO. [1]

FACTS: Zacchini, the "human cannonball," is shot from a cannon into a net 200 feet away at a county fair. A news reporter videotapes the entire fifteen-second act without Zacchini's consent. The film clip is shown on the eleven o'clock news program that night. Zacchini brings an action for damages, alleging that the reporter unlawfully infringed upon his right of publicity. The reporter claims that the news broadcast is protected under the First Amendment.

ISSUE: Does the news reporter have the right to broadcast Zacchini's act without his consent?

HOLDING: No. Zacchini prevails.

RATIONALE: The First Amendment does not immunize the press from infringing on the right of publicity. By broadcasting the whole segment, the press threatened the economic value of Zacchini's performance.

---

[1] 433 U.S. 562, 97 S. Ct. 2849 (1977).

THE FIRST
AMENDMENT
AND THE
RIGHT OF
PUBLICITY

293

Here Zacchini's right of publicity is considered more important than the First Amendment rights of the news reporter. So
the First Amendment is not always the paramount right.

The court cited three factors in support of its position:

1) the news reporter knew that Zacchini objected to having
   his entire act televised,

2) the entire act was broadcast,[1] and

3) Zacchini did not seek to enjoin the press; he just wanted
   to be paid for his performance.[2]

MOTSCHENBACHER V. R.J. REYNOLDS TOBACCO CO.[3]

FACTS: Motschenbacher (P), an internationally known
racing-car driver, is paid by manufacturers of commercial
products for his endorsement. Since 1966 his cars have
been painted red with distinctive narrow white pinstriping
and the number eleven on an oval white background.

In 1970 Reynolds Tobacco (D) produced and televised a
cigarette commercial. It depicted several cars on a race-
track, one of which appeared to belong to P. The car's
number had been changed to seventy-one and a spoiler
device attached to the car. The car had the same white
pinstriping, oval medallion and red color as the P's car.
Several persons who saw the commercial immediately
recognized P's car and believed that Winston was spon-
soring the car.

ISSUE: Is P's interest in his identity afforded legal protection?

HOLDING: Yes. These markings were peculiar to P's cars
and they caused some person to think the car in question
was his and to infer that the person driving the car was P.

Recently Bette Midler successfully sued the Ford Motor Co.
and its ad agency. They had hired a singer to imitate Midler's
distinctive voice. The Midler case is[4] discussed on pages 35-37.

---

[1] If the news reporter had stood outside the performance arena and merely informed
viewers of the nature of Zacchini's act, the result would be different. Likewise, if only
a portion of Zacchini's act was broadcast, the holding might differ.

[2] Courts are reluctant to issue injunctions when they prevent people from expressing
themselves. They often prefer to allow the defendant to express himself and compensate the plaintiff with monetary damages for any wrong.

[3] 498 F.2d 821 (9th Cir., 1974).

[4] *Bette Midler v. Ford Motor Company*, 849 F.2d 460 (1988).

DEALMAKING
IN THE
FILM AND
TELEVISION
INDUSTRY

294

Questions and Answers

1. If I shoot a documentary film and interview a subject without obtaining a written release, can I be held liable?

Answer: The First Amendment would likely protect this use. Moreover, a subject who sits still for an interview may have impliedly consented to the use of his name and likeness. However, it never hurts to get a signed release. You should make it a practice to get one whenever possible.

2. How does the right of publicity differ from a copyright?

Answer: You can copyright a work of authorship, such as a book, play or other literary or artistic work. You cannot copyright your personality, name or likeness per se. Simply put, copyright law protects writings (things that people create), while the Right of Publicity protects the value of one's name and likeness (persona).

CHAPTER 14

DEFAMATION OF PERSONS DEPICTED IN LITERARY WORKS

Defamation is a communication that harms the reputation of another so as to lower him in the opinion of the community or to deter third persons from associating or dealing with him. For example, those communications that expose another to hatred, ridicule or contempt, or reflect unfavorably upon their personal morality or integrity are defamatory. One who is defamed may suffer embarrassment and humiliation, as well as economic losses such as loss of a job or the ability to earn a living.

CONSTITUTIONAL LIMITATIONS

The law of defamation can be very confusing. That is because the common-law[1] rules that have developed over the centuries are subject to constitutional limitations. To determine the terms

---

[1] The common law is the law of precedent that arises from cases decided by courts. Another type of law is statutory, or law that has been enacted by a legislative body, like Congress.

DEALMAKING
IN THE
FILM AND
TELEVISION
INDUSTRY

296

of the law, one must read a state's defamation laws in light of various constitutional principles. For example, recent U.S. Supreme Court decisions have imposed significant limitations on the ability of public officials and public figures to win defamation actions. If a state's law is inconsistent with a constitutional principle, the law is invalid.

TYPES OF DEFAMATION

There are two types of defamation. Libel is defamation by written or printed words, or defamation embodied in some physical form. Slander is spoken defamation.

There are historical reasons for the distinction. Libel has been considered the more damaging form of defamation. Printed defamation generally has greater permanency and reaches more people than oral defamation. At least that was the rationale several hundred years ago, in the days before microphones, amplifiers and broadcasting. Today, however, an oral remark can be heard by millions. Surely a slanderous remark uttered on a popular national talk-show would reach far more people than a libelous one printed in an obscure journal.

To take account of the damage that can be done by slanderous broadcasts, California treats all broadcasts as libel.[1] Why is the difference between libel and slander important? The criteria for liability are different. Plaintiffs have to prove more to win a slander action. They must prove special damages. Special damages are specific identifiable economic losses, such as lost wages. General harm to one's reputation is not enough.

There is, however, a form of slander that is actionable without special damages. This is called slander per se, and it occurs when the defamatory remark carries an imputation in one of the following areas:

1) a criminal offense,

2) a loathsome disease,

3) a matter incompatible with the proper exercise of the

---

[1] California Civil Code section section 46.

plaintiff's business, trade, profession or office, or

4) sexual misconduct.

DEFAMATION
OF PERSONS
DEPICTED
IN LITERARY
WORKS

297

PUBLICATION

In order for a plaintiff to prevail in a defamation action, she must prove that the matter was "published." Publication is a term of art. A statement is published when it has been communicated to at least one person other than the plaintiff. The statement need not be in writing or printed.

For example, suppose I was in a room with you alone, and I said, "You dirty lowdown rotten bicycle thief." I could not defame you unless there was someone else in the room. That is because, unless a third party heard the remark, there was no publication.

The reason for this limitation makes sense when you understand that the gist of a defamation action is harm to one's reputation. People do not possess their own reputations. Your reputation is held by the community, and if the community is not exposed to a defamatory remark, your reputation can't possibly suffer.

DEFENSES AND PRIVILEGES

There are number of defenses and privileges to defamation. In other words, sometimes a person can publish a defamatory remark with impunity. Why? Because protecting people's reputation is not the only value we cherish in a democratic society. When the right to protect one's reputation conflicts with a more important right, the defamed person may not recover for harm to his reputation.

The most important privilege, from a filmmaker's point of view, is truth. If your remarks hurt someone's reputation, but your statement is true, you are absolutely privileged. An absolute privilege cannot be lost through bad faith or abuse. So even if you maliciously defame another person, you will be privileged if the statement is true.[1] Truth is an absolute privilege

---

[1] Truth is not a privilege, however, against invasion of privacy.

DEALMAKING
IN THE
FILM AND
TELEVISION
INDUSTRY

298

because society values truth more than it values protection of peoples' reputations.

Keep in mind that while truth is an absolute defense, the burden of proving truth will sometimes fall on the defendant. So if you make a defamatory statement, you should be prepared to prove its truth. And that may not be easy to do.

Another absolute privilege covers communications that occur during judicial, legislative and executive proceedings. Statements made in a court of law are absolutely privileged.[1] Why? Again, as a matter of public policy, the courts have found that it is more important that witnesses speak freely and candidly without fear of being sued than that we protect the reputation of others. Similarly, statements made in a Congressional hearing or in executive proceedings will be privileged.

Conversations between husbands and wives are also privileged. In other words, all pillow talk is protected. If you come home from a hard day at work and make disparaging remarks about your boss to your spouse, you cannot be sued for defamation. This policy encourages candid conversations between spouses. But the privilege does not extend beyond the marriage. So if your spouse the next day communi-

---

HOW DOES THE LAW OF DEFAMATION AFFECT WRITERS, DIRECTORS AND PRODUCERS?

HERE ARE SOME GUIDELINES TO AVOID LIABILITY:

1) BE ESPECIALLY CAREFUL ABOUT PORTRAYING LIVING INDIVIDUALS WHO ARE NOT PUBLIC OFFICIALS OR FIGURES.

2) MAKE SURE YOU CAN PROVE THAT ANY DEFAMATORY STATEMENTS ARE TRUE. ANNOTATE YOUR SCRIPT WITH THE SOURCES OF YOUR INFORMATION SO THAT YOU CAN DOCUMENT ITS TRUTH AND SHOW THAT YOU ACTED WITHOUT "ACTUAL MALICE."

3) OBTAIN RELEASES WHENEVER POSSIBLE. IT NEVER HURTS TO HAVE A RELEASE EVEN IF IT IS NOT LEGALLY REQUIRED.

4) HAVE YOUR ATTORNEY CLOSELY REVIEW YOUR SCRIPT FOR POTENTIAL LIABILITY BEFORE PRODUCTION. IF YOU CAN CHANGE THE NAMES OF SUBJECTS AND THE SETTING WITHOUT DETRACTING FROM THE DRAMATIC VALUE OF THE STORY, DO SO.

5) MAKE SURE THE PRODUCTION OBTAINS AN ERRORS AND OMISSIONS (E & O) INSURANCE POLICY WHICH INCLUDES YOU AS A NAMED INSURED.

---

[1] Provided the remarks are relevant to the proceedings.

cates the disparaging remark to a friend, that statement would not be privileged.

There is also a conditional common law privilege of fair comment and criticism. This privilege applies to communications about a newsworthy person or event. Conditional privileges may be lost through bad faith or abuse. This privilege has been largely superseded, however, by a constitutional privilege for statements about public officials or public figures.

PUBLIC FIGURES AND PUBLIC OFFICIALS

Public figures,[1] such as celebrities or public officials (a Senator), have a much higher burden to bear to prevail in a defamation action. They must prove that the defendant acted with "actual malice." Actual malice is a term of art that means that the defendant intentionally defamed another or acted with reckless disregard of the truth.

Plaintiffs find it difficult to prove that a defendant acted with actual malice. That is why so few celebrities bother suing *The National Enquirer*. To successfully defend itself, the *Enquirer* need only show that it did not act with malice. In other words, the newspaper can come into court and concede that its report was false, defamatory and the result of sloppy and careless research. But unless the celebrity can prove that the *Enquirer* acted with actual malice, the court is obliged to dismiss the case. Mere negligence is not enough for liability.

There is also a constitutional privilege for the mass media. The Supreme Court has said that liability without fault can never be imposed upon the mass media. Even private individuals need to show that the mass media was at least negligent to recover in a defamation action. The court reasoned the mass media must be allowed a certain amount of breathing room to exercise its First Amendment rights. If *The New York Times* was strictly liable for any mistakes it made, the paper would be inhibited from the robust debate essential to a vital democracy.

---

[1] There are two types of public figures: 1) persons of pervasive fame or notoriety, such as a celebrity sports figure, and 2) persons who voluntary inject themselves into a particular public controversy and become public figures for that limited range of issues.

DEALMAKING
IN THE
FILM AND
TELEVISION
INDUSTRY

300

CASES

YOUSSOUPOFF V. MGM (1934)[1]

FACTS: MGM produced a movie in which a character named Princess Natasha resembled real-life Russian Princess Irina Youssoupoff. In the movie the princess is ravaged or seduced by Rasputin, a despicable character. Rasputin is murdered by several men, including the prince whom the princess intended to marry.

Princess Irina brought suit for libel claiming that the public had come to identify her as a female of questionable repute because of the movie. Before the release of the movie, Irina's husband had published a book discussing his participation in the murder of Rasputin. As a result, viewers were likely to perceive that the prince character in the film, Prince Chegodieff, was Prince Youssoupoff and consequently that Natasha was Irina.

MGM described the film as factual, although it was a fictionalized account, and the studio said that some principal characters were alive. The jury concluded that reasonable people would perceive the princess Natasha character to be Princess Irina.

ISSUE: Can one be defamed unintentionally and without being named?

HOLDING: Yes.

RATIONALE: You don't need to name the defamed person if reasonable people could identify the person from the facts and circumstances.

Princess Irina contended that, although she wasn't mentioned by name in the movie, she was defamed. She asserted that viewers thought she was portrayed by the Princess Natasha character and that she had slept with Rasputin. The inference was possible because her husband had published a book recounting his role in Rasputin's death.

The court found that although the MGM movie never mentioned Princess Irina by name, viewers would reasonably conclude that the movie was about incidents in her life. This

---

[1] Eng. Ct of App., 50 Times L.R. S81, 99 A.L.R. 864 (1934).

deduction was likely since MGM billed the movie as a true story and said some people involved were still alive.

Thus, a filmmaker cannot insulate himself from defamation merely by changing the names of people depicted in a movie. If the person depicted is identifiable from the circumstances, liability may result. Similarly, a disclaimer in the credits such as "Any resemblance to people, living or dead is purely coincidental . . ." will not protect the filmmaker if viewers nevertheless

DEFAMATION
OF PERSONS
DEPICTED
IN LITERARY
WORKS

301

believe the movie is depicting a real person.

Suppose a writer published a novel about the widow of an American president who was assassinated in office during a visit to Dallas, and the widow later marries a Greek shipping tycoon. The book is clearly labeled a novel, and there is a prominent disclaimer on the first page saying that everything in it is fiction. Nevertheless, readers believe the book reveals true incidents in the life of Jackie Kennedy and dismiss the disclaimer as a device to protect the author from a lawsuit. Under such

DEFAMATION

DEFINITION: A COMMUNICATION THAT HARMS THE REPUTATION OF ANOTHER AS TO LOWER HIM IN THE ESTIMATION OF THE COMMUNITY OR TO DETER THIRD PERSONS FROM ASSOCIATING OR DEALING WITH HIM.

Types of Defamation

LIBEL: PUBLICATION BY WRITTEN OR PRINTED WORDS.

SLANDER: SPOKEN WORDS, TRANSITORY GESTURES.

Slander Per Se

NO RECOVERY ALLOWED IN A SLANDER ACTION ABSENT SHOWING OF SPECIAL DAMAGES UNLESS THE SLANDER CARRIES AN IMPUTATION IN ONE OF THE FOLLOWING AREAS:

1) CRIMINAL OFFENSE

2) A LOATHSOME DISEASE

3) A MATTER INCOMPATIBLE WITH THE PROPER EXERCISE OF THE PLAINTIFF'S BUSINESS, TRADE, PROFESSION OR OFFICE.

4) SEXUAL MISCONDUCT

Defenses and Privileges[1]

1) TRUTH

2) JUDICIAL, LEGISLATIVE AND EXECUTIVE PROCEEDINGS

3) CONVERSATIONS BETWEEN HUSBANDS AND WIVES

4) CONDITIONAL COMMON-LAW PRIVILEGE OF FAIR COMMENT AND CRITICISM

5) CONSTITUTIONAL PRIVILEGE: PUBLIC OFFICIALS AND PUBLIC FIGURES MUST PROVE ACTUAL MALICE

[1] This list is not exclusive. There are other privileges.

DEALMAKING
IN THE
FILM AND
TELEVISION
INDUSTRY

302

circumstances, the disclaimer will not be sufficient to shield the author from a defamation action.

Filmmakers can protect themselves from liability by:

1) changing the names and circumstances so that the people depicted are not identifiable,

2) obtaining a depiction release from those persons portrayed, or

3) excising any potentially defamatory material.

Of course, a filmmaker could defend a defamation action by raising one or more defenses or privileges, such as truth. But the burden may be on the filmmaker to prove the truth of his statements.

NEW YORK TIMES CO. V. SULLIVAN (1964)[1]

FACTS: Sullivan was one of three elected commissioners of the city of Montgomery, Alabama. His duties included supervision of the police department.

In 1960 a group of black clergymen took out a full page ad in *The New York Times* discussing the plight of black students involved in the civil-rights movement. The ad claimed that the students were terrorized by the Montgomery police. It described various abuses, some of which never occurred.

Sullivan felt that Montgomery residents would believe these statements reflected poorly on himself as Commissioner of the police department. He sued for libel.

ISSUE: Are the clergymen who took out the ad liable for defamation? Is *The New York Times* liable for defamation?

HOLDING: Judgment for the defendants.

RATIONALE: You can't defame a public official for statements about his official conduct unless the statements were made with actual malice (i.e., knowledge of falsity or reckless disregard of the truth). Here the *Times* was at most negligent in failing to discover the misstatements. Also evidence was insufficient to establish that the statements were made "of and concerning" Sullivan.

---

[1] 376 U.S. 254 (1964).

This is the landmark decision that established the actual malice standard required of public officials in defamation suits. Subsequent cases have extended the New York Times Co. v. Sullivan rule to public figures.

The court also ruled against Sullivan because the defamatory statements were not "of and concerning" Sullivan. In other words, Sullivan himself was not defamed, only the police officers he supervised. This was not considered direct enough to be actionable. Similarly, if someone said, "The New York Yankees stink," a die-hard New Yorker could not sue because such a statement reflected poorly on him.

DEFAMATION
OF PERSONS
DEPICTED
IN LITERARY
WORKS

303

CASES

GERTZ V. ROBERT WELCH, INC. (1974)[1]

FACTS: In 1968, a Chicago policeman shot and killed a youth. The policeman was later convicted of murder in the second degree. The family of the slain boy retained attorney Gertz (P) to represent them in a civil action against the policeman.

A John Birch Society publication published by Welch (D) portrayed Gertz as having framed the policeman and said Gertz was a communist. Because these statements constituted libel per se under Illinois law, Gertz received a jury award of $50,000. The District Court, however, overturned the jury verdict and entered judgment for D because P should have been required to meet the N.Y. Times Co. v. Sullivan standard that requires a showing of actual malice.

ISSUE: Does the New York Times Co. standard apply?

HOLDING: No. A newspaper or broadcaster that publishes defamatory falsehoods about an individual, who is neither a public official nor public figure, may not claim a constitutional privilege against liability for the injury inflicted by those statements.

RATIONALE: Public figures, by virtue of their public status, have more of an opportunity to counteract false statements.

[1] 418 U.S. 323, 94 S. Ct. 2997 (1974).

DEALMAKING
IN THE
FILM AND
TELEVISION
INDUSTRY

304

This case is instructive for three reasons. First, it establishes that an attorney involved in a prominent case is not necessarily a public figure. The status of an individual can often be difficult to determine. Another Supreme Court case[1] held that a socially prominent person involved in a celebrated divorce trial was not a public figure.

Second, the Gertz case says that a plaintiff must show actual malice to recover more than actual damages. Thus, if liability is predicated on negligence, a plaintiff ordinarily cannot recover presumed or punitive damages.[2]

Third, the Gertz court held that the mass media can never be held strictly liable for defamation. If a newspaper could be held strictly liable for any misstatement, the paper's exercise of its First Amendment Right of free expression would be greatly inhibited.

STREET V. NBC (1981)[3]

FACTS: In 1931 nine black youths were accused of raping two young white women while riding a freight train. The youths were promptly tried in Scottsboro, Alabama, found guilty and sentenced to death. The case was the subject of widespread media coverage.

In reversing the convictions, the United States Supreme Court said that the defendants were denied the right to counsel. The defendants were retried separately after a change in venue. In a trial before Judge Horton, the jury found defendant Patterson guilty and sentenced him to death. Judge Horton then set the verdict aside. Upon retrial Patterson and several other defendants were convicted and sent to prison.

The case against the Scottsboro defendants was based on the testimony of Victoria Price. She gave some press interviews at the time but then disappeared from sight.

Forty years after the case, NBC televised a historical drama entitled *Judge Horton and the Scottsboro Boys*. The movie was based on a book by a historian who portrayed

---

[1] *Time, Inc. v. Firestone*, 424 U.S. 448, 96 S. Ct. 958 (1976).

[2] An exception occurs when no public issues are involved. See *Dun & Bradstreet, Inc. v. Greenmoss Builders, Inc.*, 472 U.S. 749, 105 S. Ct. 2939 (1985).

[3] 645 F.2d 1227 (1981).

Price in a derogatory light. She was shown to be a perjurer, a woman of bad character, and a person who falsely accused the Scottsboro boys of rape knowing that the verdict would likely condemn them to the electric chair. Witnesses who corroborated Price's version of the facts were omitted from the movie. Portions of the trial that showed her to be a perjurer and a promiscuous woman were emphasized. NBC incorrectly stated in the movie that she was no longer living. After the first showing, Price informed NBC that she was living and sued. NBC rebroadcast the dramatization omitting the statement that she was no longer living.

DEFAMATION
OF PERSONS
DEPICTED
IN LITERARY
WORKS

305

ISSUE: Is Price a public figure?

HOLDING: Yes.

RATIONALE: Price remains a public figure notwithstanding the passage of time.

The defendant NBC prevailed because the *New York Times* standard applies and the P could not prove that NBC acted with actual malice. There is no evidence that NBC had knowledge that its portrayal of Price was false or that NBC recklessly disregarded the truth. The author of the history and the producer of the movie may have had their facts wrong, but the law will not punish them unless they acted with actual malice.

CHAPTER 15

THE RIGHT OF PRIVACY

The United States Constitution does not mention a right of privacy. According to the United States Supreme Court, however, such a right is implicit in the Constitution and the Bill of Rights.

The right of privacy has been defined as the right to live one's life in seclusion, without being subjected to unwarranted and undesired publicity. In other words, it is the right to be left alone.

Like defamation, the right of privacy is subject to constitutional restrictions. The news media, for example, is not liable for defamatory statements that are newsworthy unless they are made with knowing or reckless disregard of the truth (i.e., actual malice). Unlike defamation, a cause of action for invasion of privacy does not require any injury to one's reputation.

Suppose you were in your backyard sunbathing in the nude. Your backyard is surrounded by a solid wood fence preventing passersby from seeing you. Suddenly a photographer for *The National Enquirer* hops over the fence and snaps your picture. Soon the photograph is displayed in newspaper tabloids near supermarket check-out stands across the nation. Can you sue for defamation?

No, because you were sunbathing in the nude and truth is an

DEALMAKING
IN THE
FILM AND
TELEVISION
INDUSTRY

308

absolute defense to defamation. Could you sue for invasion of privacy? Yes. You have a reasonable expectation of privacy in your enclosed backyard.

Suppose you were sunbathing in the nude on your front porch, in open public view. Could you bring a successful action for invasion of privacy? No, because you do not have a reasonable expectation of privacy under these circumstances. Thus, whether an intrusion into your privacy will be actionable de-

THE WRITER/FILMMAKER AS INVESTIGATOR

Entering Private Premises

WRITERS AND FILMMAKERS WISHING TO ENTER PRIVATE PROPERTY NEED PERMISSION. THERE IS NO FIRST AMENDMENT RIGHT TO TRESPASS ON PRIVATE PROPERTY. CONSENT MAY NOT BE EFFECTIVE IF YOU EXCEED THE SCOPE OF THE CONSENT GIVEN. JUST BECAUSE SOMEONE LETS YOU INTO THEIR LIVING ROOM DOES NOT MEAN YOU CAN RIFLE THROUGH THEIR DESK DRAWERS.

Receiving Private Documents From Inside Sources

GENERALLY A WRITER WILL NOT BE LIABLE FOR INVASION OF PRIVACY IF HE DID NOT PARTICIPATE IN, ENCOURAGE OR SUGGEST ANY UNLAWFUL ACTS TO OBTAIN THE PROPERTY BUT IS MERELY A PASSIVE RECIPIENT OF THEM. THIS HOLDS TRUE EVEN IF THE WRITER KNOWS THAT PAPERS ARE STOLEN.

Taping Telephone Calls (Federal)

WIRETAPPING IS PROHIBITED BY FEDERAL CRIMINAL STATUTE 18 U.S.C. § 2511. THE LAW DOES NOT PROHIBIT, HOWEVER, TAPING OF PHONE CALLS BY A PARTY TO A CONVERSATION IF THE RECORDING IS NOT DONE FOR AN ILLEGAL PURPOSE.[1]

FEDERAL LAW GOVERNS ONLY INTERSTATE PHONE CALLS.

State

LAWS VARY BY STATE. MANY STATES REQUIRE CONSENT OF BOTH PARTIES.

CALIFORNIA PENAL CODE § 632 PROHIBITS RECORDING TELEPHONE CALLS WITHOUT THE CONSENT OF ALL PARTIES TO THE CONVERSATION. AN EXCEPTION IS PROVIDED FOR CONVERSATIONS WHICH ARE NOT CONFIDENTIAL.

CONSENT SHOULD BE OBTAINED IN WRITING OR RECORDED ON TAPE

CONTINUED.

[1] U.S. v. Wright, 573 F. 2d 681 (1978).

pends on whether you have a reasonable expectation of privacy.

Many defenses to defamation apply to invasion of privacy. But truth is not a defense, and revealing matters of public record cannot be the basis for an invasion of privacy action. Express and implied consent are valid defenses. If you voluntarily reveal private facts to others you cannot recover for invasion of your privacy.

Privacy actions typically fall into four factual patterns.[1]

THE WRITER/FILMMAKER AS INVESTIGATOR
(CONTINUED)

Obtaining Government Information

CITIZENS ARE GENERALLY PERMITTED ACCESS TO GOVERNMENT RECORDS UNDER STATE OR FEDERAL FREEDOM OF INFORMATION ACTS (FOIA).

Federal FOIA[1]

EXEMPT AREAS:

1) NATIONAL SECURITY—FOREIGN AFFAIRS

2) INTERNAL PRACTICES OF AN AGENCY

3) INTERAGENCY MEMORANDA

4) INVESTIGATORY FILES

5) TRADE OR COMMERCIAL SECRETS

6) PERSONNEL AND MEDICAL FILES

7) REPORTS ON REGULATION OF FINANCIAL INSTITUTIONS

8) GEOLOGICAL DATA

9) DATA SPECIFICALLY EXEMPT FROM DISCLOSURE UNDER OTHER LAWS

EXEMPTIONS UNDER CALIFORNIA'S FREEDOM OF INFORMATION ACT ARE SET FORTH IN CALIFORNIA GOVERNMENT CODE § 6254.

---
[1] Title 5, U.S.C. § 552.

---
[1] Privacy actions need not fall within one of these four categories to be actionable.

DEALMAKING
IN THE
FILM AND
TELEVISION
INDUSTRY

310

INTRUSION INTO ONE'S PRIVATE AFFAIRS

This category includes such activities as wiretapping and unreasonable surveillance. The intrusion must be highly offensive. Whether an intrusion is highly offensive depends on the circumstances. Most people would find it offensive to discover a voyeur peering through their bedroom window. On the other hand, a salesman knocking on your front door at dinner time may be obnoxious but will not be sufficiently offensive to state a cause of action.

PUBLIC DISCLOSURE OF EMBARRASSING PRIVATE FACTS

One who gives publicity to a matter concerning the private life of another is subject to liability for invasion of privacy, if the matter publicized is of a kind that:

a) would be highly offensive to a reasonable person, and

b) is not of legitimate concern to the public. In other words, it is not newsworthy.

An example of this type of invasion of privacy would occur if someone digs up some dirt on another person, publicizes it and the information is not of legitimate interest to the public.

APPROPRIATION

An action for appropriation of another's name or likeness is similar to action for invasion of one's right of publicity. The former action seeks to compensate the plaintiff for the emotional distress, embarrassment and hurt feelings that may arise from the use of one's name or likeness on a product. The latter action seeks to compensate the plaintiff for the commercial value arising from the exploitation of one's name and likeness.

As with the right of publicity, a person cannot always control the use of his name and likeness by another. While you can prevent someone from putting your face on their pancake mix, you cannot stop *Time* magazine from putting your face on its cover. Thus the use of someone's name or likeness as part of a newsworthy incident would not be actionable.

FALSE LIGHT

Publicity placing a plaintiff in a false light will be actionable if the portrayal is highly offensive. This type of invasion of privacy is similar to defamation but harm to reputation is not required. An example of false light invasion of privacy could entail a political dirty trick such as placing the name of a prominent Republican on a list of Democratic contributors. Although this person's reputation may not be harmed, he has been shown in a false light.

CASES

MELVIN V. REID (1931)[1]

FACTS: In 1925, Reid (D) released a motion picture entitled *The Red Kimono.* The movie told the true story of the unsavory incidents in the life of Melvin (P). The film portrayed Melvin as a prostitute who was tried and acquitted of murder in 1918. The film used the real maiden name of Melvin, who had since reformed, married, assumed a place in respectable society, and made many friends who were unaware of her previous activities. She sued Reid for invasion of privacy.

ISSUE: Did Reid invade Melvin's privacy?

HOLDING: Yes. Plaintiff wins.

RATIONALE: Publication of past unsavory incidents after she has reformed, coupled with use of her real name, is an invasion of privacy. This incident was no longer newsworthy.

---

[1] 112 Cal. App. 285, 297 P. 91 (1931).

DEALMAKING
IN THE
FILM AND
TELEVISION
INDUSTRY

312

While the public has a legitimate interest in Melvin's illegal activities, these incidents happened some time ago, and there was no good reason for revealing her identity now. The story could have been told just as well without using her real name. Had the producer changed the character's name, the court's decision would likely be different. Thus, changing the identity of a character can sometimes insulate a film-maker from liability.

Note that material taken from court records is privileged. However, the filmmaker here went beyond the public record. Writers usually find it difficult to tell a true story without going beyond the public record since it is rare for subjects' lives to be so fully documented. Of course, if one presented a courtroom drama limited to the trial transcripts, the material would be completely privileged.

Why didn't the plaintiff file a defamation action? Because the events were true, and truth is an absolute defense to defamation.

BERNSTEIN V. NBC (1955)[1]

FACTS: In 1919, Bernstein (P) was convicted of bank robbery and sentenced to prison for forty years. After serving nine years, he was paroled and pardoned. In 1933, Bernstein, under another name, was tried and convicted of first-degree murder and sentenced to death. Later the sentence was commuted to life imprisonment. In 1940, Bernstein received a conditional release and in 1945 a presidential pardon. After that, Bernstein lived an exemplary, quiet and private life, shunning publicity.

In 1952, NBC (D) telecast a fictionalized dramatization of Bernstein's conviction and pardon. The movie did not mention Bernstein's real name. He alleges, however, that the actor who portrayed him resembled him physically, and that his words and actions were reproduced creating a portrayal recognizable to his friends and identifying him in the public mind. Bernstein alleged that the program was a willful and malicious invasion of his right of privacy.

ISSUE: Did NBC invade Bernstein's right of privacy?

[1] 129 F. Supp. 817 (D.D.C. 1955).

HOLDING: No.

RATIONALE: The events in question were already known by the public from the prior publicity. The passage of time was not enough to make them private facts. Also, the program did not identify Bernstein. Bernstein conceded that only those people who already knew about the story would recognize him.

The facts of this case are not much different from *Melvin v. Reid*. However, here defendant NBC fictionalized Bernstein's name and moved the events from Minneapolis to Washington, D.C.

Why didn't Bernstein sue for defamation? First, because the story was true. Second, it is appears his reputation was not damaged. He was portrayed sympathetically, as a man unjustly convicted of a crime. Note that this movie focused most of its attention on the crusading news journalist who proved Bernstein's innocence. The journalist found an eyewitness who revealed that Bernstein wasn't the killer. The journalist also deduced that a witness against Bernstein couldn't possibly have seen the murder because leaves on a tree at that time of year blocked her view.

GILL V. HEARST PUBLISHING (1953)[1]

FACTS: As part of an article in *Ladies' Home Journal* entitled *Love*, Hearst (D) published a photo of Mr. and Mrs. Gill (P) taken without their permission. The photo captured the Gills in an affectionate pose, at their place of business, a confectionery and ice cream store in the Farmer's Market in Los Angeles.

ISSUE: Is publication of a photo without the consent of the subjects, an invasion of their privacy?

HOLDING: No.

RATIONALE: Persons do not have an absolute legal right to prevent publication of any photo taken of them without their permission. If every person had such a right, no photo could be published of a street scene or a parade. Liability exists only if publication of a photo would be offensive to people of ordinary sensibilities. Here the Gills voluntarily assumed this pose in a public place. The

---

[1] 40 Cal. 2d 224 (1953).

DEALMAKING
IN THE
FILM AND
TELEVISION
INDUSTRY

314

photo merely permitted others to see them as they publicly exhibited themselves.

The Gills were not a subject of *The Ladies' Home Journal* article. The magazine did not interview them or mention them by name. The magazine merely bought a stock photo of them taken by a photographer who happened to snap their picture one day. This photograph was taken inside the Gill's store in open public view.

This case stands for the principle that people do not have an absolute right to control the use of their name and likeness. A television news reporter could broadcast footage of an individual without his permission. It is always a good idea, however, to get a release, to preclude any possibility of a lawsuit.

The decision would be different if the Gills were photographed in a place where they had a reasonable expectation of privacy, such as their bedroom, or if the Gill's picture was used on a commercial product.

SPAHN V. JULIAN MESSNER, INC. (1967)[1]

FACTS: Spahn, a well-known baseball player, sued over the publication of an unauthorized biography, alleging that his rights under New York's misappropriation (privacy) statute had been invaded. In the purported biography, the author took great literary license, dramatizing incidents, inventing conversations, manipulating chronologies, attributing thoughts and feelings to Spahn and fictionalizing events. The invented material depicted the plaintiff's childhood, his relationship with his father, the courtship of his wife, important events in their marriage and his military experience.

The defendant argues that the literary techniques he used are customary for juvenile books. The defendant never interviewed Spahn, any members of his family or any baseball player who knew him. The author's research was comprised of newspaper and magazine clippings, the veracity of which he rarely confirmed.

ISSUE: Did the defendant invade P's privacy?

HOLDING: Yes.

RATIONALE: The New York privacy statute protects a

---

[1] *Spahn v. Julian Messner, Inc.*, 21 N.Y. 2d 124, 233 N.E. 2d 840 (1967).

public person from fictionalized publication only if the work was published with knowledge of the falsification or with reckless disregard for the truth (actual malice). D acted with at least reckless disregard of the truth in incorporating so much fictional and false material.

Factual reporting of newsworthy persons and events is in the public interest and is protected. The fictitious is not. The Plantiff does not seek an injunction and damages for the unauthorized publication of his biography. He seeks only to restrain the publication of that which purports to be his biography.

New York has enacted a statute protecting the privacy of its citizens.[1] The court found the law to be constitutional provided actual malice was shown because Spahn is a public figure. Since the defendant writer invented large portions of the book, he obviously knew his statements were not true. Spahn could not prevent publication of an unflattering biography simply because he didn't like its contents.

LEOPOLD V. LEVIN (1970)[2]

FACTS: In 1924, Nathan Leopold (P) and a partner pleaded guilty to kidnapping and murdering a young boy. Because of the luridness of the crime, the case attracted international notoriety, which did not wane over time. In 1958, a paroled Leopold published a publicized autobiography.

In 1956, Levin (D) wrote a novel, *Compulsion*, whose basic framework was the Leopold case, although Leopold's name did not appear in it. The book was described as a fictionalized account of the Leopold murder case. A motion picture based on the book was released with fictitious characters who resembled actual persons in the case. The promotional materials referred to the crime but made it clear that the story was a work of fiction suggested by the case. Leopold sues for invasion of privacy.

ISSUE: Does a person who fosters continued public attention, after having engaged in an activity placing him

---

[1] New York Civil Rights Law §§ 50, 51.

[2] *Leopold v. Levin*, 45 Ill.2d 434, 259 N.E. 2d 250 (1970).

DEALMAKING
IN THE
FILM AND
TELEVISION
INDUSTRY

316

in the public eye, have a right of privacy in fictitious accounts of that activity or in the use of his name in promoting such account?

HOLDING: No.

RATIONALE: Books, magazines, newspapers and motion pictures are forms of public expression protected by the first amendment, even if they are sold for profit. While the book and movie were "suggested" by Leopold's crime, they were evidently fictional and dramatized works. The core of the novel and film were a part of Leopold's life that he had caused to be placed in public view. The fictionalized aspects, minor in offensiveness, were reasonably conceivable from the facts of record from which they were drawn. Similarly, reference to Plaintiff in advertising materials concerned his notorious crime. His participation was a matter of public and historical record so that his conduct was without benefit of privacy.

The court noted that a documentary account of the Leopold case would be constitutionally protected. Also, a completely fictional work inspired by the case would be protected if matters such as locale were changed and there was no promotional identification with the plaintiff.

CHAPTER 16

TRADEMARKS AND UNFAIR COMPETITION

TRADEMARKS

A trademark or service mark[1] is a brand name that can be a word, a symbol, or a device used by a business to distinguish its goods or services from those of others. "Coca-Cola" written in its distinctive script is a trademark, as are "IBM," "Disney" and thousands of other marks used to identify the source of goods or services. In the entertainment industry, titles of television series and some movies may be trademarked.

Trademarks can theoretically last forever as long as they are used to distinguish goods. They can be abandoned by non-use or can fall into the public domain if they become the generic term of a product. For example, former trademarks "zipper," "thermos," "aspirin," and "brassiere" are now considered generic names for all such products, regardless of their manufacturer.

Unlike patents and copyrights,[2] protection of trademarks is

---

[1] A trademark is used on a product; a service mark designates a service. Unless otherwise noted, all references to the rights of trademark holders apply as well to service marks.

[2] Before 1978, unpublished works were protected under state law. Since then, federal copyright law has largely preempted the field.

317

DEALMAKING
IN THE
FILM AND
TELEVISION
INDUSTRY

318

not based exclusively on federal law. State law may provide important remedies. Note also that federal trademarks can be obtained only for products or services used in interstate commerce (i.e., sold in more than one state).

Federal trademark law provides for a registration system administered by the U.S. Trademark Office. You are not required to register a trademark to establish your right to use it. Simply using a particular mark to distinguish your goods from those manufactured by others may prevent third parties from using the mark. Registration of a mark confers several advantages such as allowing the trademark owner to obtain triple

CREATION OF TRADEMARK RIGHTS

TRADEMARK RIGHTS ARISE FROM 1) USE OF THE MARK OR 2) A BONA FIDE INTENTION TO USE A MARK, ALONG WITH THE FILING OF AN APPLICATION TO FEDERALLY REGISTER THAT MARK.

THEREFORE, BEFORE A TRADEMARK OWNER MAY FILE AN APPLICATION FOR FEDERAL REGISTRATION, THE OWNER MUST 1) USE THE MARK ON GOODS THAT ARE SHIPPING OR SOLD, OR SERVICES THAT ARE RENDERED IN INTERSTATE COMMERCE (OR COMMERCE BETWEEN THE U.S. AND A FOREIGN COUNTRY) OR 2) HAVE A BONA FIDE INTENTION TO USE THE MARK IN SUCH COMMERCE IN RELATION TO SPECIFIC GOODS OR SERVICES.

THE FEDERAL REGISTRATION PROCESS

WHEN AN APPLICATION HAS BEEN FILED, AN EXAMINING ATTORNEY IN THE PATENT AND TRADEMARK OFFICE WILL REVIEW THE APPLICATION AND DECIDE WHETHER THE MARK MAY BE REGISTERED. THE OFFICE WILL MAKE AN INITIAL DETERMINATION ABOUT THREE MONTHS AFTER THE APPLICATION HAS BEEN FILED. THE APPLICANT MUST RESPOND TO ANY OBJECTIONS WITHIN SIX MONTHS OR THE APPLICATION WILL BE DEEMED ABANDONED.

ONCE THE EXAMINING ATTORNEY APPROVES A MARK, THE MARK IS PUBLISHED IN THE *TRADEMARK OFFICIAL GAZETTE*. THIRTY DAYS ARE ALLOWED FOR ANYONE TO OBJECT TO THE REGISTRATION. IF NO OPPOSITION IS FILED, THE REGISTRATION WILL ISSUE ABOUT TWELVE WEEKS LATER FOR MARKS IN USE IN COMMERCE. FOR APPLICATIONS BASED ON INTENT TO USE, A NOTICE OF ALLOWANCE WILL ISSUE ABOUT TWELVE WEEKS AFTER PUBLICATION. THE APPLICANT THEN HAS SIX MONTHS TO EITHER USE THE MARK IN COMMERCE OR REQUEST A SIX-MONTH EXTENSION OF TIME TO FILE A STATEMENT OF USE.

damages and reimbursement of attorneys' fees.

To federally register a mark, one must submit an application. An examiner in the Trademark Office reviews the application to verify:

1) that the mark is not deceptive;

2) that the mark is not confusingly similar to another mark; and

BENEFITS OF REGISTRATION

THE BENEFITS OF FEDERAL REGISTRATION INCLUDE THE FOLLOWING:

1) THE RIGHT TO SUE IN FEDERAL COURT FOR TRADEMARK INFRINGEMENT;

2) THE RIGHT TO RECOVER PROFITS, DAMAGES AND COSTS FROM AN INFRINGER, AND UP TO TRIPLE DAMAGES AND ATTORNEYS' FEES;

3) GIVES OTHERS CONSTRUCTIVE NOTICE OF YOUR MARK;

4) ALLOWS THE USE OF THE FEDERAL REGISTRATION SYMBOL, ®;

5) ALLOWS ONE TO DEPOSIT COPIES OF THE REGISTRATION WITH THE CUSTOMS SERVICE TO STOP IMPORTATION OF GOODS BEARING AN INFRINGING MARK;

6) PERMITS ONE TO SUE FOR COUNTERFEITING THE MARK, PROVIDING CIVIL AND CRIMINAL PENALTIES;

7) ENABLES ONE TO FILE A CORRESPONDING APPLICATION IN MANY FOREIGN COUNTRIES.

STATE REGISTRATION GIVES ONE IMPORTANT ADDITIONAL BENEFIT—IT PREVENTS ANOTHER FROM REGISTERING THE SAME MARK WITH THE STATE.

GROUNDS FOR REFUSING FEDERAL REGISTRATION

1) IT IS SCANDALOUS OR DISPARAGING.

2) IT IS AN INSIGNIA OF A GOVERNMENTAL ENTITY.

3) WITHOUT CONSENT IT IDENTIFIES A LIVING INDIVIDUAL OR A DECEASED PRESIDENT DURING THE LIFE OF HIS WIDOW.

4) IT IS CONFUSINGLY SIMILAR TO A PREVIOUSLY REGISTERED MARK, OR TO A MARK PREVIOUSLY USED IN THE UNITED STATES BY ANOTHER AND NOT ABANDONED.

5) IT IS MERELY DESCRIPTIVE OR DECEPTIVELY MISDESCRIPTIVE OF GOODS OR SERVICES. OR IT IS PRIMARILY A SURNAME AND IS NOT DISTINCTIVE OF SUCH GOODS OR SERVICES.

DEALMAKING
IN THE
FILM AND
TELEVISION
INDUSTRY

320

3) that the mark is not merely descriptive of goods or misdescriptive, geographically descriptive or misdescriptive, or is primarily a surname.

Whether one mark infringes another is determined by whether use of the two marks would cause consumers to be mistaken or confused about the origin of manufacture.

MAINTENANCE OF THE MARK

Continued use of the mark is necessary to avoid abandonment of the mark. Federal registrations must be renewed every ten years. Moreover, between the fifth and sixth year after the date of the registration, you must file an affidavit stating that the mark is currently in use in commerce. If no affidavit is filed, the registration will be canceled.

UNFAIR COMPETITION

Section 43 of the federal Lanham Act, 15 U.S.C. § 1125, provides:

> (a) Any person who shall affix, apply, or annex, or use in connection with any goods or services, or any container or containers for goods, a false designation of origin, or any false description or representation, including words or other symbols tending falsely to describe or represent the same . . . shall be liable to a civil action . . . by any person who believes that he is or is likely to be damaged by the use of any such false description or representation.

Under the law of unfair competition, a person cannot open a hamburger stand and name it "McDonald's" if they are not affiliated with the well-known chain. A competitor would also be barred from displaying golden arches or using any device that would mislead and confuse consumers and make them think his burgers are genuine McDonald's burgers when they are not.

Placing a misleading title on a movie could be actionable as unfair competition. Suppose a sleazy movie producer decides to release his low-budget movie with the title *Raiders of the <u>Last</u> Ark* soon after George Lucas has released his *Raiders of the Lost Ark*. Since the public has come to identify the title with the work of George Lucas, the words have acquired a secondary meaning. Thus consumers would likely be confused about the origin of *Raiders of the Last Ark*.

CASE

ALLEN V. NATIONAL VIDEO (1985)[1]

FACTS: National Video, a video-rental chain, placed a series of ads in which a Woody Allen look-alike is portrayed in a picture as one of its customers. The look-alike appears at a counter checking out the videotapes of *Annie Hall, Bananas, Casablanca* and *The Maltese Falcon*. He is holding a National Video V.I.P. card and the woman behind the counter is smiling and gasping in exaggerated excitement at the presence of a celebrity.

The copy reads, "Become a V.I.P. at National Video. We'll make you look like a star," and, "You don't need a famous face to be treated to some pretty famous service." A small disclaimer stating that a celebrity double was being used appeared in one ad. Allen sued, claiming that his portrait was used without permission and that the ads were misleading and likely to confuse consumers and lead them to believe he had endorsed National Video.

ISSUE: Does Allen have a cause of action?

HOLDING: Yes.

RATIONALE: Consumers are likely to be confused. There is a likelihood of confusion even with the ad containing the disclaimer. The disclaimer is small and says only that a celebrity double is being used which doesn't by itself dispel the inference that Allen may be involved with National's products or services. The disclaimer must be bold and make clear Allen in no way endorses the service.

Allen also sued on Invasion of Privacy and infringement of his

---

[1] *Allen v. National Video*, 610 F. Supp. 612 (S.D.N.Y., 1985).

DEALMAKING
IN THE
FILM AND
TELEVISION
INDUSTRY

322

Right to Publicity. The court said that since the defendant didn't use Allen's name or likeness, there was no privacy cause of action. Whether Allen stated a cause of action for invasion of his Right of Publicity was a question for the jury to decide. They would need to decide whether the look-alike created the illusion of Woody Allen's actual presence.

CHAPTER 17

GLOSSARY OF TERMS

Above-the-line costs Portion of the budget that covers major creative participants (writer, director, actors and producer), including script and story development costs.

Below-the-line costs The technical expenses and labor including set construction, crew, camera equipment, film stock, developing and printing.

Advance Money obtained up front in anticipation of profits or royalties. Maybe be non-coupable or refundable, the former sometimes called a guarantee.

Answer print The first composite (sound and picture) motion picture print from the laboratory with editing, score and mixing completed. Usually color values will need to be corrected before a release print is made.

Art theater Shows specialized art films, generally in exclusive engagements, rather than mass-marketed studio films.

DEALMAKING
IN THE
FILM AND
TELEVISION
INDUSTRY

324

Auteur A French term, the auteur theory holds that the director is the true creator or author of a film, bringing together script, actors, cinematographer, editor and molding everything into a work of cinematic art with a cohesive vision. Anyone who has worked on a movie knows what complete nonsense this is. Filmmaking is a collaborative endeavor and the director is only one of the contributors.

Back end Profit participation in a film after distribution and/or production costs have be recouped.

Between projects Out of work.

Blind bidding Requiring theater owners to bid on a movie without seeing it. Several states and localities require open trade screenings for each new release. Guarantees and advances may also be banned.

Blow-up Optical process of enlarging a film, usually from 16mm to 35 mm.

Box office gross Total revenues taken in at movie theater box offices before any expenses or percentages are deducted.

Break To open a film in several theaters simultaneously, either in and around a single city or in a group of cities, or on a national basis.

Breakout To expand bookings after an initial period of exclusive or limited engagement.

Completion bond A form of insurance which guarantees completion of a film in the event that the producer exceeds the budget and is unable to secure additional funding. Completion bonds are sometimes required by banks and investors to secure loans and investments in a production. Should a bond be invoked, the completion guarantor will assume control over the production and be in a recoupment position superior to all investors. But, do you really want an insurance company finishing your film?

Cross-collateralization Practice by which distributors offset financial loses in one medium or market against profits derived from others. For example, the rentals obtained from France are combined with those from Italy, and after the expenses for both are deducted, the remainder, if any, is profit. Filmmakers don't like to have the markets for their films cross-collateralized because it may reduce the amount of money they are likely to see.

Crossover film Film that is initially targeted for a narrow specialty market and achieves acceptance in a wider market.

Day and Date The simultaneous opening of two or more movie theaters in one or more cities.

Day Player An actor who works a day at a time on a film. In other words, actors with bit parts.

Deferred payment Writers, directors, actors and others may take only part of their salary up front in order to reduce the budget of the picture. The rest of their fee is paid from box-office and other revenues that may, or may not, accrue later.

Development The process by which an initial idea is turned into a finished screenplay. Includes optioning the rights to an underlying literary property and commissioning writers to create a treatment, first draft, second draft, rewrite and polish.

Distributor A company that markets a motion picture, placing it in theaters, advertising and promoting it. The major studios nowadays are mostly in the business of financing and distributing films, leaving production to smaller independent companies.

Direct advertising Mailing fliers and direct outreach to consumers, usually targeted to a specific interest group.

Display advertising Advertising which features art work or title treatment specific to a given film in newspaper and magazine advertising.

DEALMAKING
IN THE
FILM AND
TELEVISION
INDUSTRY

326

Domestic rights Rights within U.S. and Canada only.

Downbeat ending A story that ends unhappily or in a depressing manner.

Exclusive opening A type of release whereby a film is opened in a single theater in a major city, giving the distributor the option to hold the film for a long exclusive run or move it into additional theaters based on the film's performance.

Feature film Full length, fictional films (not documentaries or shorts) generally for theatrical release.

Film noir Dark, violent, urban, downbeat films, many of which were made in the '40s and '50s.

Final Cut The last stage in the editing process. The right to final cut is the right to determine the ultimate artistic control over the picture. Usually the studio or the financier of a picture retains final cut.

First money From the producers point of view, the first revenue received from the distribution of a movie. Not to be confused with profits, first monies are generally allocated to investors until recoupment, but may be allocated in part or in whole to deferred salaries owed talent or deferred fees owed the film laboratory.

First run The first engagement of a new film.

Floors In distributor/exhibitor agreements, the minimum percentage of box office receipts the distributor is entitled to regardless of the theater's operating expenses. Generally decline week by week over the course of an engagement. Generally range from 70% to 25%.

Foreign sales Licensing a film in various territories and media outside the U.S. and Canada. Although Canada is a foreign country, American distributors typically acquire Canadian rights when they buy U.S. domestic rights.

Four-Walling   Renting a theater and its staff for a flat fee, buying your own advertising, and receiving all the revenue. The exhibitor is paid a flat fee regardless of performance and receives no split of box office receipts.

Front office   The top executives, the people who control the money.

General partners   Management side of a limited partnership (the position usually occupied by the film's producers) which structures a motion-picture investment and raises money from investors who become limited partners. General partners control all business decisions regarding the partnership.

Grassroots campaign   Using fliers, posters, stickers and building word-of-mouth with special screenings for local community groups.

Gross Box Office   Total revenue taken in at theater box office for ticket sales.

Hot   Anyone whose last picture was a big hit, won an Academy Award or is being lionized by the media. A transitional state.

House nut   Weekly operating expenses of movie theater.

Hyphenates   Persons who fulfill two or more major roles such as producer-director, writer-director or actor-director.

Key Art   Art work used in posters and ads for a movie.

Limited Partnership   Instrument of investment commonly used to finance movies. General partners initiate and control the partnership; limited partners are the investors and have no control of the running of the partnership business and no legal or financial liabilities beyond the amount they have invested.

Merchandising rights   Right to license, manufacture and distribute merchandise based on characters, names or events in a picture.

DEALMAKING
IN THE
FILM AND
TELEVISION
INDUSTRY

328

Mini-multiple Type of release that falls between an exclusive engagement and a wide release, consisting of quality theaters in strategic geographic locations, generally a prelude to a wider break.

Multi-tiered audience An audience of different types of people who find the film attractive for different reasons, and who must be reached by different publicity, promotion or ads.

Negative cost Actual cost of producing a film through to the manufacture of a completed negative (does not include costs of prints or advertising).

Negative pickup A distributor guarantees to pay a specified amount for distribution rights upon delivery of a completed film negative by a specific date. If the picture is not delivered on time and in accordance with the terms of the agreement, the distributor has no obligation to distribute it. A negative pickup guarantee can be used as collateral for a bank loan to obtain production funds.

Off-Hollywood American independent films made outside the studio system.

Original A screenplay that has not been adapted from an article, book, play, old movie etc.

On spec Working for nothing on the hope and speculation that something will come of it.

Platforming A method of release whereby a film is opened in a single theater or small group of theaters in a major territory and later widening the run to a greater number of theaters.

Playoff Distribution of a film after key openings.

Regional release As opposed to a simultaneous national release, a pattern of distribution whereby a film is opened in one or more regions at a time.

Rollout Distribution of film around the country subsequent to either key city openings or an opening in one city, usually New York.

Run Length of time that a feature plays in theaters or territory.

Scale The minimum salary permitted by the guilds.

Shooting script A later version of the screenplay in which each separate shot is numbered and camera directions are indicated.

Slicks Standardized ad mechanical, printed on glossary paper, which includes various sizes of display ads for a given film, designed to receive local theater information as needed.

Sleeper A film not expected to be a hit which audiences fall in love with and make into a success.

Specialized distribution As opposed to commercial distribution, distribution to a limited target audience, in a smaller number of theaters with limited advertising budget and reliance upon publicity, reviews and word-of-mouth to build an audience for the picture.

Stills Photographs taken during production for use later in advertising and/or publicity. Stills should be in a horizontal format and should list below the photo such information as film title, producer/director and cast.

Story analyst or reader A person employed by a studio or producer to read submitted scripts and properties, synopsize and evaluate them; often young literature or film school graduates who don't know a great deal about story or filmmaking—but then again their bosses sometimes know even less.

Story conference A meeting at which the writer receives suggestions as to how to improve his/her script.

Sub-distributor In theatrical releases, distributors who handle a specific geographic territory. They are sub-contracted by the main distributor, who co-ordinates the distribution campaign and marketing of all sub-distributors.

Syndication Distribution of motion pictures to independent commercial television stations on a regional basis.

DEALMAKING
IN THE
FILM AND
TELEVISION
INDUSTRY

330

Talent The word used to describe those involved in the artistic aspects of filmmaking (i.e., writers, actors, directors) as opposed to the business people.

Target market The defined audience segment a distributor seeks to reach with its advertising and promotion campaign, such as teens, women over thirty, yuppies, etc.

Test marketing Pre-releasing a film in one or more small, representative markets before committing to an advertising campaign. The effectiveness of the marketing plan can thereby be assessed and modified as needed before the general release.

Trades The daily and weekly periodicals of the industry such as *Variety* and *The Hollywood Reporter*.

Treatment A prose account of the storyline of a film. Usually between twenty and fifty pages. Comes after outline and before first-draft screenplay.

Wide release The release of a film in numerous theaters (800 to 2,000).

Window Period of time in which a film is available in a given medium. Some windows may be open-ended, such as theatrical and home video, or limited, such as pay television or syndication.

CHAPTER 18

APPENDIX

BOOKS AND PUBLICATIONS

Reel Power, The Struggle for Influence and Success in the New Hollywood. Mark Litwak (New York: William Morrow & Co., 1986; reprinted in paperback, Los Angeles: Silman-James Press, 1994). A comprehensive look at how Hollywood works—who has the power and how deals are made.

Off-Hollywood, The Making and Marketing of American Specialty Films. David Rosen with Peter Hamilton (New York: Grove/Weidenfeld, 1990). A study of American independent feature films commissioned by the Sundance Institute and The Independent Feature Project. Case history profiles of the making and marketing of nine narrative and two documentary films including *The Ballad of Gregorio Cortez, Eating Raoul, El Norte, My Dinner with Andre, Wild Style,* and *The Return of the Secaucus Seven*.

Independent Feature Film Production. Gregory Goodell (New York: St. Martin's Press, 1982).

Adventures in the Screen Trade. William Goldman (New York: Warner Books, 1983). A writer's view of the industry.

***Final Cut: Dreams and Disaster in the Making of* Heaven's Gate**. Steven Bach (New York: William Morrow & Co., 1985). All about the *Heaven's Gate* debacle. Good insights into how decisions are made within a studio.

DEALMAKING
IN THE
FILM AND
TELEVISION
INDUSTRY

332

Indecent Exposure: A True Story of Hollywood and Wall Street. David McClintock (New York: William Morrow & Co., 1982). Explores the Begelman scandal and sheds light on studio boardroom politics and high finance.

Hollywood, The Dream Factory. Hortense Powdermaker (Boston: Little Brown & Co., 1950). This book is difficult to find since it is out-of-print. Try second-hand bookstores. Powdermaker was an anthropologist who decided to study Hollywood, its mores, customs, etc. It provides a sociological perspective on industry people and on industry practices that is remarkably relevant today, thirty-five years after this book was published. And it's amusing to read her comments comparing the behavior of the indigenous people of Hollywood with those of "primitive" cultures.

American Film Now. James Monaco (New York: Oxford University Press, 1979). The early chapters describe the workings of the industry, the latter a review of the work of top filmmakers.

What a Producer Does: The Art of Moviemaking (Not the Business). Buck Houghton (Los Angeles: Silman-James Press, 1991).

Filmmakers on Filmmaking: The American Film Institute Seminars on Motion Pictures and Television, Joseph McBride, ed. (Los Angeles: AFI/J.P. Tarcher, Inc., dist. by Samuel French Trade). Volumes I & II. These books are comprised of edited transcripts of AFI seminars held with prestigious people in the industry.

The Studio. John Gregory Dunne (New York: Touchstone, Simon & Schuster, 1968 & 1969). Stories about life inside Twentieth Century-Fox.

Anatomy of the Movies. David Pirie, ed. (New York: Macmillan Publishing Co., Inc. 1981). Collection of articles written by various journalists about the industry.

Rolling Breaks, and Other Movie Business. Aljean Harmetz (New York: Alfred A. Knopf, 1983). Collection of this *New York Times* correspondent's articles on the industry.

City of Nets: A Portrait of Hollywood in the 1940's. Otto Friedrich (New York: Harper & Row, 1986). Stories about Hollywood.

Film: An International History of the Medium. Robert Sklar (New York: Harry N. Abrams, 1993).

A History of the American Film Industry From its Beginnings to 1931. Benjamin B. Hampton (New York: Dover Publications, Inc., 1970). Gives the reader a good historical perspective of the industry. It's interesting to note how certain patterns keep recurring.

WRITING

The Art of Adaptation: Turning Fact into Film. Linda Seger (New York: Henry Holt, 1992).

Best American Screenplays, Sam Thomas, ed. (New York: Crown Publishers, 1986). A collection of screenplays.

The Craft of the Screenwriter. John Brady (New York: Simon and Schuster, 1981). Interviews with top screenwriters.

Creating Unforgettable Characters. Linda Seger (New York: Henry Holt, 1990).

Making a Good Script Great. Linda Seger (Los Angeles: Samuel French Trade, 1988).

The New Screenwriter Looks at the New Screenwriter. William Froug (Los Angeles: Silman-James Press, 1992). Froug's second collection of interviews featuring top screenwriters of the 80s and 90s.

The Screenwriter Looks at the Screenwriter. Willian Froug (Los Angeles: Silman-James Press, 1991). Twelve top screenwriters talk about their craft. Reprint of 1972 edition.

Screenwriting Tricks of the Trade. William Froug (Los Angeles: Silman-James Press, 1993).

Writing Screenplays That Sell. Michael Hauge (New York: Harper Collins, 1990).

DEALMAKING
IN THE
FILM AND
TELEVISION
INDUSTRY

334

DIRECTING

Directing the Film: Film Directors on Their Art. Eric Sherman (Los Angeles: Acrobat Books, 1988).

Film Directing Shot by Shot: Visualizing From Concept to Screen. Steven D. Katz (Los Angeles: Michael Wiese Productions, 1991).

Grammar of the Film Language. Daniel Arijon (Los Angeles: Silman-James Press, 1991).

THE BUSINESS

Contracts for the Film and Television Industry. Mark Litwak (Los Angeles: Silman-James Press, 1994). A collection of sample entertainment contracts along with discussions of the terms and ideas contained therein.

Film Finance & Distribution: A Dictionary of Terms. John W. Cones (Los Angeles: Silman-James Press, 1992).

The Movie Business Book, 2nd Edition. Jason E. Squire (New York: Simon & Schuster, Inc., 1992). Collection of articles about various aspects of the business.

Producing, Financing and Distributing Film, 2nd Edition. Paul A. Baumgarten, Donald C. Farber, and Mark Fleischer (New York: Limelight Editions, 1992).

Producing Theatre, A Comprehensive Legal and Business Guide. Donald C. Farber (New York: Limelight Editions, 1987).

REFERENCE

Academy Players Directory. Published triannually by The Academy of Motion Picture Arts and Sciences, 8949 Wilshire Blvd., Beverly Hills, CA 90211-1972, (310) 247-3000.

The Blu-Book Directory. Comprehensive industry directory published annually by The Hollywood Reporter, 5055 Wilshire Blvd., Los Angeles, CA 90036-4396, (213) 525-2000.

Film Directors: A Complete Guide. Michael Singer (Los Angeles: Lone Eagle Publishing). Published annually, this reference book lists film directors with their credits and contact information. Other similar books published by Lone Eagle include

Cinematographrs, Production Designers, Costume Designers & Film Editors Guide; *Film Actors Guide; Film Composers Guide*; *Film Producers, Studios, Agents & Casting Directors Guide*; *Film Writers Guide*; *Special Effects and Stunts Guide*; and *Television Writers Guide*. .

Hollywood Creative Directory. Published triannually by Hollywood Creative Directory, 3000 Olympic Blvd., Santa Monica, CA 90404, (310) 315-4815. This "Who's What and Where" in motion picture and TV development and production, contains production companies, studios, and networks. The Hollywood Creative Directory publishes several other directories including, *Hollywood Distributors Directory*.

L.A. 411. Published annually by LA411, P.O. Box 480495, Los Angeles, CA 90048, (213) 460-6304. Contact information for everything you need to produce commercials, film or video in Los Angeles.

The Whole Film Sourcebook. Leonard Maltin (New York: New American Library, 1983). Listing of film schools, grants, archives, film festivals, books and libraries.

Who's Who in the Motion Picture Industry. Rodman Gregg (Beverly Hills: Packard Publishing).

MAGAZINES

Broadcasting Magazine (weekly), 1680 N. Vine St., Los Angeles, CA 90028. (213) 463-3148.

Daily Variety, 5700 Wilshire Blvd., Ste. 120, Los Angeles, CA 90036. (213) 857-6600.

Drama-Logue (weekly), P.O. Box 38771, Los Angeles, CA 90038. (213) 464-5079.

Emmy Magazine (Bimonthly), 5220 Lankershim Blvd.,North Hollywood, CA 91601. (818) 754-2800.

Hollywood Reporter (daily), 5055 Wilshire Blvd., Los Angeles, CA 90036-4396, (213) 525-2000.

Women in Film Newsletter (monthly), 6464 Sunset Blvd., Ste. 530, Los Angeles, CA 90028. (213) 463-6040.

DEALMAKING
IN THE
FILM AND
TELEVISION
INDUSTRY

336

BOOKSTORES

Samuel French Theatre & Film Bookshops, 7623 Sunset Blvd., Hollywood, CA 90046, (213) 876-0570, fax (213) 876-6822 and 11963 Ventura Blvd, Studio City, CA, 91604, (818) 762-0535.

Larry Edmunds Bookshop, 6644 Hollywood Blvd., Hollywood, CA, 90028, (213) 463-3273.

Drama Book Shop, 723 Seventh Ave., New York, NY 10019, (212) 944-0595.

Cinema Books, 4753 Roosevelt Way, N.E., Seattle, WA 98105, (206) 547-7667.

Theatrebooks, Ltd., 11 St. Thomas Street, Toronto, Ont., Canada M5S 2B7, (416) 922-7175.

Contacts Librairie du Cinema, 24 Rue du Colisee, 75008 Paris, France, 14-359-1771.

LIBRARIES

The American Film Institute, 2021 North Western Ave, (213) 856-7600.

University of Southern California, Doheny Memorial Library, U.S.C., University Park, Los Angeles, CA 90089-0182, (213) 740-8906.

Academy of Motion Picture Arts & Sciences, Margaret Herrick Library, 333 S. La Cienega Blvd., Beverly Hills, CA 90211, (310) 247-3020.

GUILDS, ASSOCIATIONS & UNIONS

Actor's Equity Association (AEA), 6430 Sunset Blvd., Ste. 700, Los Angeles, CA 90028, (213) 462-2334.

American Federation of Musicians (AFM), 1777 N. Vine St., Ste. 500, Hollywood, CA 90028-5218, (213) 461-3441.

American Federation of TV and Radio Artists (AFTRA), 6922 Hollywood Blvd., P.O. Box 4070, Hollywood, CA 90078-4070, (213) 461-8111.

Directors Guild of America (DGA), 7920 Sunset Blvd., Los Angeles, CA 90046, (310) 289-2000. Info. Line: (213) 851-3671.

Screen Actors Guild (SAG), 7065 Sunset Blvd., Los Angeles, CA 90028-6065, (213) 465-4600.

Producers Guild of America, 400 S. Beverly Dr., Ste. 211, Beverly Hills, CA 90212, (310) 557-0807.

Writers Guild of America, west, 8955 Beverly Blvd., Los Angeles, CA 90048, (310) 550-1000.

PROTECTING TITLES

Non-member title registration agreement: MPAA, 1133 Avenue of the Americas, New York, N.Y. 10036, (212) 840-6161.

MUSIC RIGHTS CLEARANCE

Write for a free copy of *A Producer's Guide to Music Clearance*, Clearing House, Ltd., 6605 Hollywood Blvd., Ste. 200, Hollywood, CA 90028, (213) 469-3186.

FILMMAKER ORGANIZATIONS

Independent Feature Project, 21 West 86th Street, New York, N.Y. 10024, (212) 496-0909.

Independent Feature Project/West, 309 Santa Monica Blvd., Ste. 422, Santa Monica, CA 90401, (310) 451 8057. A non-profit organization dedicated to supporting and promoting quality American independent films.

Sundance Institute, 4000 Warner Blvd., Burbank, CA 91522, (818) 954 4776. The Sundance Institute was founded by Robert

DEALMAKING
IN THE
FILM AND
TELEVISION
INDUSTRY

338

Redford to assist independent filmmakers. Sundance selects ten scripts each year for its script development program and assigns veteran screenwriters to work with the project participants. The June Laboratory is a month-long residency fellowship at the Sundance Resort in Provo Canyon, Utah.

Association of Independent Video and Filmmakers (AIVF), 625 Broadway, 9th floor, New York, N.Y. 10012, (212) 473-3400. AIVF is a national association of independent producers and individuals involved in independent video and film. Publishes *The Independent* ten times a year.

International Documentary Association, 1551 Robertson Blvd., Los Angeles, CA 90035, (310) 284-8422, fax (310) 785-9334. Publishes *International Documentary*.

EDUCATION

The American Film Institute (AFI), 2021 N. Western Ave., Los Angeles, CA 90027, (213) 856-7627.

Boston Center for Adult Education, 5 Commonwealth Ave., Boston, MA 02116, (617) 267-4430.

California Institute of the Arts (Cal Arts), School of Film and Video, 24700 McBean Parkway, Valencia, CA 91355, (805) 255-1050.

Columbia University, Film Division, School of the Arts, 513 Dodge Hall, 116th Streets & Broadway, New York, NY 10027, (212) 854-2815.

Florida State University, Conservatory in Motion Picture, Television & Recording Arts, 5555 N. Tamiami Road, Sarasota, FL 34243, (813) 355-6611.

Hollywood Film Institute, 5225 Wilshire Blvd., Los Angeles, CA 90036, (213) 933-3456.

New School for Social Research, 66 W. 12th Street, New York, NY 10011, (212) 229-5613.

New York University (NYU), School of Arts, 51 W. 4th Street, New York, NY 10003, (212) 998-1212.

911 Media Arts Center, 117 Yale Ave. N., Seattle, WA 98109, (206) 682-6552.

Northwest Film Center, 1219 S.W. Park Ave., Portland, OR 97205, (503) 221-1156.

San Francisco State University, Film and Creative Arts Interdisciplinary Dept., 1600 Holloway Ave., San Francisco, CA 94132, (415) 338-111.

San Francisco State Extended Education, Downtown Center, 425 Martket St., San Francisco, CA 94105, (415) 543-4250.

University of California, Los Angeles (UCLA), 405 Hilgard Ave., Los Angeles, CA 90024, (310) 825-5761.

UCLA Entension, 10995 Le Conte Ave., Los Angeles, CA 90024, (310) 206-1411.

University of Hawaii at Manoa, Film & Video Summer Institute, 2500 Dole Street, P.O. Box 11450, Honolulu, HI, 96829-0450, (808) 956-7221.

University of Southern California (USC), Division of Cinema/Television, School of Performing Arts, University Park, Los Angeles, CA 90007, (213) 740-2235.

INDEX

DEALMAKING
IN THE
FILM AND
TELEVISION
INDUSTRY

342

DEALMAKING
IN THE
FILM AND
TELEVISION
INDUSTRY

344

DEALMAKING
IN THE
FILM AND
TELEVISION
INDUSTRY

346

ABOUT THE AUTHOR

Mark Litwak is a veteran entertainment attorney known for aggressively representing independent filmmakers who have been cheated by distributors. He has won large awards in compensation for clients after distributors tried to defraud them through creative accounting. He also functions as a producer's representative assisting filmmakers in the marketing and distribution of their films.

Litwak is the author of numerous articles and several books: *Reel Power: The Struggle for Influence and Success in the New Hollywood, Courtroom Crusaders, Contracts for the Film and Television Industry*, and the upcoming *Litwak's Multimedia Producer's Guide*.

Litwak maintains his own law practice in Santa Monica, California. As a law professor he has taught entertainment and copyright law at the University of West Los Angeles, U.C.L.A., and Loyola Law School. He has lectured before many filmmakers and university audiences including presentations at the American Film Institute, Columbia University, N.Y.U., U.S.C., U.C.L.A., The New School for Social Research, the University of British Columbia, San Francisco State University, and the Royal College of Art in London.

As an authority on the movie industry, he has been interviewed on more than fifty television and radio shows, including ABC, "The Larry King Show," N.P.R's "All Things Considered," and the Cable News Network.

Critical acclaim for Mark Litwak's *Reel Power*

"...valuable, fresh information on contemporary Hollywood...breaks new ground in identifying the industry's true power brokers. The book is peppered with revealing facts, figures and opinions."—The New York Times

"[Litwak] is an astute observer of the business...filled with pertinent anecdotes, as well as with an extremely intelligent and sound analysis of the various aspects of the business."—Newsday

"A painfully accurate look at the movie business today. It is also a good read, well-written and fascinating on every level...A real eye-opener."
—James Bridges, Director, *Urban Cowboy, The China Syndrome*

"Intelligent, perceptive, rich in common sense observation."
—Steven Bach, author, *Final Cut*

"Fascinating in its pertinence and exacting in its description of the day-to-day processes involved in setting up a movie...It is a primer for anyone interested in the movie business. If you want to earn your living in Hollywood, read it and save five years apprenticeship."
—American Film

CONTRACTS ON COMPUTER DISK

Obtain all of the contracts included in *Dealmaking in the Film and Television Industry* on computer disk:

Depiction Release, reversion
Depiction Release, option
Depiction Release, documentary short-form
Location Agreement
Option & Literary Purchase Agreement
Writer Employment Agreement
Actor Employment Agreement, SAG weekly theatrical
Actor Employment Agreement, low-budget, non-union
Extra Agreement
Extra Release
Line producer Employment Agreement
Collaboration Release
TV Music Rights License
Composer Agreement, low-budget
Acquisition/Distribution Agreement

ORDER FORM

Qty	Title	Price @	Total
	***Dealmaking* Contracts**	$99.00	

Contracts are sent on 3.5 inch high-density disks formatted for IBM and IBM compatibles. Please indicate desired format:

☐ Microsoft Word

☐ Wordstar

☐ Wordperfect

☐ ASCII

Sub-total _____

Sales Tax
(Los Angeles County residents add 8 1/4 %. Other California residents add 7 1/4 %) _____

Shipping & handling $ 3.00 _____

TOTAL _____

Ship to:

_____
(Name)

_____
(Company)

_____
(Street Address)

_____
(City/SAtate/Zip)

Send check or money order payable to **Fast Forward Production** to **P.O. Box 3226, Santa Monica, CA 90408.**

Orders are shipped via UPS (we cannot ship to P.O. boxes). Prices are subject to change without notice. All sales are final. Allow 2-4 weeks for delivery.